YEARS

A GERRY ANDERSON PRODUCTION

THUNDERBIRDS

YEARS

A GERRY ANDERSON PRODUCTION

THUNDERBIRDS

THE VAULT

MARCUS HEARN

To Emma Woods
fondly remembered, forever young

1 3 5 7 9 10 8 6 4 2

Virgin Books, an imprint of Ebury Publishing,
20 Vauxhall Bridge Road,
London SW1V 2SA

Virgin Books is part of the Penguin Random House group of companies
whose addresses can be found at global.penguinrandomhouse.com

First published in the United Kingdom by Virgin Books in 2015.

www.eburypublishing.co.uk

A CIP catalogue record for this book is available from the British Library.

ISBN: 9780753556351

Printed and bound in Italy by L. E. G. O. SpA

Penguin Random House is committed to a
sustainable future for our business, our readers
and our planet. This book is made from Forest
Stewardship Council® certified paper.

ABOUT THE AUTHOR

Since beginning his career at Marvel Comics in 1993, Marcus Hearn has written for *The Times*, *The Guardian* and *The Independent*, as well as contributing booklet notes, audio commentaries and documentaries to nearly a hundred DVDs and Blu-rays. His numerous books include the *New York Times* bestseller *Doctor Who: The Vault*, the Rondo Award-winning *The Art of Hammer*, *The Cinema of George Lucas* and *Eight Days a Week*, the story of The Beatles' final world tour. He is an associate research fellow at De Montfort University's Cinema and Television History Research Centre, and is the official historian of Hammer Film Productions.

PICTURE CREDITS

Original photography from *Captain Scarlet and the Mysterons*, *Danger Man*, *Fireball XL5*, *Joe 90*, *The Saint*, *The Secret Service*, *Space: 1999*, *Stingray*, *Supercar*, *Thunderbirds*, *Thunderbirds Are Go* (1966), *Thunderbird 6* and *UFO* is copyright © ITC Entertainment Group Limited.

Pictures from *Come Into My Parlour*, *Coronation Street*, *Four Feather Falls*, *Sergeant Musgrave's Dance* and *Val Parnell's Sunday Night at the London Palladium* are copyright © ITV Ventures Limited.

The author and publisher gratefully acknowledge the permission granted to reproduce the copyright material in this book. Every effort has been made to trace copyright holders and to obtain permission for the use of copyright material. The publisher apologises for any errors or omissions in the below list and would be grateful if notified of any corrections that should be included in future reprints or editions of this book.

20th Century-Fox (page 47), Anderson Entertainment (10, 14), Anglo Amalgamated (27), Associated-Rediffusion (8, 11), BBC Television (93), Katie Bleathman (239), Charles Buchan's Publications (39, 83), Katie Daines (224, 225, 231), DMG Media (99), Getty Images (46, 76, 119, 133), Barry Gray Archive (198, 199, 204), Guardian Media Group (95), Mick Hall (40), Marcus Hearn (32, 36, 41, 51, 63, 72, 80, 81, 97, 106, 127, 129, 144, 147, 148, 150, 153, 155, 158, 162, 163, 164, 201, 202, 203, 210, 217, 219, 226, 227), IPC Media (26), Mike Jones (75, 104), Mastermodels (173), Newtrade Publishing (215), Northern & Shell Media Group (44), Polystyle Publications (175), Rex Features (107, 184), Keith Shackleton (208), Alan Shubrook (166), *Television Mail* (83), Mike Trim (140) and Universal Pictures (234).

CONTENTS

AUTHOR'S NOTE AND ACKNOWLEDGEMENTS

Appropriately enough, we'd just entered the 21st century when I was asked to write the authorised biography of *Thunderbirds* creator Gerry Anderson. We became friends as well as colleagues and this proved to be the first of many collaborations over the next ten years. Gerry passed away in 2012, so *Thunderbirds: The Vault* is the first time I've attempted a major appraisal of his career without his fresh input or guidance.

While I miss our regular meetings and phone calls, Gerry's absence has provided an opportunity to introduce many other voices. My thanks to the following, all of whom gave their time to be interviewed: Jamie Anderson, the late John Blundall, Cathy Ford, Ben Foster, Ken Holt, Brian Johnson, David Lane, Robin McDonald, Mike Noble, Alan Perry, Shane Rimmer, Keith Shackleton and Ralph Titterton. Quotes from Gerry are taken from the extensive interviews I conducted with him in 2001.

My work on Gerry's biography was partly an effort to complete a manuscript compiled by Simon Archer before his tragic death in 1993. I'm grateful to Simon's sister, Sue Harman, for preserving Simon's tapes and allowing me to listen to them for the first time. These recordings have enabled me to quote previously unpublished extracts from Simon's interviews with Bob Bell, Arthur 'Wag' Evans, Alan Fennell, Christine Glanville, Derek Meddings and Alan Pattillo, almost all of whom are no longer with us. Gerry was a great admirer of Simon's talents, and I'm pleased that some of this material can now be shared in a book about a television series that Simon loved.

I would also like to thank Chris King for his permission to use extracts from a 2014 interview he conducted with Sylvia Anderson, and Ian Fryer for permission to use an extract from his 2012 interview with Nicholas Parsons. All other interview sources are referenced in the text.

Sylvia's autobiography *Yes M'Lady* was one of the books I consulted, along with *The Complete Book of Thunderbirds* and *The Complete Gerry Anderson* (both by Chris Bentley), *Filmed in Supermarionation* (Stephen La Rivière), *21st Century Visions* (Derek Meddings and Sam Mitchell), *The Gerry Anderson Memorabilia Guide* (Dennis Nicholson) and the *Gerry Anderson Complete Comic History* website, edited by Shaqui Le Visconte.

Below: This game was manufactured by Peter Pan Playthings in 1965 and was part of the first wave of *Thunderbirds* merchandise. The player manoeuvred a ball bearing to 'rescue sites' around a maze, avoiding the various pitfalls.

The following kindly allowed us to photograph and scan some of the rarest items from their collections: Graham and Katie Bleathman, Stephen Brown and Lynn Simpson, Steve Cambden, Sam Denham, Vaughan Herriott, Chris King, Steve Kyte and Helen McCarthy, and the curators of the Barry Gray Archive, Ralph Titterton and Cathy Ford. My thanks to them, and to Theo de Klerk, Chris McHugh and Dennis Nicholson for their priceless contributions to our picture research.

For the provision of additional images, my thanks to Anderson Entertainment, Andrew Barr (of Mastermodels), Tony Clark, Fanderson, Chris Gamm and Chris Rolfe (of Newtrade), Mick Hall, Derek Handley, the Doug Luke Archive, Tim Mallett and Nick Williams, Alistair McGown, Will Shackleton, Alan Shubrook and Mike Trim. For help with other aspects of the book's research, my thanks to the BBC Written Archives Centre, the British Film Institute, Michele Fabian Jones, Ian Fryer, Melvyn Hiscock, Adam Jezard, Joe McIntyre, the National Archive, the late Ian Scoones and Rorie Sherwood. At ITV, Najmie Allette and Maggy Harris made the project possible, while at Random House my editors Yvonne Jacob and Lorna Russell guided it to completion.

Chris Bentley answered many of my queries, Jonathan Rigby made valuable

Lady Penelope and Parker: Thunderbirds, Thursday 7.0

comments on the manuscript and Peri Godbold advised on technical aspects of the image restoration. At home, Sharon and our beautiful children, Leo and Niamh, kept my spirits high during the long months of research, photography and writing.

My closest colleague throughout was the designer, Mike Jones. He rose to the considerable challenge of creating a 'virtual museum' dedicated to *Thunderbirds*, and has been a pillar of strength. We hope that our joint effort does justice to Gerry's remarkable legacy.

Marcus Hearn
July 2015

Above left: A 1963 advertisement from trade magazine *Kinematograph Weekly*, listing recent productions and a new series from Gerry Anderson's company AP Films.

Above right: Parker and Lady Penelope promote *Thunderbirds* in this 1965 issue of listings magazine *TV World*.

1

THE TOMORROW PEOPLE

Although closely identified with a culturally pioneering decade, *Thunderbirds* has been revered by successive generations of children and adults. More than 50 years after it first appeared in 1965, the programme is considered a landmark in the history of television entertainment.

This enduring achievement can be traced back to the fertile imagination of its creator, Gerry Anderson. The producer had a career that spanned six decades, sustained by a genius for devising innovative, family-friendly series.

Thunderbirds is at the heart of Anderson's legacy, a totem of all the extraordinary shows that bear his name. Anderson had the foresight to turn himself into a brand, prompting speculation that he could be Britain's answer to Walt Disney. But he was the first to admit that the series produced by his companies were the sum of their parts, and that many of his colleagues played invaluable roles in realising his ideas.

The board of AP Films included its original art director Reg Hill, director of photography John Read and Gerry's wife, Sylvia. The creative spark of APF's science-fiction shows largely came from Gerry, much of the practical ingenuity was supplied by Reg and the camera expertise was John's. It was a *Boy's Own* adventure, both on and off the screen, but Sylvia sprinkled stardust on the designs and did much to humanise the puppet characters.

Some of the technicians who joined APF after its formation made a comparable contribution to the inimitable style of its programmes, but it was this core group that steered the company through its golden age.

Below: Gerry Anderson, pictured in 1963. By this time he was, by his own admission, "obsessed with trying to make puppets look like live-action."

Below right: Gerry (foreground) with his older brother Lionel and their parents, Deborah and Joe. Gerry and his parents narrowly survived the wartime bombing raids, but Flight Sergeant Lionel Anderson was not so lucky.

Below inset: In 1955 Gerry became a director of production company Pentagon Films. It was while making a television commercial for Pentagon that he and his future business partner Arthur Provis first worked with puppets.

Gerry Anderson was born Gerald Alexander Abrahams in Hampstead, London, on 14 April 1929. His was a working class, occasionally impoverished upbringing, but the first great hardship of his life was being caught between his unhappily married parents, Joe and Deborah. In 1939 Deborah changed the family name to Anderson as an act of rebellion against her husband's Jewish faith.

The biggest trauma in Gerald's childhood was the death of his older brother Lionel, an RAF pilot who was killed during a mission on 27 April 1944. Already an isolated and unhappy boy, Gerald's neurosis was compounded when his distraught mother told him that the wrong son had died.

"This must have been a devastating thing to hear from your own mother," says Jamie Anderson, Gerry's youngest son. "When I met Dad's first wife, Betty, she told me this set him up in all the right and all the wrong ways. He spent the rest of his life trying to live up to the character of Lionel that he'd created in his head, trying to impress his mum and trying to create replacement family units. I think we can see this in the fictional families he created, most obviously the Tracy brothers in *Thunderbirds*."

TELEPHONE: MAIDENHEAD 140

PENTAGON FILMS
LIMITED

STOCKWELLS
BERRY HILL, TAPLOW
MAIDENHEAD, BERKS

G. A. ANDERSON
DIRECTOR

Keith Shackleton became friends with Gerry during their national service in the late 1940s, and he remembers both Joe and Deborah. "Our parents must have some responsibility for us," he says. "Alexander Pope said something to the effect that many people think they've drawn the short straw, and that it's always somebody else's fault. There was a bit of that in Gerry. He was carrying a burden."

Gerry was a single-minded career man throughout his adult life, although his earnest demeanour was frequently punctuated by flashes of dry wit. The only thing tempering his ambitious nature was a nagging insecurity. "We're all inexperienced when we're young, and in some ways Gerry was naïve," says Shackleton, who stayed in touch with Anderson throughout the 1950s. "He didn't have the confidence to do it by himself; he needed someone to hold his hand."

Anderson's first business partner was Arthur Provis, a camera operator he met while directing the television series *You've Never Seen This!* for Polytechnic Studios

in 1955. The series was barely screened by broadcaster Associated-Rediffusion, and towards the end of that year Gerry and Arthur joined the board of a new company, Pentagon Films.

Gerry and Arthur spent more than 18 months at Pentagon, making television commercials for a wide variety of products. Commercials advertising a Kellogg's breakfast cereal gave them their first experience of working with puppets. Neither men could have predicted that a writer of romantic fiction was about to present another.

Roberta Leigh was the pen-name adopted by author Rita Lewin for a string of novels with such melodramatic titles as

Above left: "Perhaps we'd better begin at the best place for a story – at the beginning..." stated the narration for the opening episode of *The Adventures of Twizzle*, the first series Gerry Anderson and Arthur Provis produced for Roberta Leigh. The voice-over went on to describe the toy shop that the eponymous doll called home.

Above right: Roberta Leigh with Torchy and Pom-Pom the poodle. *Torchy the Battery Boy* was the second series she commissioned from Anderson and Provis.

Above left: Filming *Torchy the Battery Boy* on the ballroom stage at Islet Park House. Camera operator John Read and continuity girl Sylvia Thamm can be seen far left. Director of photography Arthur Provis and director Gerry Anderson are in the centre.

Above right: Roberta Leigh pays a visit to the Frutown set of *Torchy*.

Below: This 7" EP was based on *The Adventures of Twizzle* and released by HMV in 1958.

Dark Inheritance and *The Vengeful Heart.* Leigh was reportedly the country's highest-paid writer of women's fiction when she decided to launch a new career, adapting her children's stories as puppet shows for television. "I didn't know one end of a camera from another when John McMillan [of Associated-Rediffusion] gave me my first start," she admitted in the 16 January 1964 issue of *The Stage and Television Today*. "I sent him a manuscript; he loved it, told me to make a film, and put up the money for it. I blithely said 'yes' because I was quite determined to do it and I wanted to see my characters come alive."

Leigh may have been naïve about certain aspects of television production but she was an astute businesswoman who only passed a fraction of Associated-Rediffusion's fee to the company she sub-contracted to make *The Adventures of Twizzle.* Anderson and Provis had already decided to leave Pentagon Films when Leigh visited the company with her offer of 52 episodes. A low budget puppet series about a doll that could magically extend its arms and legs was not a prospect that Anderson relished, but he recognised the commission as a valuable opportunity. In summer 1957 Anderson and Provis left Pentagon and set up their own company to make Roberta Leigh's series.

The name AP Films reflected the major shareholdings of Anderson and Provis, but the company directors also included three former Pentagon employees. Reg Hill was a former RAF airframe fitter who had contributed models and special effects to recruitment films after the war. John Read was an animator and titles artist with experience in rostrum camerawork. This was a broad base of expertise, but Anderson admitted there were more pragmatic reasons for inviting his colleagues onto the board. "Arthur and I were very short of money, which was why we made Reg and John partners."

The fifth director in this breakaway group was Sylvia Thamm, a secretary from Pentagon who borrowed £100 from her mother as a contribution to APF's start-up capital. "Arthur and I both fell in love with Sylvia from day one," said Gerry. "She used to drive us both mad – we would break for lunch and Sylvia would go to get into Arthur's car and then change her mind and say 'I'll go with Gerry.' Or vice versa. This rivalry never caused tension between Arthur and myself because we got on so well, but it was desperately upsetting for both of us. Little by little, Sylvia decided for whatever reason that I was her man."

In common with other production companies of the era such as Hammer, APF found a large private property and rented rooms which they converted as studio space. *The Adventures of Twizzle* began filming in the ballroom of Islet Park House in Maidenhead, Berkshire, at the end of August 1957. By pursuing a strict schedule of punishing shifts, APF completed the series in January 1958. At the wrap party, Gerry and Sylvia set aside thoughts of their respective spouses and began an adulterous affair. "The point came when I couldn't live without Sylvia, so I left my wife," said Gerry. "There's no justification for the way I behaved, but I was head over heels in love with Sylvia and found her very attractive. That sort of thing plays havoc with the mind."

Below left: Reg Hill, John Read and assistant art director Bob Bell on the set of the AP Films' series *Four Feather Falls* in 1959. Reg Hill invited Bell to join APF during the production of *Torchy*.

Below right: The former ballroom at Islet Park House in Maidenhead was APF's studio for *Twizzle*, *Torchy* and the pilot episode of *Four Feather Falls*. When Gerry left his first wife, Betty, he moved in for a while.

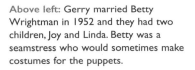

Above left: Gerry married Betty Wrightman in 1952 and they had two children, Joy and Linda. Betty was a seamstress who would sometimes make costumes for the puppets.

Above right: Sylvia Thamm discusses the filming of *Four Feather Falls* with David Elliott, one of the series' directors. Elliott had been an editor on *Twizzle* and *Torchy*, and would remain with APF until the second series of *Thunderbirds*. On the far right is camera operator Kumar Soni.

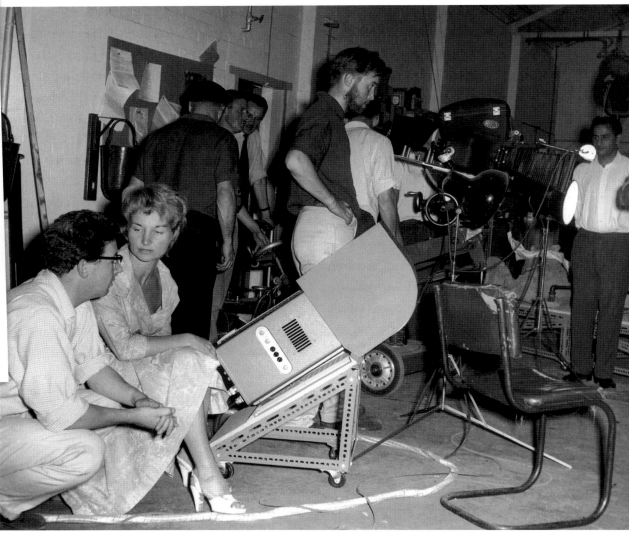

Keith Shackleton has fond memories of Gerry's first wife. "Betty was a sweet girl," he says, "but Gerry had aspirations and she didn't grow with him. I think that was part of the problem. When Gerry met Sylvia, Betty was sidelined."

A dearth of commissions forced APF to return to puppetry later in the year, when Anderson and Provis accepted a contract from Leigh to produce her next series, *Torchy the Battery Boy*. Torchy was another walking, talking doll endowed with special powers – in this case a hat that projected a magical beam of light.

Leigh's budget for *Torchy* increased the allowance to APF. This facilitated Reg Hill's more complex sets and Gerry Anderson's relatively ambitious direction. But Anderson was growing uncomfortable about his business relationship with Leigh, and felt undermined by Provis' more cautious nature. APF completed the first series of *Torchy* in March 1959, after which Leigh offered the company another 26 episodes. Provis felt it would

be wise to accept, but by now Anderson had decided that APF should no longer be dependent on Leigh's creativity or patronage.

Leigh hired another director, Vivian Milroy, to make the second series of *Torchy*, while Anderson and Provis pursued their own project at Islet Park. Shortly afterwards, the owner of the house offered APF the opportunity to buy the building and the Thameside grounds it stood in. Anderson was keen to accept so he could turn the property into a permanent studio, but Provis told him it was an unwarranted risk. "Arthur, while a delightful man and a brilliant cameraman, was a great worrier and didn't share my belief in investing in the future expansion of the company," said Anderson. "I wanted to push forward and he wanted to take things more steadily."

In October, Anderson assumed sole leadership of APF as the majority shareholder, while Provis returned to Roberta Leigh. "Arthur saw in Roberta Leigh a better bet than what we had," says Sylvia. "She had money and she had ideas. We literally had no money."

Splitting from Gerry Anderson might have seemed prudent in 1959, but in later life Provis described the decision as the greatest mistake he ever made.

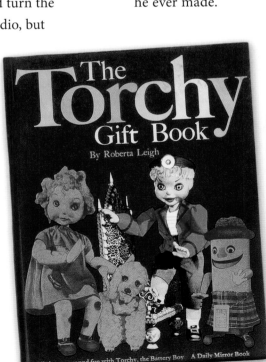

Below left: Art director Reg Hill (seated) with his assistant Bob Bell, working on designs for *Torchy the Battery Boy* at Islet Park House. Behind them is a model of the rocket Mr Bumble-Drop builds for Torchy in the first episode.

Below right: Hill had a penchant for expensive cars. This picture was taken in 1965, when he was the associate producer of *Thunderbirds*.

APF's reorganisation promoted Anderson to chairman, while Hill and Read became joint managing directors. In the late 1950s Hill fast emerged as Anderson's right-hand man.

"As well as creating fictional families on screen, I think Dad would try to create family units in his working life," says Jamie Anderson. "He would tend to find one person who would be the 'best mate' replacement for Lionel. It went from person to person: there was Keith Shackleton, Arthur Provis, Reg Hill... all these thick as thieves male partners. I suppose that when your self-belief and your confidence have been undermined so much by your mother, then perhaps you feel you can't trust yourself to do something by yourself.

"Dad would put pressure on these people to live up to Lionel," continues Jamie. "Of course nobody could. People would start to resent Dad for expecting them to behave in a certain way, and then Dad would be disappointed in them. All these things are educated guesses, and I don't think this behaviour was conscious."

Keith Shackleton joined the board of APF in 1960 and got to know Reg Hill well. "Gerry didn't have a monopoly on the ideas," he says. "Reg was brilliant. Gerry and Reg were great confidants, and they worked hand in glove. I had a warm regard for Reg and we had quite a good relationship. He was incredibly creative, and his skill as an artist was remarkable."

Shackleton remembers Hill as a reserved, inward-looking character. "If you asked him a question he was always of the mindset to say 'no' before he'd really considered the proposition. That was his style, but I learned how to get round this. If I knocked on Reg's door and went into his office I'd have a little warm-up conversation before I got round to the subject. That was a reasonably hopeful way of getting a consensus."

As APF expanded, Hill took a special interest in what would now be described as health and safety, flying into a panic if a fire extinguisher was covered up or displaced. Gerry appreciated Reg's diligence, but claimed that "Sylvia used to take the mickey out of him for it, calling him 'Mrs Hill'. I thought this was terribly unkind."

Alan Perry joined APF as a clapper/loader in 1960 and recalls a more affectionate nickname. "We used to call him 'Meat and Veg Reg'," he says with a smile. "If we had any problems Reg would encourage us to go to him and not Gerry, as Gerry was usually busy on the next project. Reg had a habit – when you saw him he'd rub his hands together and say, 'All right mate!'"

David Lane was also recruited by APF in 1960, initially as an assistant editor. "Reg was a real gent," he says fondly. "A lovely man, married to a lovely lady, Lily. But nobody really knew what he did at the studio, except taking the flak for Gerry. If Gerry got angry about something Reg would soak it up. Reg was the closest friend Gerry had, and Reg always stuck by him, offering him companionship and advice on art direction. Gerry got rid of Reg in the end, but in the 1960s he was Gerry's soul mate."

Below left: An example of the first headed paper to bear the APF logo.

Below right: A portrait of Hill, taken in his office at the APF studio in 1965. He is holding a copy of the original press book for *Thunderbirds*.

A. P. FILMS LIMITED   ISLET PARK, MAIDENHEAD, BERKSHIRE
TELEPHONE MAIDENHEAD 5043

Above left and below: When Arthur Provis resigned from APF, John Read became the company's director of photography. He is pictured here on the set of *Four Feather Falls.*

Above right: Read was featured in this 1963 advertisement from *Kinematograph Weekly.* In the background is puppeteer Mary Turner, who joined APF on *Torchy the Battery Boy.*

Much less is known about John Read, who seemed to keep a lower profile than APF's other executive directors, both in the studio and the pages of the trade press. "John was a private person, but very helpful if you had a problem," says Perry. "If you wanted to discuss how to shoot a scene he'd always be ready to suggest using a particular lens or so on."

Anderson's relationship with Read ended acrimoniously, but in 2001 he acknowledged that his former colleague was "a great nuts and bolts guy" who oversaw the engineering and mechanical aspects of many APF projects. "John wasn't at all ambitious like me and Reg, but he was a great partner. I can't speak too highly of him."

The junior partner on the board was Sylvia Thamm. Gerry's muse worked her way up from secretary to continuity girl, dialogue director, writer and eventually producer. "I was lucky," she says, referring to the fact that she married the boss, "but nothing was ever handed to me. I've never had any problem talking about women's rights. I think if you just do your own thing, do what you feel you're good at doing, then people will ignore whether you're a man or a woman."

Keith Shackleton has remained friends with Sylvia since 1960. "There's no doubt about it, Gerry was a driven man," he says. "I think we all deferred to that ambition and his position. Gerry was in charge, but both he and Sylvia ran the company in its heyday because Sylvia had Gerry's ear at times when we didn't."

David Lane admires Sylvia's showbusiness instinct and sense of humour. "Sylvia was the glamour; she was the front of house. She had such a bubbly personality, and she could take a joke. If you were at a party, Sylvia would make an entrance and take centre stage. She was the publicity person really, because Gerry wasn't charismatic."

What Gerry may have lacked in 'personality' he compensated for with formidable technical skills honed at Gainsborough and other post-war studios. "Gerry was a guru in everything – scriptwriting, editing and directing," says Lane. "He once said to me that he could tell a story about anything – even something as mundane as two people sitting on a park bench."

In 1959 Anderson, Hill, Read and Thamm pooled their talents in an initial effort to do nothing more ambitious than stay in business. During the 1960s they would, of course, achieve much more. "We were all young," says Sylvia. "And when you're young you can aspire to anything and do anything."

Below left: Gerry Anderson shows a journalist around the APF studio in 1963. The egg boxes glued to the walls were an effort by Reg Hill to baffle the sound during the filming of live-action television commercials.

Below right: Sylvia inspects one of the props for an APF production in 1963.

2
ROCKET SCIENCE

The road to *Thunderbirds* was defined by a dogged determination to survive and innovate. A sense of camaraderie prevailed in AP Films' early years, as the company struggled with a lack of resources and indifferent distributors.

After short-lived agreements with Granada Television and Anglo Amalgamated, Gerry Anderson and his colleagues found a more sympathetic ally in ATV. Under Lew Grade's patronage, the homespun western *Four Feather Falls* gave way to *Supercar*, the technological fantasy that would serve as the blueprint for all Anderson's puppet adventures in the 1960s. *Fireball XL5* and *Stingray* were similarly named after the miraculous vehicles that overshadowed their intrepid crew members. Series were either set in the future or a more scientifically advanced version of the present day.

Each series was more ambitious than the last, and the company's studios were upgraded to keep pace. This was a journey that took APF from the ballroom stage at Islet Park House to a modest but dedicated building on the Slough Trading Estate. The pioneering move into colour filmmaking on *Stingray* was achieved when APF moved to another part of the trading estate and its biggest premises to date.

APF borrowed advanced techniques from cinema and invented systems of its own to create television films of unprecedented complexity. Anderson's vision may have been miniaturised, but the sweep of his storytelling was epic and his standards were unforgiving.

Anderson was keen to promote his company's collective ingenuity as a proprietary process. In 1960 he gave that process a name: Supermarionation.

Following the split from Roberta Leigh, AP Films embarked on *Four Feather Falls*, an endearing series that can best be described as a supernatural western with musical interludes. Singing sheriff Tex Tucker defends a pleasant frontier town with the help of magic feathers that enable his horse and dog to talk, and his pistols to spontaneously fire in their holsters.

When filming began in April 1959, Gerry Anderson was still content to define himself primarily as a technician – the original format for the series had been devised by composer Barry Gray and the initial scripts were written by Mary Cathcart Borer. Anderson's ingenuity was channelled towards a feat of engineering that would do more than anything else to define the nebulous puppetry technique that his company was to become renowned for.

Anderson had the idea for the process APF called Automatic Lip Synch while he was directing *Torchy the Battery Boy* the previous year. Put simply, this was a method of automatically animating puppets' faces in synchronisation with pre-recorded dialogue or songs. The puppets in *Torchy* had chins or lower lips that were opened or closed by the puppeteers, but Anderson noticed that "It was very difficult to get the mouth to open and close in synch with the pre-recorded dialogue that was being played back on the stage. We used to do take after take after take trying to get that right."

In an effort to fix the problem, APF adapted two background puppets to a new system. The steel wires suspending a puppet would carry electrical impulses that activated a solenoid inside its head, dropping its chin or opening its lower lip. When the current was interrupted, a spring inside the puppet's mouth returned it to the closed position.

Anderson wanted to extend Automatic Lip Synch to all the major characters in *Four Feather Falls*. He took his requirements to two Birmingham-based electronics companies: RTC Wright & Co created the internal mechanisms for the puppets' heads, while recording specialists Hollick & Taylor constructed the control console which became known as the Four-channel Natterer. This technology enabled up to four characters to be lip-synched to pre-recorded dialogue via a bank of key switches. Reacting to the consonants on the dialogue tapes, the machine operated 50 volt DC relays, sending activating pulses to the puppets' heads when the respective switches were flicked forward.

While this freed up puppeteers to concentrate on more expressive aspects of the puppets' movements, the shortcomings of the process sometimes required them to intervene. The sound activation from the tapes could be insensitive, failing to recognise the duration of long vowels or the difference between 'narrow' words such as "he" or "me" and 'open' sounds such as "Ah!" When Automatic Lip Synch failed, it once again fell to the puppeteers to ensure that subtle lip movements were

visible to viewers, while ensuring that exclamations didn't leave the puppets looking like ventriloquists' dolls. The introduction of an electrical current to the puppets' wires added a new occupational hazard. "The bridges were made of metal, and in hot weather with sweaty hands it was quite usual for us to get a shock," remembered puppetry supervisor Christine Glanville.

Above: Merchandise licensed from Granada Television in 1960. These cards show Tex Tucker, his magic feathers and Mexican bandit Pedro.

Left: The camera tracks towards Tex Tucker in the *Four Feather Falls* title sequence.

Below: Director David Elliott, Reg Hill and Sylvia Thamm at the controls of the original Four-channel Natterer.

Above left: Michael Holliday duets with Tex Tucker in a publicity photo from *Four Feather Falls*. Holliday became a television and recording star in the late 1950s with a style that was clearly influenced by Bing Crosby and Perry Como. He suffered from a troubled private life, which may have contributed to his early death in 1963.

Above right: Holliday was under contract to EMI's Columbia label, which issued this EP in 1960.

Below: *Four Feather Falls* was APF's only production for Granada, and received a complete first run network transmission in the UK. No Gerry Anderson series would match this feat until *Lavender Castle* in 1999.

APF raised £6000 to produce the pilot episode of *Four Feather Falls*, £2000 of which went to singer Michael Holliday for performing some of the series' vocal numbers. "Michael was the first big star I had signed," recalled Anderson, who offered Holliday his contract after a recording session at Elstree's Gate Studios. "I started to read Clause One only to be interrupted by Michael asking me if I had the money on me! I gave him the cheque, at which point he took the contract and turned straight to the last page and signed it. He was so interested in the money that he didn't want to waste time checking that I hadn't signed him up for life."

Anderson's investments paid off when the pilot was eventually picked up by Granada Television, who commissioned a further 38 episodes. This commitment, and its

attendant budget, prompted the company to move the Four-channel Natterer and all its other kit from Islet Park to new premises on the Slough Trading Estate. The building they rented was a former electrical warehouse in Ipswich Road. Its previous tenant was Les Bowie, the renowned special effects expert for Hammer and numerous other companies.

"We took up the option and had four walls and a roof and nothing inside," Anderson told the trade paper *Television Today* in 1962, recalling how he, Reg Hill, John Read and Sylvia Thamm had transformed the building. "All four of us got down to turning the empty place into a studio. We worked all day and pretty well all night. We hardly even stopped to eat, which was just as well because we were living a hand-to-mouth existence."

Anderson recalled that it was Reg Hill who first suggested moving to Slough, and it was Hill who gave *Television Today* a guided tour of the new premises in February 1960. He began by describing Anderson's innovative system to show puppeteers and other crew members the camera operator's view as each scene was being shot. "The Arriflex [camera] we use has a mirror shutter," said Hill. "The [closed circuit] TV camera works through that like a reflex, so we see the scene actually being shot through the lens. This is important for puppet photography for, in many shots, we get right in to about two feet, six inches – much closer than close-ups in live studios.

"Our problems are quite different from normal TV filmmaking," he continued. "We have to 'think small'... think all the time in terms of a Lilliputian world. We have to condense our vision. For example, the saloon of *Four Feather Falls* is only five feet high. Yes, it is a permanent set, and does not have to be struck. That's an advantage over 'live' full-size sets. But in every shot we have the difficulty of working in a very confined space."

Anderson directed the shows from a control room that overlooked the stage. On the desk in front of him were a Pye TV monitor relaying the image from the film camera and an EMI TR90 tape recorder linked to a puppet head fitted with the Automatic Lip Synch mechanism. To communicate with the puppeteers and other studio staff he would speak into a microphone.

"I would set up a scene and use the public address system to talk to the crew on the stage," he said. "In the meantime, Sylvia would rehearse the scene we were about to shoot by passing the tape backwards and forwards through the automatic mouth movement and watch the head and mouth to see how accurate it was. In fact, we achieved about 90 per cent accuracy. All this went on while we were setting up a shot and lighting it. When the shot was ready, a switch was thrown and instead of the pulses of DC going to the puppet's head on the desk, it would go out

Below: One of Gerry Anderson's original APF business cards from the early 1960s.

Bottom left: APF's Ipswich Road studio was approximately four times larger than the ballroom at Islet Park House.

Bottom right: Filming a scene from *Four Feather Falls* at Ipswich Road. John Read is on the far left of the picture and Arthur Provis is seated towards the right. Puppeteers Mary Turner, Roger Woodburn and Christine Glanville (foreground) are on the bridge.

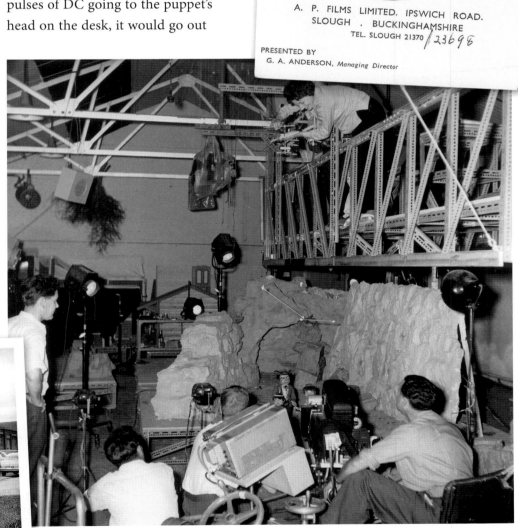

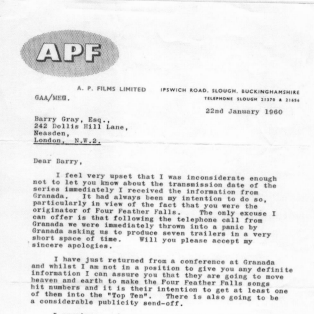

Above left: Voice artists Nicholas Parsons and Kenneth Connor with the characters they played in *Four Feather Falls* – Dusty the dog, Sheriff Tex Tucker and Rocky the horse.

Above right: Barry Gray kept this letter of apology from Gerry Anderson. The crossed-out section at the bottom indicates Arthur Provis' departure from the APF board.

Below: Granada's "considerable publicity send-off" included securing this front cover of *TV Times* in February 1960.

onto the stage, up the bridge and onto power lines running in front of the puppeteers. I would inform them which puppet was on which particular channel and, with the use of crocodile clips, the appropriate channel would be selected, being careful of course not to touch the wires as there was 50 volts going through them. From the control room each character's dialogue would be switched manually to the appropriate channel and by the time the current had reached the puppet heads, it was reduced to about 12 volts, enough to actuate the mouth movements."

Heading the voice cast of *Four Feather Falls* was Carry On actor Kenneth Connor, with other roles played by David Graham and Denise Bryer. Starring as Tex Tucker was Bryer's then husband Nicholas Parsons. "We all sat around a table and recorded the voices together,"

he recalls. "With a radio play you have a part to perform, a character to create, and you do it to a microphone or to the unseen audience and that's what you concentrate on: creating a character for the play. There is a huge difference in technique when you're creating a character to fit a puppet... You have to think of it as adding a voice to a character which already exists."

Independent television was relatively new, and the nine franchise-holders that comprised ITV at that time were still jostling for position. *Four Feather Falls* was unusual in being purchased by all of them, beginning its simultaneous screening across the whole network on Thursday 25 February 1960. Soon afterwards Anderson devised a follow-up series called *Supercar*, about a vehicle that could travel on land, in the air, underwater or even in space. This miraculous invention was designed by Reg Hill, who gave it a striking red-and-yellow livery for a sales brochure promoting the new series. Sylvia Thamm was impressed, describing *Supercar* as Gerry and Reg's "schoolboy dream". Unfortunately it was not a dream shared by Granada.

Undaunted, Anderson took the company in a new direction. An opportunity from distributor Anglo Amalgamated enabled him to fast track his ultimate ambition to make a live-action film. The money on offer was reportedly £16,500 – a pittance, even by the standards of 1960 – but the quality of *Crossroads to Crime* can't be entirely blamed on its budget. Anderson's clumsy direction, Alun Falconer's convoluted script and Barry Gray's inappropriate score all conspire to make this prosaic tale of lorry hijacking one of the most unappealing B movies of its era.

Rather more accomplished was APF's collaboration with Nicholas Parsons and Denise Bryer on three television commercials for the Blue Cars travel agency. In 1961 all three films would receive major recognition at the *Television Mail* Advertising Awards, with the Martian-themed commercial taking the Grand Prix in the Consumer Services category. However APF and Parsons' company DN Productions were cold-shouldered by the industry for committing a cardinal sin: they had produced commercials for their client without using an advertising agency as an intermediary. Parsons and an APF crew led by John Read subsequently shot *Blue Skies Ahead*, a 25-minute travelogue for Blue Cars, but the prestige of the *Television*

Mail awards failed to excite any further advertising business.

Crossroads to Crime did nothing to enhance APF's reputation or bank balance, and although the Blue Cars contract enabled Anderson to keep the Ipswich Road studio open a while longer, by late summer 1960 he had instructed the company accountant to put APF into voluntary liquidation. In the hope of finding jobs after the dissolution, Gerry and Sylvia met with an old colleague called Frank Sherwin Green. During an emotional meeting, Sherwin Green argued that they had come too far to give up on APF. He put them in touch with Connery Chapel, a friend who could effect an introduction to ATV's deputy managing director Lew Grade.

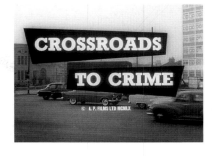

Above: The original title screen for *Crossroads to Crime*. The title sequence was later replaced by Anglo Amalgamated when the film's negative was re-edited for inclusion in the *Edgar Wallace* series of thrillers.

Below: Part of the crew of *Blue Skies Ahead*, on location in Switzerland – director John Read (second from left), director of photography Kumar Soni (second from right) and art director Bob Bell (right). APF's finances were in a perilous state in 1960 and Read recalled that the budget for the shoot wouldn't even stretch to a round of drinks.

Above left: "None but a fool makes television films for the British market alone," said Lew Grade, seen here celebrating the sale of his series *Danger Man* to French television in the early 1960s.

Above right: Grade (right) with Val Parnell, the managing director of ATV, in 1957.

Below: Lew Grade's company logo, which was often accompanied by the slogan 'ITC Entertains the World'.

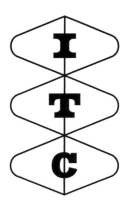

When independent television began in 1955, ATV (Associated TeleVision) held the franchise to broadcast to the Midlands on weekdays and London at weekends. In 1957 ATV expanded with the addition of production and distribution arm ITP (the Incorporated Television Programme Company), changing its name to ITC (the Incorporated Television Company) soon afterwards.

In 1958 another company with the initials ITC (the Incorporated Television Corporation) was founded in the United States as a joint venture between ATV and wealthy American producer Jack Wrather. In 1960 ATV bought Wrather's shares in the group, giving them a wholly-owned subsidiary that could syndicate filmed television series produced by the British ITC. The American ITC was run by Walter Kingsley, while the British company's managing director was Lew Grade.

Arguably British television's greatest mogul, Lew Grade was born Louis Winogradsky in Tokmak, southern Crimea, on Christmas Day 1906. The Winogradskys moved to Bethnal Green in London when Lew was five. While their father worked as a tailor's presser and sewing machine mechanic, Lew and his brothers – Leslie Grade and Bernard Delfont – forged careers in showbusiness. Lew joined a double-act called Grade and Gold, enjoying early recognition when he won the title World Charleston Champion. Realising his opportunities as a performer would be limited, he then established the Grade Organisation theatrical agency with Leslie. From 1931 to 1955, with a gap for his war service, Lew was one of the most successful agents in the country. "I seemed to have the knack of knowing which acts would succeed," he said. This was a talent which, combined with a nose for business, made him an ideal choice to help develop commercial television.

Anderson's first meeting with Grade was happily timed. Grade was seeking to expand the ATV group's portfolio of innovative series he could sell to US broadcasters. And with seats on the boards of both ATV and the British ITC he was in a good position to back his instincts. Anderson soon became aware that he was pitching to an executive with considerably more clout than his previous clients at Associated-Rediffusion or Granada. "There was no capital gains tax. There was no tax on television advertising," he explained. "This was a wonderful situation for entrepreneurs, and Lew's company was swimming in money. Lew built his reputation by advertising his honesty and living up to it. If he said to you, 'You've got a deal,' then yes, you'd go to your lawyer, but the money would probably be with you three days later, before the contract was even drawn up and signed.

But that wasn't the only thing about Lew. Although he was tough in business he had a great big heart. He was a generous man who had a wonderful way with people."

Anderson presented Grade with a copy of the sales brochure that he and Reg Hill had prepared for *Supercar*. Grade was intrigued by the idea, and encouraged by the fact that APF shot their productions on film, a prerequisite for American distribution. He agreed to place an order for 26 25-minute episodes, on the condition that APF halved the proposed fee of £3000 per episode. The following morning a desperate Anderson protested that over the course of a sleepless night he hadn't been able to cut the costs by more than a third. Grade appreciated his sincerity and the two men shook hands on a deal. It was the beginning of the most important business partnership of Anderson's career, and one of the greatest friendships of his life.

Above: Supercar's test pilot Mike Mercury. The character was voiced by Graydon Gould.

Below left: Artist Harold Tamblyn-Watts illustrated this preview of *Supercar* in issue 482 of *TV Comic*, cover-dated 18 March 1961. The strip supplanted *Muffin the Mule* and would run in *TV Comic* until September 1964.

Below right: Eric Eden's endpaper illustration from the *Supercar Annual* published by Collins in 1962.

Above: This *Supercar* story book was published by World Distributors in 1962.

Below left: Members of *Supercar*'s puppet cast, pictured against one of the soundproofed walls at Ipswich Road. From left to right: Pablo, Colonel LaGuava, Judd, Harper, Bill Gibson, Felicity Farnsworth, Masterspy, Jimmy Gibson, Mitch, Professor Popkiss, Dr Beaker and Mike Mercury.

Below right: Supercar takes to the air, flying against back projection footage shot by John Read and Gerry Anderson.

Supercar entered production at Ipswich Road in September 1960. The star of the show was the powerful vehicle that enabled a faster pace and more rapid editing than the predominantly talking heads of *Four Feather Falls*. In the first episode, written by Martin and Hugh Woodhouse, we learn that Supercar was developed by elderly Austrian boffin Professor Rudolph Popkiss (voiced by George Murcell) and his absent-minded English colleague Dr Horatio Beaker (David Graham). In the driving seat is test pilot Mike Mercury (Graydon Gould), who recruits youngster Jimmy Gibson (Sylvia Thamm) and his mischievous pet chimpanzee Mitch (David Graham) to the team. From their base in the Black Rock laboratory in the Nevada Desert, this motley crew embark on scientific research and rescue missions. Prevailing Cold War concerns were embodied by the rotund Albanian villain Masterspy (George Murcell) and his snivelling accomplice Zarin (David Graham).

The filming of one particular sequence was a vivid memory for Anderson, as it coincided with the day of his wedding on 22 November. As Gerry and Sylvia drove home from the ceremony they noticed some unusual activity from the circular pool outside the Ipswich Road studio. The crew were clearly having problems trying to convincingly launch Supercar from the water, so Gerry decided to get out of the car and help them. "I didn't do it lightly, but we were really up against it," he said, adding that he didn't return home to his new bride until 2.00 am. "It wasn't a wedding night in any traditional sense. There certainly wasn't any question of the marriage being consummated that night because we'd been living together for a long time."

Inside the studio, *Supercar* benefited from refinements in Automatic Lip Synch (which was now fitted with bias controls) and the introduction of a more traditional special effect. Supercar's high speed and versatility on and off land demanded moving backgrounds that couldn't be faked using the static painted backdrops of *Four Feather Falls*. The answer was to use back projection, a system that placed actors (or in this case, puppets and models) in front of a translucent screen displaying an image that was projected from behind. The process was widely used in film and television, usually as an economical way of showing actors

in driving scenes, and its inherent problems made it easily detectable to audiences. One of the most obvious was a difference in saturation between the sharp foreground object and the background, which could appear slightly washed out due to the translucent screens.

When filming started, the budget wouldn't even run to a proper back projection screen – for the earliest episodes the footage appeared on a huge sheet of tracing paper. If a puppet or a model slipped, the paper would tear, leading to a delay while a new sheet could be attached to the wooden frame.

For the process to work effectively there had to be a certain distance between the lens of the projector and the screen. This distance was achieved in the confines of the Ipswich Road studio by projecting the footage down a corridor and onto a mirror, which reflected the image at a right angle along another corridor, on to the back of the tracing paper.

Budget constraints extended to the closing titles. Episodes two to 11 were directed by either

David Elliott or Alan Pattillo and on-screen credits were prepared accordingly. The first episode was directed by Anderson, but he gave the credit to Elliott rather than going to the expense of creating an extra title screen.

This paucity was naturally overlooked during publicity for the series' ATV London debut, on Saturday 28 January 1961. Sixteen episodes were in the can by the time Anderson spoke to the 2 February edition of *Television Today*. "We didn't even know what our problems would be at first," he admitted. "One proved to be back projection. Now while most BP problems in full-size working have been solved, we began to discover unique problems when we applied BP technique for the first time to this 'small-world' scale filming... When photographing puppets and models you have to get the camera close in, and this reduces depth of focus. It also becomes difficult to light small figures properly against the back projection."

Above left: Dr Beaker in his laboratory. The set was placed on a rostrum constructed from Dexion steel strips.

Above right: Mike Mercury and Supercar, surrounded by Dr Beaker, Mitch, Jimmy Gibson and Professor Popkiss in the Black Rock facility.

Below: Part of the end titles from *Supercar*'s first series.

Above left: Reg Hill's art department created this promotional material for distributor ITC in 1961.

Above right: The Beverley Sisters take a ride in a replica Supercar for the 25 February 1962 edition of ATV variety show *Val Parnell's Sunday Night at the London Palladium*.

Below: This deluxe Supercar toy cost 9s 11d and was manufactured by Plaston in 1961.

Anderson credited Walturdaw, projection specialists based in Kingston-upon-Thames, for their help in solving APF's unique problems. He then described his and John Read's efforts in a customised Airspeed Oxford, shooting real-life sky and air-to-ground footage for the back projection plates. They came away with around 20,000 feet of aerial footage, but the seven hours they spent in the air proved particularly arduous to Read. When they were at high altitude Anderson noticed his friend was having difficulty breathing. It was at this point that Read revealed he only had one lung.

Despite these admirable efforts, Anderson couldn't help but be embarrassed when strangers asked about his line of work. "Whenever I met people socially, if they asked me what I was doing, I would say I was making such and such a series. When I said I was making them with puppets I knew they were thinking that I was working with the sort of puppets that were used in pre-school programmes on television. I thought that somehow I had to separate my puppets from any other show being made."

To this end, he came up with a new word that allied his productions with Hollywood photographic techniques such as CinemaScope and VistaVision. "I combined the words 'super', 'marionette' and 'animation' to make 'Supermarionation.'"

The term was unveiled in the 2 February edition of *Televison Today*. "Science-fiction with a difference. And what a difference!" exclaimed reporter Kenneth Ullyett. "But while watching don't forget this isn't a puppet film, or cartoon stuff. This is Super Marionation (marionettes with an electronic 'kick'). The technique uses electronically-controlled model characters, plus lip-synchronised speech, with screened back projection... Super Marionation is the quintessence of puppetry and model-craft, an entirely British TV development."

Supermarionation encompassed the full panoply of APF's expertise – production values in model-making, photography, special effects, editing and orchestral music that had never been so consistently applied to any type of children's programme, let alone those featuring puppets.

Supercar was so successful in the United States that it apparently saved the ailing American ITC, grossing the company $750,000 in its first eight weeks. Grade ultimately syndicated the series to 107 stations across the country. In July Anderson told the trade press that he was contemplating a second series to join the 26 episodes that had already been completed. Following a commission from Grade, production on *Supercar* resumed in October 1961.

Supercar's second series ran to an additional 13 episodes – a half-season to American broadcasters – and featured a number of changes. There was a new arrangement of Barry Gray's theme tune, and Cyril Shaps replaced George Murcell as the voice of Popkiss and Masterspy. The end titles of these episodes were the first to boast that the series was 'Filmed in Supermarionation'.

It has been suggested that APF's immediate response to the success of *Supercar* was to propose an extension of the concept that would have seen more spacebound adventures. The first *Supercar* annual, published in 1962, shares its cover and a number of inside pages with Super-R, a rocket developed by Popkiss and Beaker with funding from the US government. The final page of the book hints at further adventures with Super-R, but by the time it had been published the APF team had already turned their attention to another space vehicle of an almost identical design.

Above left: The cover of this 1962 annual featured an illustration of Supercar and Super-R by Eric Eden.

Above right: Alan Fennel (sic) was credited with the stories in the 1963 annual. Fennell would become one of APF's television writers from *Fireball XL5* onwards, later becoming the managing director of the company's publishing division.

Below: Two examples from the second series of *Supercar* sweet cigarette cards issued by Como Confectionery Products in 1962.

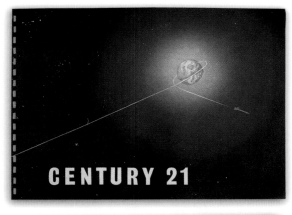  

Leaving VENUS behind, STEVE ZODIAC crashes through the barrier of flames on his Jet-mobile.

Above: Pages from the *Century 21* brochure Gerry Anderson presented to Lew Grade in early 1962. The illustrations were by Reg Hill and APF's special effects director Derek Meddings. Anderson felt it was impossible for the puppets to walk in a lifelike way, so Hill depicted the crew of Century 21 accelerating towards the action aboard Jetmobiles.

Grade felt it would be easier to sell an entirely new Supermarionation concept, rather than further instalments of a series that now had sufficient episodes for a syndication package. Anderson duly presented him with a choice of formats. *Century 21* was a colour science-fiction adventure named after a United States Space Patrol ship with a detachable nose cone that could land on alien planets. The series was set a thousand years in the future and would be shot in colour. The other format would combine live-action and Supermarionation in the story of Little Joe, an American boy who dreamed of being Joe 90, the pilot of Space Patrol Vehicle 1 Zero. The beginning of each imaginary adventure would mark the transition from actors to puppets.

Grade played it safe and commissioned the first concept, stipulating that it would have to be filmed in black and white. The

format went through a number of changes in pre-production: the date was moved to the Universal Astronomic Year 2062 and, in the first sign that Anderson's predictions for the future included globalisation, the United States Space Patrol became the World Space Patrol.

In February 1962 the title of the new series was briefly reported as *Nova X 100* before Gerry settled on *Fireball XL5*. In later years he cheerfully admitted that the 'XL' was a pinch from Castrol XL, a well-known brand of engine oil.

In August 1962 *Television Today*'s Kenneth Ullyett returned to Ipswich Road to describe APF's progress. "Hardened by spacemen Colonel Glenn and Yuri Gagarin, TV-conditioned to outer space by Telstar, you are now ready for the TV sequel to *Supercar*. It is *Fireball XL5*, Britain's first truly adult exploration into science-fiction in a dramatic TV series."

While it was stretching things a bit to describe this as anything more mature than family viewing, APF had been moving further away from the nursery with every series since *Torchy*. *Fireball*'s scripts – largely written by Alan Fennell, Anthony Marriott and Dennis Spooner – were enlivened by postmodern asides and the introduction of futurist slang such as 'tootie'. This mildly derogatory term was possibly inspired by Arthur Provis' habit of describing someone as "an old toot."

Added sophistication could be detected in the episodes directed by Alan Pattillo. "*Fireball* was an interesting series for me," he remembers. "We tried to do all kinds of experimental angles with deep focus photography, with the big heads in the foreground and other characters talking to them in the distance, to give the feel of a comic strip format. Sometimes it worked well, other times they ended up looking rather pretentious. It was a real challenge for the lighting cameraman John Read, but he knew how to do it."

The main characters were all grown-ups and included Venus, Supermarionation's first female lead. This blonde doctor of space medicine was voiced by Sylvia Anderson in an 'ow-you-say French accent that evoked Brigitte Bardot and the copycat sex kittens adding Continental glamour to contemporary cinema. By Venus' side in the XL5 control cabin was Colonel Steve Zodiac (Paul Maxwell), another square-jawed American from the Mike Mercury school of heroics. Professor Matthew Matic (the dependable David Graham) was XL5's navigator and the series' resident boffin. There were further echoes of *Supercar* in Zoony the Lazoon (David Graham), Venus' mischievous alien pet. The crew was completed by Robert, XL5's robotic automatic pilot. Robert's few lines of dialogue were voiced by Gerry Anderson himself, using the type of throat device designed to aid speech in those who had undergone a laryngectomy.

Fireball XL5 was based at Space City, a glass-and-steel metropolis on a Pacific island. Following a rocket-powered take-off from a horizontal ramp (as per Super-R) Fireball's space manoeuvres were enhanced by the application of front projection. The process was invented in the late 1940s, but *Fireball*

Following the super success of **SUPERCAR** ITC are pleased to announce **FIREBALL XL5**

produced by AP Films for ATV, distributed throughout the world by ITC

LONDON ITC NEW YORK

XL5

A SERIES OF 52
(1st Series Numbers 1-26)

No. 1

FIREBALL Junior is the detachable nose cone, that explores unknown planets while FIREBALL XL5 stays in orbit.

See back of packet for wonderful album offer!
Issued by
COMO CONFECTIONERY
PRODUCTS(London)LTD
91 Regent St., London W.1

Above: Sylvia Anderson with Venus, *Fireball XL5*'s doctor of space medicine. The puppet was sculpted by Christine Glanville, but initially failed to meet with Sylvia's approval. It was only when Glanville took her father's advice and modelled the puppet on Sylvia that it was finally accepted.

Right: Now rather moth-eaten, this Steve Zodiac trophy was created by APF's puppet workshop and presented to a *Fireball XL5* ten-pin bowling team.

Below: The cover of Collins' 1964 *Fireball XL5 Annual* was illustrated by Eric Eden.

XL5 was the first production to use it for television. APF used Alekan-Gerard axial projection equipment supplied by the Rank Organisation for their experiments. Filming took place through a semi-transparent mirror that reflected footage from a projector placed at right angles to the camera. The image was bounced from the mirror onto a glass-beaded screen. The intensity of the reflected light produced a more luminous picture than back projection, and nullified shadows thrown by foreground objects.

"Supermarionation is not an easy medium," Reg Hill told the 23 August 1962 edition of *Television Today*. "So when *Fireball* was planned in a 26 [episode] series we realised it might take a fortnight for each episode, thus occupying a whole year for the series. This has many disadvantages apart from cost spread over so long a time; for one thing, you are producing a very long way from actual screen dates. So Gerry Anderson decided on a full-time second unit, with two film directors working at once. For example, after the first week on episode A, it goes to the second unit to clear up inserts, then the second director takes over to start episode B. So though in effect each episode still takes a fortnight, production of two episodes at once is overlapped. In fact we now have virtually a third unit for special effects, BP and other technical work. And we have a second Four-channel Natterer in continual use."

The first episode of *Fireball XL5* was broadcast by ATV London on Sunday 28 October 1962. Lew Grade commissioned an additional 13 instalments and, unlike *Supercar*, the ultimate collection of 39 episodes was produced in a single production block. The series was a great success in the UK, but its popularity in the US exceeded all expectations. Grade scored a major coup by selling *Fireball XL5* to the NBC network. "Each network, such as NBC, would have around 200 affiliate stations which were under contract," said Anderson. "At a certain time every evening, each of those stations would have to finish their own programming bang on time and join their network. At that point, the whole country had the opportunity to watch whatever they were transmitting. This is how *Fireball XL5* was transmitted – for Lew it meant one deal, one contract and one print. And NBC paid a fortune for it."

Over the last two years, Grade's relationship with APF had become crucial to ITC's American operation. Rather than hiring APF on a series-by-series basis, and running the risk that they could be wooed by another distributor, Grade decided to bring the company in-house. Anderson was summoned to a 7.30 am meeting in Grade's office and told unequivocally that ATV was going to purchase AP Films. Grade would become the new chairman, with Anderson, his partners and staff becoming his employees. Anderson was rendered speechless by Grade's audacity, but when he discovered that ATV was prepared to pay £110,000 for the company's shares his attitude soon mellowed. As a further sweetener, ten per cent of ATV's profits from the shows would go to the Andersons, Hill and Read. As the major shareholder of APF Anderson stood to benefit the most, but the sale represented a windfall for all four executive directors, as well as holding the promise of significant further investment. Not everybody on the board agreed the deal was a good idea, but APF was sold to ATV on 20 December 1962.

Just two years after what Gerry had described as a "hand-to-mouth existence", he and Sylvia were now a wealthy couple with generous salaries. In 1963 they bought a new house in Gerrards Cross. Parked in the drive was a gift from Lew – a Rolls-Royce Silver Shadow.

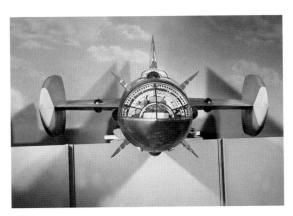

Top: Puppeteers Judith Shutt, Christine Glanville and Phyllis Fisher operate Dr Venus, Professor Matic and Colonel Zodiac aboard Fireball XL5.

Above: The *Fireball XL5 Quiz Paint Book* was published by Collins in 1963.

Left: Two shots of a large Fireball XL5 model, taken as reference for licensees.

Above: The *Stingray* series overview booklet published by ITC in 1964.

Below left: The Stirling Road water tank employed a weir system at the front and back. This picture was taken during the production of the *Stingray* episode *The Disappearing Ships*.

Below right: In 1963 APF moved to a new building on the Slough Trading Estate. The Stirling Road studio would be the company's base of operations until the end of the decade.

APF's next series stayed in the universe of the 2060s, effectively transferring the format of *Fireball XL5* to an underwater setting. ITC's brochure for *Stingray* revealed "The wonder underwater craft of the future. A super submarine that plunges into the depths, meeting new and fascinating creatures and vegetation, discovering underwater cities and finding people never before known to man. Hazards amid scenes of breathless beauty."

At the helm of the atomic-powered submarine was Captain Troy Tempest (voiced by Don Mason) and his navigator 'Phones' (Robert Easton). Also on board was the beautiful but mute Marina, a liberated slave from the undersea kingdom of Pacifica. Back at base, the crew included Commander Shore (Ray Barrett) and his daughter Atlanta (Lois Maxwell), Marina's rival for Troy's affections. This time round the inevitable pet was a seal pup called Oink (David Graham), but he would be quietly forgotten long before the 39-episode series was over.

Anderson felt that APF had outgrown the studio at Ipswich Road, so asked Grade if the company could have larger premises. APF remained on the Slough Trading Estate, but moved to a new unit half a mile away on Stirling Road. The art department occupied offices in the nearby Edinburgh Avenue. The burgeoning merchandise division had already relocated to an office in Bayswater.

The Stirling Road studio was big enough to accommodate an initial three stages, measuring 40 x 45 feet, with a height of 12 feet 6 inches to the eaves. Two were designated for puppet filming – enabling different units to shoot episodes in tandem – while the third was reserved for special effects. Reg Hill oversaw all construction, including production offices, workshops, a props department, a preview theatre and 12 cutting rooms. "Everything was done in a huge panic," remembered Anderson. "We were designing, writing and preparing for *Stingray* as the work was going on. But, clearly, we weren't able to start work until the studio was ready."

R Howard Cricks wrote about the new facility in the 27 June issue of trade magazine *Kinematograph Weekly*: "I saw a number of sets for *Stingray* nearing completion – highly imaginative concepts of future construction, built with immense skill to present realistic appearance. The scale is eight feet to the inch. The Stingray itself is a submarine, embodying a method of propulsion not yet known to our shipbuilders. The film is based on a town, Marineville, which is the headquarters of the World Aquanaut Security Patrol – the WASPs. All the buildings are built on hydraulic ramps, so that they drop below ground for security."

Underwater scenes would be achieved with a piece of trickery Hill had first devised for *Supercar*. A narrow aquarium was placed between the dry models and the film camera. By shooting through the glass, it was possible to create the illusion that Stingray and the other undersea craft were mingling with bubbles and schools of tropical fish. The first *Stingray* aquarium exploded under the pressure of the water, so new ones were built using half-inch plate glass walls.

KINE PRODUCTION REVIEW

SUPERMARIONATION

A NEW DIMENSION IN ENTERTAINMENT

THE PROCESS OF SUPERMARIONATION IS EXCLUSIVE TO A.P. FILMS LIMITED

Top left: Sweet cigarette cards showing Marineville and one of Titan's mechanical fish. The set of 50 *Stingray* cards was issued by Cadet Sweets in 1964.

Left: An Aquaphibian puppet from *Stingray*. The Aquaphibians were inspired by a creature that had appeared in the *Fireball XL5* episode *XL5 to H$_2$0*.

Top right: A publicity shot of Stingray, launching from its Marineville tunnel into the Pacific Ocean.

Above: The Supermarionation supplement included with the 27 June 1963 issue of *Kinematograph Weekly*.

TV WORLD 6d

Complete Midland ITV programmes SATURDAY MAY 15 – FRIDAY MAY 21

Troy Tempest and Marina: Stingray, Wednesday, 5.25—see page 32

Free inside!
HOLIDAY KNITTING for the family

TOP STAR TALKING
EAMONN ANDREWS

The Queen in Germany
SPECIAL ITV COVERAGE

Above left: Gerry answers the call for a publicity photo, with Sylvia and Troy Tempest at the Stirling Road studio.

Above right: *Stingray*'s Marina and Troy Tempest featured in this 1965 issue of *TV World*.

Below: Like most of the Supermarionation puppets, El Hudat – from the *Stingray* episode *Star of the East* – had a panel in the back of his head allowing access to the lip-synch mechanism.

Puppets and models only got wet when they had to appear on the sea surface. For these sequences an interior tank was constructed to a lens angle. The front and far edges of the tank were set at a slightly lower level than the other two sides. The overflowing water was collected out of shot and pumped back into the tank. "This gave us a perfect horizon without the edge of the tank showing," said Anderson. "While it was my idea, Reg employed a lot of expertise in designing and building it."

By this time only 30 per cent of NBC's prime time shows were broadcast in black and white, so Grade needed little persuading to authorise Anderson's next major innovation. *Stingray* became the first British television series shot entirely in colour, and over the ten months of production APF struggled to find enough Eastmancolor stock for their needs.

Stingray was first screened by ATV London and four other ITV regions on Sunday 4 October 1964. "Stand by for action!" announced Commander Shore at the beginning of each episode, echoing the American radio and television drama *Stand By For Crime*. The title sequence that followed is a thrilling showreel for APF's peerless artistry, expertly scored by Barry Gray's clamorous theme music. "I would work out the main titles in my mind," said Anderson. "Then I would brief Barry: 'Twenty seconds of this… Crash… Anything can happen in the next half hour… Into the music… Overall length: 75 seconds.' Then I would describe the speed of cutting that I would want to do. I didn't attempt to translate any of this brief into musical terms, I just gave him the general scenario of the titles and the breakdown. He would then record the music and when we shot the material we would cut it to the music, which would work because the music was prepared and awaiting the final assembly."

Shortly before *Stingray* made its debut Lew Grade predicted that it would earn at least three million dollars for ITC in the United States. While the series wasn't networked, it proved to be a huge hit in the UK and in syndication across the US.

Anderson and Grade held bi-monthly progress meetings at ATV House in Great Cumberland Place. During one such conversation at the end of 1963 Grade asked what the next format

would be. Anderson was ready with an idea that he warned "might be expensive." It would be the zenith of APF's achievements in Supermarionation, and one of the most extraordinary television series ever made.

Above: Atlanta, Troy and Marina in a publicity shot from *Stingray*.

Far left: *Stingray* was filmed in Eastmancolor.

Below: The packaging of this 1964 Plaston toy doubled as a 'Playorama Pack' with cardboard figures that could be cut out. As a consequence, boxed examples are now extremely rare.

THE *Fabulous* TV SUBMARINE

3
APPROACHING DANGER ZONE

"I don't think we knew that *Thunderbirds* was going to be such a big hit, but we certainly felt it was a great progression," said writer Alan Fennell. Sylvia Anderson similarly defines AP Films' early programmes as valuable steps towards its greatest accomplishment. "The lead up was all very practical, but *Thunderbirds* was the big thing," she says. "Personally, I thought, 'We're never going to do any better than this.'"

Prototype versions of the Thunderbird craft had appeared in previous shows – a high-speed reconnaissance vehicle in *Supercar*, a spaceship in *Fireball XL5* and a submarine in *Stingray* – but the new series would combine these elements in a concept that benefitted from all the filmmaking skills that APF had acquired since *Four Feather Falls*.

Gerry Anderson spent late 1963 and early 1964 developing his original idea for *Thunderbirds* in consultation with Sylvia and the department heads at Stirling Road. The scenario drew upon events of the 1940s, as well as taking its inspiration from the Space Race and recent advances in aeronautical engineering. The production of the series would demand a new level of technical sophistication, while the multitude of diverse characters suggested ways to extend the appeal of Supermarionation to an older audience. Gerry's format would be authentically cinematic in both its ambition and realisation, with production values that were unprecedented in the history of television.

"*Thunderbirds* was the high," said Gerry, reflecting on the creation that came to define his entire career. "As important as characterisation is, I think the sheer action and adventure of that series was unbeatable."

The catalyst for *Thunderbirds* was a tragedy in Germany that made global headlines.

The Mathilde mine in Lengade, Lower Saxony, was serviced by artificial lakes that provided water to wash its iron ore. On the evening of Thursday 24 October 1963 a dam collapsed and the mine was flooded by water and mud from one of the lakes, threatening to drown or crush 129 of the miners. Seventy-nine men made their way to the surface, but the remainder were trapped.

Gerry Anderson followed the progress of the rescue operation from the day the news broke until 7 November, when the last 11 survivors were finally brought to the surface. Twenty-nine men had died underground, but the eventual recovery of the others became known as the 'Wunder von Lengade' (the 'Miracle of Lengade').

Anderson was fascinated by the bravery of the rescue teams, the plight of the victims and the ingenious technology that enabled them to escape. "The rescuers needed a huge drill that was big enough to hoist a man from 300 feet down below," he told Chris Bentley in 2000. "Such a drill existed, but it was in Bremen, so it had to be brought by rail and was going to take eight hours to arrive. Little by little, I started to think that there really ought to be dumps around the world with rescue gear standing by, so that when a disaster happened, all these items of rescue equipment could be rushed to the disaster zone and be used to help people get out of trouble."

As production of *Stingray* drew to a close, Anderson presented his idea for a follow-up series to Lew Grade. *International Rescue* would revolve around wealthy philanthropist Jeff Tracy and his five sons, all of whom operate from a secret location. The organisation would be first on the scene with the most advanced equipment wherever disaster struck – from the bottom of the sea to the depths of outer space.

Previous Supermarionation series had each been named after a central vehicle, but *International Rescue* boasted a fleet of five. Anderson's outline also described Jeff's sons,

Below left: Newspapers all over the world, including England's *Daily Express*, provided regular bulletins on the rescue operation at Lengade.

Below right: The emblem of International Rescue was reproduced on this badge, manufactured by Plastoid in 1966.

Left: Gerry and Sylvia Anderson join *Stingray*'s Troy Tempest and Marina on the set of *Thunderbirds* in early 1965.

Above: The set as it appeared in the episode *The Perils of Penelope*.

Below: This promotional image of Stingray in front of Tracy Island was published months before *Thunderbirds* made its television debut.

each one named after a member of NASA's elite Mercury Seven crew: Scott (Malcolm Scott Carpenter), Virgil (Virgil Grissom), Alan (Alan Shepard), Gordon (Leroy Gordon Cooper) and John (John Glenn). Each Tracy brother commanded his own vehicle:

RESCUE 1, the 15,000 mph rocket piloted by Scott Tracy, comes out of the swimming pool, palm trees swaying and smoke billowing from its tail.

RESCUE 2, transporter of heavy rescue equipment, is piloted by Virgil Tracy and housed in a hangar behind a cliff face. It is comparatively slow, travelling at a maximum speed of 2,000 mph, and is the heavy-duty arm of the International Rescue fleet.

RESCUE 3, the spacecraft, awaits pilot Alan Tracy down in the heart of Tracy Island. There is an eruption of sound as three giant engines kick into thunderous life. As they scream louder, the craft begins to shudder and then she is away, roaring through the Round House for the emptiness of space.

RESCUE 4, the underwater scout, is carried aboard Rescue Two and piloted by Gordon, who is also Virgil's co-pilot.

RESCUE 5, the super-satellite, appears. Its function is to orbit Earth and monitor global communications.

Top: It's unclear when *Thunderbirds* was set. In *30 Minutes After Noon* this edition of the *Spoke City Tribune* is dated 2007…

Above: … while this calendar in *Give or Take a Million* shows the year to be 2026. Gerry Anderson and art director Bob Bell dismissed such references as mistakes.

Above right: Lew Grade holds court at ATV House in 1964.

Despite on-screen evidence to the contrary, Anderson maintained that International Rescue commenced operations in 2065. The futuristic setting and epic potential for stories made him anxious that Grade would consider it too expensive. When he expressed this concern, Grade reacted in a surprising way. "Lew jumped out of his seat, came round to my side of the desk, grabbed me by the scruff of the neck and dragged me into the centre of the room," said Anderson. "He pointed to the ceiling and said, 'You see that light bulb, Gerry? If you told me you wanted to make a television series about that light bulb I'd back it!'"

Following a pattern that had been established on *Fireball XL5* and *Stingray*, Gerry and Sylvia collaborated on the new series' pilot script. The couple retreated to their holiday villa in Albufeira, Portugal, where Gerry outlined a story that drew upon a vivid memory from his national service. While at RAF Manston, he had witnessed a plane making an emergency landing with its undercarriage jammed in the retracted position. For the first *International Rescue* story, the stricken plane became a nuclear-powered, supersonic airliner, sabotaged with a bomb on its maiden flight from London to Tokyo.

"I had already devoted a lot of time to thinking about the plot and the basic structure," said Gerry, "but the only way I was able to write was by dictating every word of the script as it unfolded in my head. Sylvia was very good at shorthand, and she sat by my side, writing down everything I said. She would stop every now and then, when the commercial break was supposed to occur for example, and ask if we could go swimming. This used to annoy me intensely because it would interrupt my train of thought. When I finished dictating the final scene she looked up from her notepad and I told her to write '*Trapped in the Sky*, by Gerry and Sylvia Anderson' on the front page of the script."

When Gerry and Sylvia returned to England the draft script was circulated to executives at ATV and the staff at Stirling Road. Alan Pattillo was completing work on his episodes of *Stingray* when Gerry asked him to direct *Trapped in the Sky*. "Gerry invited me up to see him and Sylvia," he remembers. "I was told that the next series was going to be called *International Rescue* and that there would be a family of sons controlling the craft. I remember saying to Gerry, 'Oh fine,' and thinking it wouldn't catch on. How wrong I was."

The concept was not quite ready, however. *International Rescue*'s emphasis on flight-based adventure once again betrayed Gerry's admiration for his late brother, but this was the series on which Lionel may have had the greatest influence of all. During the war, Lionel spent 18 months stationed at Falcon Field near Mesa, Arizona. His frequent letters home described not only his flying exploits but off-duty activities that seemed impossibly exciting. The young Gerry had been deeply impressed to read that Lionel had danced with Hollywood pin-up Gene Tierney, met her co-star Preston Foster, and even secured a walk-on role in their new film. This colourful melodrama was released in England in 1943. Its title was *Thunder Birds*.

Gerry never discussed whether this was the direct inspiration for the name of his new television series and its vehicles, but in 1964 there was broad agreement that *Thunderbirds* was a much better title.

Pattillo was in complete sympathy with the new series' aspirations. "I don't count *Thunderbirds* as science-fiction," he says. "It's too *nice*, its values are too human... science-fiction is a cold description for such warm-hearted stuff. The pilot script that Gerry and Sylvia wrote really is excellent. It shows you all the characters, what their functions are, what craft they manipulate and at the same time it tells an exciting story. To do all those things and dovetail them so well was very good."

Above: An insert poster promoting the American release of *Thunder Birds* in 1942. Gerry Anderson's brother, Lionel, took part in the filming as an extra.

Left: Director Alan Pattillo on the Marineville Tower set of *Stingray*.

Top: A passport picture of Derek Meddings taken by AP Films' photographer Doug Luke.

Above: Meddings' original sketches for Rescue 1 and Rescue 4 can be seen on the wall of Brains' laboratory in *Sun Probe*.

Right: Thunderbird 1 in *Trapped in the Sky* and Thunderbird 2 in *Pit of Peril*. Meddings was often asked why Thunderbird 2's wings appeared to be placed the wrong way round. "I only did it because I thought it was different," he said. "All aircraft have swept back wings, so I thought I'd sweep mine forward."

Since *Fireball XL5*, Gerry Anderson had increasingly expressed his ambition to broaden the appeal of his programmes. The term 'Supermarionation' had partly been created as an effort to distance AP Films' output from less sophisticated puppet series, but the company's productions remained a staple of late afternoon broadcasting for children. *Thunderbirds* would be the first APF show to be scheduled for a family audience, with a 7.00 pm broadcast slot in many ITV regions. According to *Television Mail*, the trade magazine that published a special *Thunderbirds* supplement in December 1965, this shift in perception was premeditated. "At the end of 1963, when APF was planning a series to follow its already successful *Stingray*, it was decided to go for a more adult market," wrote Rod Allen. "The new series would be transmitted in the UK in early evening time instead of children's hour and at least as much of the potential audience would be adult as it would be children."

In a 1965 interview for the news programme *ATV Today*, Gerry suggested that he and his team's efforts to make *Thunderbirds* as believable as possible would help him to court a wider audience. "We very much want the films to have adult appeal," he said.

This increased sophistication of *Thunderbirds* was reflected in the detailed designs of Derek Meddings. The special effects expert had first worked for Gerry Anderson as a freelance on *The Adventures of Twizzle*, joining APF full-time towards the end of *Supercar*. Meddings collaborated with Reg Hill on the blueprints for Fireball XL5, but when Hill stepped aside as APF's art director Meddings assumed sole responsibility for major vehicles. "The reason I designed these things was that I was the one who was going to make them fly, go underwater and do everything they needed to do," he said in 1992. "I didn't want to be landed with something the art department gave me, something that might have been too heavy to fly on wires.

"Gerry, Sylvia, Reg Hill, all of us got together at the beginning," he said, remembering how pre-production began. "Gerry explained the series outline, and what the vehicles would do. They weren't called Thunderbirds to start with – they

were called Rescue 1, 2, 3 and so on. I just sat down and doodled."

The results of Meddings' doodles were the swing-winged reconnaissance scout Rescue 1, the Soyuz-inspired rocket Rescue 3, the diminutive submarine Rescue 4 and the surveillance satellite Rescue 5. Meddings' favourite, however, was International Rescue's multi-purpose freighter. "I didn't get to Thunderbird 2 straight away – I did a few sketches that weren't quite right. But when I settled on the one I liked I never showed anybody the other sketches. Never give them a choice, in case they go for something you don't like!

Above: Some of Meddings' pre-production sketches found their way into this advertisement, which featured in the January-February 1966 issue of trade magazine *Toys International*.

Right: "I used to let my imagination run wild," said Meddings, recalling how he designed the International Rescue vehicles. "I'd sit at home in the evenings and doodle until I came up with something." Meddings' original painting of Rescue 3 is almost identical to his ultimate design.

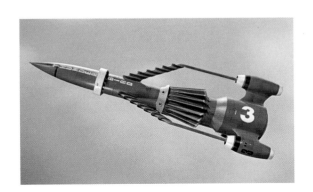

Left: Thunderbird 3, as it appears in the show's opening titles, and Thunderbird 4 in *The Mighty Atom*.

Left and above: Meddings' design for Thunderbird 5 was inspired by sketches he had already made for the Tracy family's Round House. "I enjoyed designing Tracy Island," he said, "because it was one of those places I imagined living when I was a kid. A bit like Robinson Crusoe."

"I drew it up, showed it to Gerry and everybody and I don't think anybody said they didn't like it. There may have been a few little comments from Reg, but he had to do that because he had been the art director and he had to put his mark on it, a bit like a cat peeing up a door and marking its territory. I respected Reg, but I didn't take any notice, because I thought, 'Reg, you are now elevated up to the managerial side. You stick to that, I'll do the designing.' I never said that, of course. I used to say, 'Yes, I will,' when he made those suggestions but I never did unless I genuinely thought he had a point."

In 1992 Meddings compared filming special effects miniatures to working with actresses. "Like women, they have good sides and bad sides," he said. "But I still think

Right: When Meddings designed the Fireflash he took the unusual decision to place the cockpit in the tail fin and passenger lounges in each of the wings. These elements were preserved when the airliner reached the screen in *Trapped in the Sky* (below), although by this time the plane was no longer operated by BOAC.

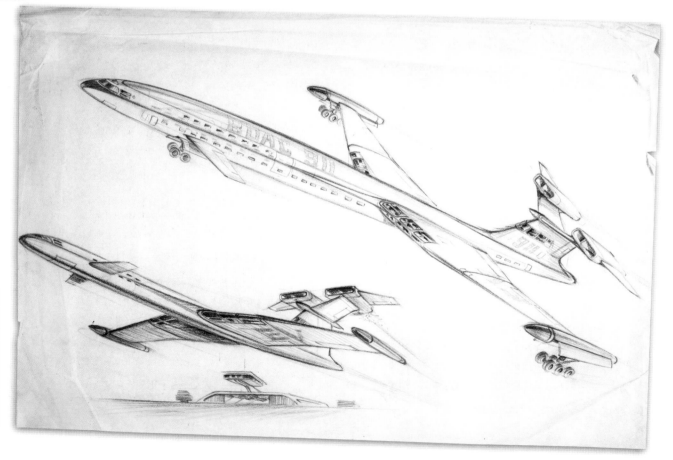

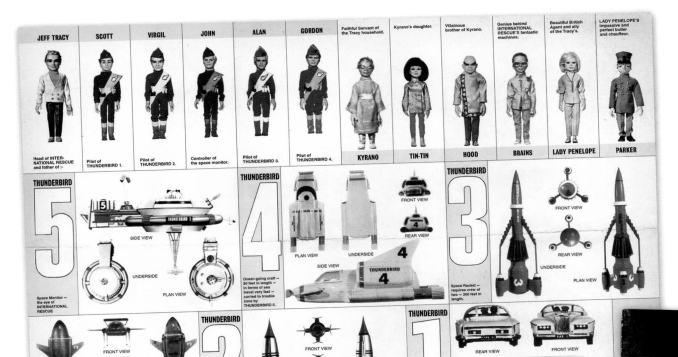

JEFF TRACY · SCOTT · VIRGIL · JOHN · ALAN · GORDON · Faithful Servant of the Tracy household. · Kyrano's daughter. · Villainous brother of Kyrano. · Genius behind INTERNATIONAL RESCUE'S fantastic machines. · Beautiful British Agent and ally of the Tracy's. · LADY PENELOPE'S impassive and perfect butler and chauffeur.

KYRANO · TIN-TIN · HOOD · BRAINS · LADY PENELOPE · PARKER

Head of INTER-NATIONAL RESCUE and father of :-
Pilot of THUNDERBIRD 1.
Pilot of THUNDERBIRD 2.
Controller of the space monitor.
Pilot of THUNDERBIRD 3.
Pilot of THUNDERBIRD 4.

THUNDERBIRD 5 · SIDE VIEW · UNDERSIDE · PLAN VIEW · Space Monitor – the eye of INTERNATIONAL RESCUE.

THUNDERBIRD 4 · FRONT VIEW · REAR VIEW · PLAN VIEW · UNDERSIDE · SIDE VIEW · Ocean-going craft – 30 feet in length – in terms of sea travel very fast – carried to trouble zone by THUNDERBIRD II.

THUNDERBIRD 3 · FRONT VIEW · REAR VIEW · UNDERSIDE · PLAN VIEW · Space Rocket – requires crew of two – 200 feet in length.

THUNDERBIRD 2 · FRONT VIEW · REAR VIEW · UNDERSIDE · PLAN VIEW · SIDE VIEW · Heavy rescue vehicle of enormous proportions – length 250 feet, wing span 180 feet, height 60 feet, speed 5,000 mph.

THUNDERBIRD 1 · FRONT VIEW · REAR VIEW · SIDE VIEW · PLAN VIEW · Designed to get to trouble zones as quickly as possible – speed 15,000 miles per hour – length 115 feet, diameter 12 feet

REAR VIEW · FRONT VIEW · PLAN VIEW · SIDE VIEW

GERRY ANDERSON'S. THUNDERBIRDS CHARACTER MERCHANDISE SPECIFICATION SHEET

Left and below: The Character Merchandise Specification Sheets created by APF for *Thunderbirds* and other series were forerunners of the style guides issued by modern licensors. Although primarily designed to assist toy manufacturers, this fold-out chart was also used as reference by the special effects department at Stirling Road.

Bottom: These models, given away free inside packets of Kellogg's Sugar Smacks in 1967, were faithful representations of Meddings' designs.

Thunderbird 2 is a good shape. You could shoot it from almost any angle and it looked great. If I was designing it now I think it would end up with more air intakes and it would be a chunkier vehicle. It would be like the Apache helicopter and all these gunships that don't have to be streamlined because they have to carry various armaments."

The Character Merchandise Specification Sheet compiled by APF for toy manufacturers and other licensees elaborated on the capabilities of each vehicle. Thunderbird 1 was "designed to get to trouble zones as quickly as possible" and was 115 feet in length. Thunderbird 2 was a "heavy rescue vehicle of enormous proportions", 250 feet in length with a wingspan of 180 feet and a revised top speed of 5,000

mph. Thunderbird 3 was described as a "space rocket", 200 feet in length (although in the 1966 episode *Give or Take a Million* we learn that it is actually 287 feet tall). Thunderbird 4 was "an ocean-going craft" that was 30 feet in length, and Thunderbird 5 was the "space monitor – the eye of International Rescue."

Thunderbird 2's impressive air-speed was achieved in spite of stubby wings that appeared to have been attached back-to-front. Meddings dismissed concerns that the vehicle didn't look as if it could fly. "*I* made it fly," he said. "I could make *anything* fly."

Above: Jeff Tracy studies a map showing his international network of agents in *The Imposters*.

Below: The first *Thunderbirds* annual was published by City Magazines and AP Films (Merchandising) in 1966. The book included this profile of Jeff and his five sons.

The Thunderbird fleet would become scene-stealers, but the show's cast was extensive compared to its predecessors and played a major part in its success. Back stories were created for all the major characters to help with publishing and other licensed merchandise, but sticking strictly to the television episodes of *Thunderbirds* reveals plenty about the stars of the series.

The show's patriarch is Jeff Tracy, the retired astronaut who runs International Rescue from the Pacific island bearing his surname. Jeff didn't want the highly advanced vehicles and technology he was developing to be used for anything other than humanitarian purposes, so maintained a policy of strict secrecy while planning the organisation. In the episode *The Imposters* it's revealed that Jeff's ambitions took shape during his service in the US Air Force,

at which time he took the hillbilly Jeremiah Tuttle into his confidence. Tuttle was one of the workers at Jeff's base, but would later be recruited as one of International Rescue's agents. When Jeff later joined the space programme, even some of his closest colleagues remained unaware of his plans. In *Edge of Impact*, Jeff's old friend Colonel Tim Casey visits Tracy Island, where great efforts are made to ensure he remains ignorant of Jeff's new vocation.

By the time the space missions came to an end, Jeff was using his wealth and connections in the aeronautics industry to assemble the Thunderbird fleet. No mention is ever made of Jeff's wife, but his mother and five sons joined him on Tracy Island to help him run International Rescue.

Jeff's sons maintain absolute deference to their father. He is generous with his praise when

A CENTURY 21 PRODUCTION ▶ SUPER 33 R.P.M.

JEFF TRACY INTRODUCES
INTERNATIONAL RESCUES CENTURY 21 Records

THUNDERBIRD 2
in the Episode
END OF THE ROAD

THUNDERBIRD 1
in the Episode
TRAPPED IN THE SKY

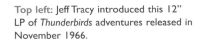

1-24 THUNDERBIRDS

their rescue missions succeed, but quick to criticise what he considers to be poor judgement or a lack of discipline. When two of his sons argue over the salvage potential of a damaged tanker in *Danger at Ocean Deep* he reminds them that: "For many years now, man has worked to perfect the material things in this world, and he's done pretty well for himself. If a building falls down he can soon build it up again. With life, it's different. And this is why the object of International Rescue will never change – your job is to save lives that are in danger. And that's how it's going to be. Always."

Although Jeff doesn't take part in missions, his responsibilities as International Rescue's commander give him little time off. He occasionally relaxes with a Scotch and a cigar, but the other members of his family recognise that he is a workaholic and in *Atlantic Inferno* they urge him to take a holiday.

In most episodes, Jeff's discipline and absolute dedication help to define International Rescue, but he occasionally reveals a sentimental side to his character. In *The Imposters* he sends two of his sons to save a technician stranded in space, even though he knows that launching Thunderbird 3 will reveal the location of International Rescue to the authorities. And in *Cry Wolf*, he waives the usual rules about secrecy when he welcomes youngsters Tony and Bob Williamson to Tracy Island – possibly because they remind him of his own boys.

Top left: Jeff Tracy introduced this 12" LP of *Thunderbirds* adventures released in November 1966.

Top right: Tracy Island, International Rescue's secret headquarters, as seen in *The Imposters*.

Above left: Some of the most unusual items of *Thunderbirds* merchandise included this Belgian cigar band, which was part of a collection issued in 1968.

Above right: "Here's mud in your automated eye." Jeff toasts Wilbur Dandridge III in *The Duchess Assignment*.

Above: Postcards of Thunderbird 1 pilot Scott (left) and Thunderbird 2 pilot Virgil (right), published by Dutch company Vita Nova in 1965.

Far right: A cardboard figure of Alan Tracy, given away with Dutch sugared lollies in the mid-1960s.

Below left: Gordon, Virgil and Scott relax between missions in *Operation Crash-Dive*.

Below centre: Scott comes a cropper in *Cry Wolf*.

Below right: Virgil entertains the International Rescue team at the end of *Trapped in the Sky*.

of action in his father's absence, ultimately winning Jeff's respect.

Although one of the most level-headed members of the team, Scott is not without a sense of fun. In between missions he enjoys a game of pool with his brothers. After saving Tony and Bob from a disintegrating tin mine in *Cry Wolf*, he participates in one of the boys' games back at their house. Their reconstruction of Tracy Island's launch apparatus deposits him in a home-made Thunderbird 2 that careers through a chicken coop before crashing on the other side of a barn, leaving Scott in a dustbin. Fortunately he takes it all in good humour.

The pilot of the actual Thunderbird 2 is Virgil who, like his father, enjoys a cigar in the Tracy Island lounge. Perhaps the most serious of the brothers, he relaxes by painting and playing the piano. He doesn't mind being referred to as "Virg" by his siblings.

Thunderbird 3 is flown by Alan, the youngest Tracy brother. Alan was America's most exciting racing car driver until he announced his retirement from the

Jeff's eldest son is Scott, who is the quick-thinking pilot of Thunderbird 1. It is Scott's assessment of the danger zone that determines which specialist equipment will be needed by his brothers, who follow in the other Thunderbird craft. In *Trapped in the Sky*, Scott supervises the delicate operation to safely land the sabotaged Fireflash airliner. He is similarly resourceful in *Atlantic Inferno*, the first episode of the second series, when he takes temporary command of International Rescue. Scott agonises over the best course

sport, shortly before International Rescue commenced operations. In *Atlantic Inferno* he takes charge of Thunderbird 1 while Scott remains at their father's desk. He is also required to man Thunderbird 5, but is quietly frustrated that these stints take him away from the action on Earth.

Aquanaut Gordon Tracy is at the controls of Thunderbird 4. It seems Gordon is required on fewer missions than Scott, Virgil and Alan, but his most memorable excursions include the trip he makes accompanying Virgil to the Sahara Desert in *Desperate Intruder*. Between assignments, Gordon plays the guitar and visits the rifle range with his brothers.

The least conspicuous of all the Tracy brothers is John, largely because each of his shifts in Thunderbird 5 lasts for a month. Alan and Scott also share monitoring duties aboard the satellite, leaving John free to occasionally take part in rescues. In *Danger at Ocean Deep* he reminds his father that he has been on a dozen missions, but the only one we actually see takes place in this episode.

The engineer responsible for the design and maintenance of the Thunderbird craft is universally addressed by the affectionate

nickname Brains. In a departure from the resident boffins of *Supercar* and *Fireball XL5*, Brains is proof that age is no longer commensurate with scientific authority. He is one of the younger members of the team, although he seems to have little time for youth culture. His stutter might suggest a degree of social awkwardness, but Brains is far from shy – in *Day of Disaster* he dances with glee, and in *Alias Mr. Hackenbacker* he adopts a pseudonym in order to pursue a freelance design project for Atlantic Airlines.

Above left: Gordon attempts to fix the sabotaged Fireflash in *Operation Crash-Dive*.

Above centre: John comes to the end of a shift on Thunderbird 5 in *City of Fire*.

Above right: Brains watches the unveiling of the Skythrust airliner in *Alias Mr. Hackenbacker*.

Below: A cut-out of Thunderbird 5 was a novel feature of this birthday card published by Valentine & Sons in the mid-1960s.

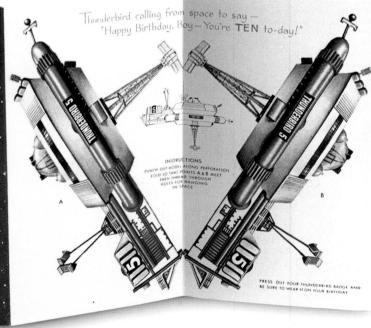

International Rescue's arch enemy is the Hood, a bald-headed mercenary with no patriotic or political allegiance. His principal aim is to steal information about International Rescue that he can sell to the highest bidder. A master of disguise, the Hood is also a powerful hypnotist whose eyes literally light up when he gets excited or places victims under his spell.

The Hood's powers rely on a mysterious form of telepathy which he practises in an exotic jungle temple. He uses this influence to remotely interrogate and manipulate his brother Kyrano – who happens to be Jeff Tracy's manservant.

The Hood's voodoo may give him an initial edge in his otherwise hapless schemes, but it makes him the most problematic character in *Thunderbirds*. In a format devoted to realistic or at least feasible presentations of scientific and engineering concepts, the episodes featuring this Oriental magician sometimes strike an incongruous note. The Hood's presence diminishes as the series progresses, possibly indicating that scriptwriters were struggling with the character.

The secrecy surrounding the Hood's relationship with Kyrano is another of *Thunderbirds*' weak links. Kyrano is understandably reluctant to reveal the source of his fainting spells and remains a poorly

Top left: The Hood establishes a psychic link with Kyrano in *Trapped in the Sky*.

Top centre: Jeff rushes to Kyrano's aid in *Trapped in the Sky*.

Top right: Tin Tin joins Alan and Scott aboard Thunderbird 3 in *Sun Probe*.

Left: The Hood, *Thunderbirds*' only recurring villain, uses magic in his efforts to undermine International Rescue.

Above: Sweet cigarette cards showing Kyrano and his daughter, Tin Tin, from the set issued by Barratt & Co in 1967.

sketched character. Nothing is known about how he and Tin Tin came to live on Tracy Island, although in *Sun Probe* he tells Jeff: "Both my daughter and I owe our lives to you." The comment is never explained or even discussed again.

Although Tin Tin Kyrano is a relatively minor player at International Rescue, she is a more accomplished creation. In *The Uninvited* she accompanies Virgil and Brains when they rescue the injured Scott, and in *Desperate Intruder* her archaeological holiday with Brains brings her face-to-face with her evil uncle. "I have never seen him before in my life," she tells Virgil, "and yet I felt I knew him in some far off way..."

Tin Tin is more commonly seen at Tracy Island, sitting at a typewriter by Jeff's side, swimming in the pool or nervously smoking a cigarette as she awaits news of a rescue. Alan is clearly falling in love with her, but she takes time to realise the depth of his feelings. Tin Tin's on-off relationship with Alan prompts fits of jealousy in the youngest Tracy brother:

in *End of the Road* she falls for civil engineer Eddie Houseman, and in *Ricochet* swoons over a DJ broadcasting from a pirate satellite station ("Isn't he just minty?"). It's probably just as well that Alan never finds out that she also has a crush on the leader of The Cass Carnaby Five in *The Cham-Cham* ("Isn't he gorgeous?").

The matchmaker between Alan and Tin Tin is Jeff's mother, who is only ever referred to as Grandma. An excellent cook, whose speciality seems to be apple pie, Grandma's role takes her little further than her well-equipped kitchen. As well as cooking for everyone on Tracy Island, she rustles up a feast for Tony and Bob in *Cry Wolf*; the boys describe it as the best meal they've ever had. Grandma is a calming influence on the house, and her own grandmother's memories of 20th-century London prove invaluable to Alan and Virgil in *Vault of Death*.

Above: This publicity session from 1965 provided the Hood with a unique opportunity to infiltrate Tracy Island.

Below: Grandma interrupts her game of cards to tell Jeff and Scott about "the old London subway" in *Vault of Death*.

The team at Tracy Island represent just part of International Rescue – the organisation has affiliates and agents all over the world, but only one has earned a framed picture alongside those of the Tracy brothers on Jeff's wall. Lady Penelope Creighton-Ward is a cool blonde who lives in an English stately home. She leads a double life as an elegant socialite and International Rescue's London agent. Even Penelope's Tracy Island portrait is glamorous: as with the Tracy brothers, the eyes on her picture light up when she wants to contact Jeff. But when she has an emergency message to relay, her necklace illuminates.

Jeff is extremely fond of Penelope: he refers to her as 'Penny' and they link arms at an art exhibition in *The Duchess Assignment*. When Jeff takes a belated holiday in *Atlantic Inferno* he spends it with Penelope at her Australian sheep farm. And in *Give or Take a Million* he returns the favour by inviting her to spend

Christmas with his family at Tracy Island.

Although Penelope is frightened of mice (*The Mighty Atom*), and can sometimes be a terrible driver (*Vault of Death*), her spying skills are not to be underestimated. Her handbag conceals a pistol, and her powder compact doubles as a receiver/transmitter. She is loyal to her friends, such as the financially embarrassed Deborah in *The Duchess Assignment*, but ruthless towards those she mistrusts ("Move a muscle and I'll blow off your head" she tells Bondson in *The Man from MI.5*).

Only sartorial pursuits get in the way of her duties – in *The Imposters* she packs more suitcases than are strictly necessary for a foreign jaunt and tries to cross some treacherous swamp land in a pair of slingbacks. It's not until *Alias Mr. Hackenbacker* that she is able to indulge her interest in fashion alongside her talent for espionage.

Fortunately for Penelope, her faithful butler and chauffeur 'Nosey' Parker is on hand for safecracking and other illegitimate necessities. A former thief, Parker is well acquainted with many members of the criminal underworld and sometimes finds it impossible

Above: Lady Penelope Creighton-Ward, International Rescue's London agent, was the subject of this mid-1960s postcard published by CG Williams.

Below left: Penelope takes Jeff's arm at an art gallery in *The Duchess Assignment*.

Below centre: Proving more than a match for secret agent Bondson in *The Man from MI.5*.

Below right: Modelling the latest fashions in *Alias Mr. Hackenbacker*.

Right: A cardboard figure of Penelope's chauffeur Parker, from the Dutch lolly promotion.

to resist the lure of his old lifestyle. In *The Man from MI.5* he secretly plans to rob the bank at Monte Carlo before losing Penelope's yacht at the gaming tables. And in *Danger at Ocean Deep* the rascal gets drunk on a purloined bottle of 1998 Champagne with another chauffeur.

Usually, however, Parker and Penelope work together as an unlikely but highly efficient team. She keeps him on just the right side of the law, disapproving of his bad behaviour until one of his dubious skills comes in useful.

The development of Penelope and Parker was arguably Sylvia Anderson's major contribution to *Thunderbirds*. As she points out, they were the only two regular characters who didn't speak with an American accent. "I wanted to give Lew Grade something he could sell in America," she says. "I felt Americans didn't know anything about us over here. You were either a posh lady of the manor, you were a crook, or you talked in a cockney accent.

Above left: *Vault of Death* includes this flashback to Nosey's incarceration at Parkmoor Scrubs.

Above centre: Getting drunk with fellow chauffeur Stevens in *Danger at Ocean Deep*.

Above right: Dressed for the beach in *Lord Parker's 'Oliday*.

Below: This 1966 book exploited Penelope's reputation as a style icon.

Above left: Penelope was popular enough to inspire a series of novels, which included this paperback published in 1967.

Above right: Sylvia Anderson was meticulous about the presentation of Penelope, both within the series and in publicity shots.

Below: Studio reference photographs of Penelope's FAB 1, illustrating Derek Meddings' typically eccentric decision to position the steering wheel in the middle of the dashboard.

"One of my favourite books was *The Scarlet Pimpernel*. I was fascinated by the idea that you could be one person by day and someone completely different at night. So I thought about the lady of the manor with her lovely car, doing all her good works. And then I thought there would be someone she would give a second chance to in life; a lovable rogue who could be the driver of her pink Rolls-Royce. That's how Penelope and Parker evolved. Lew was always very good at saying, 'As long as it works, just do it.' But when I was working on Lady Penelope he rang me up and said, 'There's only one thing I want to say to you Sylvia – don't make her too posh. The Americans won't understand her.'"

Alan Pattillo was especially fond of Penelope, describing the Tracy brothers as "dull" in comparison. "All the men had to do was pilot these marvellous craft, strapped

into the cockpit saying things like 'Open Pod Three'. You got awfully sick of that, whereas Penelope was much more flexible. She wasn't living on this island in a practically all-male society. She lived a life of her own, but she enjoyed participating with International Rescue when necessary."

Penelope's luxurious car was widely known by its registration number FAB 1 and would rival Thunderbird 2 as the show's most iconic vehicle. In an effort make his design distinctive, Derek Meddings essentially reversed the chassis of a lorry. "I put four wheels at the front, two at the back and the driver in the middle," he recalled. "My excuse for putting four wheels at the front was that the engine was so big and powerful it needed them, but it wasn't done for any technical reason. It was just done for the appearance."

Meddings' sketch was submitted to Rolls-Royce, who gave APF permission to use their brand. "The only stipulation was that we always had to refer to it as a Rolls-Royce, never a 'Rolls,'" said Meddings. "At the time there was a company called Rolls Razors. Rolls-Royce didn't like that, but couldn't do anything about it."

As well as a gun that protruded from the car's radiator grille, the show's writers introduced numerous other gadgets in the style of the customised Aston Martin seen in *Goldfinger* (1964) and *Thunderball* (1965). But *Thunderbirds* went even further than James Bond in the 1966 episode *Lord Parker's 'Oliday*, when Penelope flicks a switch to activate FAB 1's hydrofoils.

Above: Water proves no obstacle to the well-equipped FAB 1 in *Lord Parker's 'Oliday.*

Below right: The first *Lady Penelope* annual, published by City Magazines and AP Films (Merchandising) in 1966, featured strip stories devoted to Penelope, Parker and *Stingray*'s Marina.

Below left: Derek Meddings examines a model of his famous creation at Stirling Road in autumn 1965.

A CENTURY 21 PRODUCTION

INTRODUCING

THUNDERBIRDS 33 R.P.M. mini album

CENTURY 21 Records

21 MINUTES OF ADVENTURE

Above: Jeff showed Parker and Penelope around Tracy Island in this original story, which was released on a 7" 'mini album' in October 1965.

Below: Each packet of Somportex *Thunderbirds* bubblegum featured two picture cards. These examples depict scenes from *Trapped in the Sky* and date from 1966.

Although Gerry and Sylvia relinquished day-to-day supervision of the scripts, Gerry in particular cast an eye across each draft of every 'teleplay'. "Whether I was fair to writers or not I don't know," he said. "There were 101 reasons why people found it difficult to write for our shows, the most common being a lack of understanding of our budgetary or technical restraints. If the writer delivered a good characterisation and a reasonably strong plot, however, then I was quite happy to commission a script."

In 1964 Alan Fennell was balancing a job writing and editing comic strips with a new career as one of APF's most prolific scriptwriters. His episodes of *Thunderbirds* began with the first four into production after *Trapped in the Sky*. "I think scripts were Gerry's first love, really," he said in 1992. "Sylvia was usually involved in the initial story discussions, but then she'd have to go off. So she had some input, but the main story discussions were with Gerry. I used to arrive at the studio at about 11 o'clock. I'd go into Gerry's office and he'd say, 'Right, tell me a story.' I'd relay the idea to him, and he'd embellish it or change it, depending on how good or bad he thought it was. A lot of the time he had other ideas he'd want you to work into the script. If we reached an impasse in the story he'd get up from his desk and go into the cloakroom next door. When he came back he always had a solution. He always managed to get the answer in the toilet. It never failed!

No. 9 HOOD IN ONE OF HIS MANY DISGUISES PLACES AN AUTO-BOMB IN THE HYDRAULIC LANDING GEAR OF THE WORLD'S FASTEST AIRLINER 'FIRE FLASH'
© A.P. FILMS LTD ISSUED BY SOMPORTEX LONDON
A SERIES OF 72 PICTURES.

No. 56 INTERNATIONAL RESCUE'S MOBILE CONTROL MONITOR IN OPERATION AT LONDON AIRPORT.
© A.P. FILMS LTD ISSUED BY SOMPORTEX LONDON
A SERIES OF 72 PICTURES.

2 PHOTO CARDS

THUNDERBIRDS
© 1965 A. P. Films Ltd.
BUBBLE GUM

"Generally speaking the story would be complete by lunchtime. We'd either go for lunch together or I'd leave the studio and go to work. I would usually work on the scripts at night, because I had a publishing job during the day. When I had a first draft script I'd go back to the studio and we'd go through it frame by frame. I'd make a note of any changes then I'd go back home and retype it."

Fennell recalled that Gerry's obsession with realistic production values began with the scripts. "In everything we did, Gerry insisted that it had to be feasible. The only real fantasy came about in how you solved the problem. The beginning of *Martian Invasion* came about because we had to keep the stories realistic – we couldn't have real Martians, so the situation you see at the beginning of the episode turns out to be a film set."

In 1965, Alan Pattillo became the series' story editor. "The writers were asked to send in an idea in the form of a single-page outline," he says. "Gerry and Sylvia would look at it, we'd discuss it, and once we'd had time to think about it the writer would come in for a meeting. We'd meet at 11 in the morning, but I remember some meetings at six o'clock in the evening. They were very amicable get-togethers."

Other writers on the first series included Martin Crump, a film editor who was recommended by director Desmond Saunders, and Donald Robertson. The latter was an ex-engineer who worked from a caravan parked at the end of his garden in Birmingham. Robertson ultimately wrote four episodes, in between making corporate films. Six episodes were written by Dennis Spooner, a veteran of *Fireball XL5* and *Stingray*, and most recently the story editor of the BBC's *Doctor Who*.

Above: Gerry and Sylvia Anderson at home in early October 1965, days after the first episode of *Thunderbirds* was broadcast.

Left: This Thunderbird 3 model included a friction motor and was manufactured by the J Rosenthal company. The toy cost 6s 11d when it was launched in 1965.

Below: An alien zombie is revealed to be a disgruntled actor in *Martian Invasion*.

Above: Gerry and Sylvia were credited as script supervisors on all bar the first episode of *Thunderbirds*.

Below left: Gordon and Virgil tease the lovesick Alan in Dennis Spooner's shooting script for *End of the Road*.

Below right: Pictures from the corresponding sequence in the episode.

"I got on with Dennis very well, but he was a terrible fraud," remembered Gerry with a smile. "I'd ask him to tell me his idea for a storyline, and he'd say, 'Well, er, there are these two fellers, and… er… they're out walking a dog… and… er…' There would be an awkward pause and I'd say, 'You haven't got a story, have you?' He'd sheepishly reply, 'Er… no.' But because it was Dennis, and because I knew his was capable of writing some very good scripts, I would chip in a few ideas of my own. We would develop some ideas together and within 20 minutes we'd have a very good story."

"Dennis Spooner was naughty sometimes," agrees Pattillo. "I often thought he made his story outlines up in the car on the way to the meetings, but he had some very amusing ideas. Dennis would always give you situations that were ingenious, somehow different."

Fennell also admired Spooner's scripts. "Dennis developed more of the humour. I think Alan Pattillo based his more on the characters. Action was really my thing, because of my background in comic strips. With kids' comics you haven't got time for dialogue, and kids don't read it anyway, so you had to keep it moving. In television there is time for the characters to talk, but you can't do that in a strip cartoon – the speech balloons would be too big."

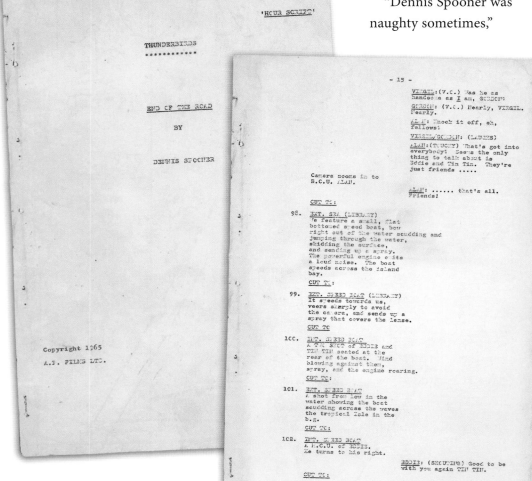

Although there are some excellent stories among the initial episodes, towards the end of 1964 Sylvia felt she had to intervene. "Someone pointed out that we'd done five episodes and Lady Penelope was hardly in any of them," she says. "She just got in her Rolls-Royce, rode around and the next thing you knew you were back on Tracy Island. This was because the writers didn't know how to write for her. So I had to get some material that was exclusive to her. I told the writers, 'Forget she's a woman – *this* is what she does.'"

Spooner rose to the challenge with the outstanding *Vault of Death*. In 1965 Pattillo wrote *The Perils of Penelope* and

Fennell contributed *The Man from MI.5*. These stories, along with Pattillo's *The Cham-Cham* and Tony Barwick's *Alias Mr. Hackenbacker* from 1966, firmly established Penelope and Parker as the series' most consistently entertaining characters.

With International Rescue's London agent and her cockney chauffeur successfully integrated into the mix, the formula for *Thunderbirds'* success was finally complete.

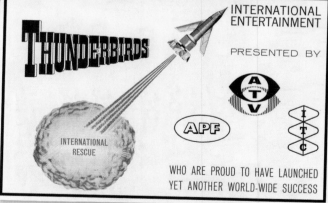

Top: Brains, Penelope, Scott, Jeff, Virgil, John, Tin Tin, Alan and Gordon in a publicity photo from *Thunderbirds'* first series.

Above: International Rescue lifts off in this advertisement from a supplement that appeared in the December 1965 issue of trade magazine *Television Mail*.

4

THE ATOMIC AGE

In 2001, *Thunderbirds*' creator was in a self-deprecating mood when he admitted that "Gerry's world of the future" had been rendered obsolete by more cynical and dystopian predictions of mankind's fate. "In my shows everybody is clean-shaven and everything is sparkling and shining and sanitised," he said. "It unfortunately destroys what people see as humanity."

Anderson was overlooking the fact that *Thunderbirds*' humanistic values are intact in Jeff Tracy's team of heroes, while beyond the organisation lies the greed, poorly conceived schemes and evil intent that provide the series with some of its most compelling frissons.

International Rescue's idealistic notions are as admirable now as they must have seemed in 1965, but AP Films' colourful and detailed extrapolations of life one hundred years hence already seem wide of the mark.

Thunderbirds was created in an era before the advent of the personal computer, the mobile phone and the internet, while its almost complete neglect of what we'd now call alternative sources of energy seems a curious omission to modern eyes.

During the production of *Thunderbirds*, Anderson, Derek Meddings and David Lane visited the British Aircraft Corporation where the Concorde, the world's first supersonic airliner, was being developed. Anderson's interest in all things mechanical was further reflected in the astonishing array of gadgetry developed by Brains and his contemporaries.

Thunderbirds was correct in imagining that our lives would be made easier by technology, but this vision of 2065 is more intriguing for what it reveals about the hopes, fears and aspirations of the era in which it was created...

Top: Thunderbirds 1 and 2 fly to the aid of drilling rig Seascape in *Atlantic Inferno*.

Above: Two examples from the first set of *Thunderbirds* bubblegum cards issued by Somportex in 1966. The Fireflash image was from *Trapped in the Sky*, but the picture of the helijet was one of many promotional shots staged by AP Films' photographer Doug Luke.

The idea of a rescue-based format was not entirely new – three years before he devised the Thunderbird fleet, Gerry Anderson had designated a similar purpose for Supercar. The touch of genius that distinguished *Thunderbirds*, however, was Anderson's realisation that his new series could provide all the pyrotechnics and destruction that youngsters craved, while avoiding the fatalities that generally ensued in more adult productions. Previous Supermarionation series dealt with exploration and conflict, but such plots are rare in *Thunderbirds*. International Rescue is an organisation devoted to a selfless, philanthropic cause, and its members are anxious to protect life wherever possible.

Throughout the series, care is taken to ensure that nobody is killed or seriously injured on screen. For example, Lady Penelope is concerned about the fate of the policeman that Parker subdues outside the Bank of England in *Vault of Death*. She nervously raises her hand to her mouth as Parker applies the chloroform, and then checks, "You haven't hurt him, have you Parker?" Even thugs have a conscience; when Victor Gomez coshes someone in *Move – And You're Dead*, his accomplice Johnny Gillespie asks, "You haven't killed the guy, have ya?" Gomez replies: "No, it was just a little tap."

Where there have been disasters that International Rescue couldn't prevent, the victims are remarked upon. *The Uninvited* begins with Scott returning to Tracy Island after attending a fire in Tokyo. Jeff contacts him for an update en route and says, "Not too many casualties, I hope?"

When deaths occur in *Thunderbirds* it's either in reported incidents or when the camera isn't looking. In *Operation Crash-Dive* it's a shock to discover that the destruction of a Fireflash airliner has resulted in the loss of 600 crew and passengers. This is the greatest single disaster in the series, and takes place prior to International Rescue's involvement. An incident towards the end of that episode illustrates the rules surrounding what the scriptwriters seemed to consider a justifiable loss of life. When a saboteur is discovered aboard a subsequent Fireflash test flight, he jumps from the plane despite being warned by Gordon that his parachute won't have time to open. The assumption is that this misjudged gamble leads to his demise.

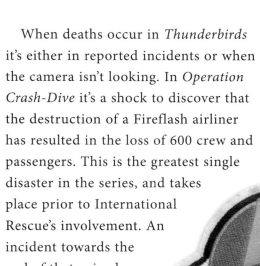

Below right: Air Terrainean's Captain Hanson (right) and his co-pilot at the controls of the seemingly doomed Fireflash in *Thunderbirds*' first episode *Trapped in the Sky*.

Below left: A replica Air Terrainean patch created by Fanderson, the Gerry Anderson Appreciation Society, in 1997.

Bottom: The atomic-powered Fireflash airliner at London Airport in *Trapped in the Sky*.

Above and right: The Fireflash, as depicted in Barratt & Co's first series of *Thunderbirds* sweet cigarette cards. This set of 50 illustrated cards was issued in 1966.

THUNDERBIRDS

A Series of 50

No. 20

FIREFLASH

Main civil aircraft is the Mach 4 atomic powered Fireflash airliner. The Fireflash carries 600 passengers and cruises at 2,800 miles per hour, covering the distance from London to New York in an hour and forty-five minutes.

Issued by
BARRATT & CO LTD
LONDON - - - ENGLAND
PRINTED IN ENGLAND

In *Move – And You're Dead*, Gomez and Gillespie are presumably killed when Thunderbird 1 helps to drive their stolen car off the road. And at the end of *30 Minutes After Noon*, Scott leaves Penelope to "tidy up the details"; this involves Parker aiming FAB 1's radiator cannon on a helijet carrying members of the criminal Erdman Gang. A couple of shots are enough to bring it down with a huge explosion, thus saving the inconvenience of a trial.

The message of *Thunderbirds* is clear about the sanctity of life, but it seems that certain criminals exempt themselves from this rule.

More than any other Supermarionation series, *Thunderbirds* preaches a philosophy of better living through engineering. In *Give or Take a Million* Jeff explains that Thunderbird 3 is 287 feet high. The rocket is frequently introduced in low camera angles that present it as a monument to technological progress. Other large vehicles are treated with the same reverence, and the series is famous for fetishising Thunderbirds 1 to 3, especially during their lengthy launch sequences. As Thunderbird 2 rolls towards its launching ramp, the palm trees of Tracy Island bend out of its way, as if nature was bowing to human achievements.

1.1 TRAPPED IN THE SKY

teleplay by **Gerry and Sylvia Anderson**
directed by **Alan Pattillo**
first broadcast 30 September 1965

The atomic-powered airliner Fireflash has been sabotaged by the Hood. If its landing gear touches down a bomb will detonate, but if the plane stays airborne for too long there will be a fatal radiation leak. With time running out, International Rescue embarks on its inaugural mission....

Towards the end of his life, Gerry Anderson singled out the opening instalment of *Thunderbirds* as his proudest achievement. Untitled on screen, but identified as *Trapped in the Sky* in its shooting script, this episode sets the tone for the series, with extraordinary special effects and a tense resolution.

The fast-paced Hollywood style was no accident – here was a production aimed squarely at the American market. The crew at the control tower of London Airport are stiff upper-lip Brits who need rescuing by the American Tracy family. Lady Penelope and her chauffeur Parker are resourceful exceptions to this rule, yet still comply with a stereotypical view of the aristocracy and its servants.

The Andersons' other predictions for a future England are ambiguous about the power of technology to both enrich and endanger our lives. The Fireflash eventually lands on Runway 29 at London Airport, but Penelope and Parker chase the Hood down a motorway with just three lanes. Most ominous is the threat to the crew and passengers of the Fireflash from radiation exposure, a topical spectre that would become a preoccupation in future episodes.

Left: A publicity photograph of Jeff Tracy, taken to promote the Barnardo Helpers' League during production of the first series. Jeff was never seen in this uniform during *Thunderbirds*.

Below: Barratt's second series of *Thunderbirds* sweet cigarette cards was issued in 1967 and compiled using photographic images, such as this scene from *Trapped in the Sky*.

Bottom: Virgil's master elevator car struggles to halt the sabotaged Fireflash in *Trapped in the Sky*.

The establishment of International Rescue, and Jeff's credentials as its founding father, are given a relatively unusual amount of back story. Jeff's enthusiasm for "interesting engineering investments" gets him a ticket aboard a dodgy monotrain in *Brink of Disaster*. He exercises more discretion in equipping International Rescue. In *Terror in New York City* he explains to Scott that the Thunderbird craft rely on components ordered from different aircraft corporations. "None of them know what they're making. It's only when they all arrive here that the jigsaw fits together."

MASTER ELEVATOR CAR

THUNDERBIRDS

A Second Series of 50
No. 2

Virgil, pilot of Thunderbird 2, is here seen at the controls of one of the elevator cars which are contained in one of the freight pods. This is the master car from which Virgil can control a string of these vehicles by remote control. You may remember how effectively these vehicles were used to bring Air Terrainean's super "Fireflash" airliner to a safe landing.

Issued by
BARRATT & CO LTD
LONDON   ENGLAND
PRINTED IN ENGLAND

Brains' assembly of that jigsaw results in equipment so advanced that it lies beyond the reach of even the major powers. When International Rescue cautiously lend their weight to the espionage affairs of *The Man from MI.5* it's because Bondson argues that their unique contribution to his mission could save the lives of millions. In *Alias Mr. Hackenbacker*, Brains applies his expertise to another admirable cause: an ejectable fuel pod that will revolutionise safety in passenger airliners.

Mechanical engineering is just one aspect of the series' broad catalogue of future technology. Everyday life in 2065 benefits from the overhead monorail that replaced the London Underground (*Vault of Death*) and the Auto-Nurse, a recycled *Stingray* prop that keeps a mechanical eye on Scott and Virgil in *City of Fire*. The development of the Penelon textile

in *Hackenbacker* promises to transform women's wardrobes, with one potential buyer exclaiming, "It's the biggest thing in fabric since the cotton mill!"

Concerns about the planet's resources were not as prevalent in the 1960s, so it's no surprise that green issues receive scant attention. In *The Perils of Penelope*, it's not clear whether the coveted formula for a rocket fuel developed from sea water was prompted by ecological or economic concerns. Similarly the solar therapy treatment being planned by the Coralville Children's Hospital in *Give or Take a Million* is presumably a medical breakthrough, and not an attempt to reduce the establishment's heating bill.

Above: The damaged Thunderbird 2 is repaired on Tracy Island, following a missile attack at the beginning of *Terror in New York City*.

Top right: "Hey, what's all this bedside manner stuff?" Tin Tin and one of the Tracy Island Auto-Nurses tend to the recovering Scott in *City of Fire*.

Above right: "Why, I could carry a whole wardrobe around with me in my handbag!" Lady Penelope is impressed by Penelon in *Alias Mr. Hackenbacker*.

Below: The miniature Mole that was packaged with some editions of the Thunderbird 2 replica manufactured by J Rosenthal in 1966.

Opposite page: The Mole, as pictured in *Thunderbirds*' end titles.

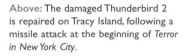

1.2 PIT OF PERIL

teleplay by **Alan Fennell**
directed by **Desmond Saunders**
first broadcast 7 October 1965

A 500-ton Sidewinder vehicle plunges into the site of a former mine containing equipment dumped after the Second World War. International Rescue employs the Mole, a giant jet-propelled drill, and specialist recovery vehicles in an effort to drag the stricken colossus out of the fiery pit...

Following the sabotage scenario of *Trapped in the Sky*, *Pit of Peril* introduces the other great staple of *Thunderbirds* – the accidental disaster. In many other respects, however, this story takes its lead from the first episode. The Sidewinder is powered by an atomic reactor, with predictable consequences if it succumbs to the 260-degree heat at the bottom of the pit. The attempts to inspect the danger zone and restore the Sidewinder recall a similar intervention in *Trapped in the Sky*; in both cases this was a means of extending the running time from 25 minutes to 50 at the behest of Lew Grade. Composer Barry Gray and editor Harry MacDonald work hard to engage the viewer, but Alan Fennell's relatively one-dimensional plot

struggles to sustain the new running time. For this reason, Gerry Anderson always regarded *Pit of Peril* as one of the least effective episodes.

There are compensations in the outstanding model work. The four-legged Sidewinder resembles a huge upturned beetle when it lies at the bottom of the pit, and the corkscrew-like Mole was such a hit that from here on it earned a place in the show's end titles.

The Tracy brothers get about on their hoverbikes (descendants of the jetmobiles from *Fireball XL5*) and *The Cham-Cham* sees the debut of Tin Tin and Penelope's nifty ski thrusts. More conventional transport seems to have changed little in the year 2065; cars and trucks resemble their 1960s' counterparts and still rely on old-fashioned fossil fuel. Car-parking facilities have, however, kept pace with the increased popularity of motoring. The automobile park in *Move – And You're Dead* is operated by Parola Stacker Inc and carefully deposits Alan's car within a

Above: Scott and Virgil emerge from the Mole and head towards the Carter family in *City of Fire*.

Right: The reverse of this Somportex bubblegum card from 1966 described the Parola Stacker system from *Move – And You're Dead* as "computer parking".

1.3 CITY OF FIRE

teleplay by **Alan Fennell**
directed by **David Elliott**
first broadcast 6 January 1966

The newly completed Thompson Tower is a self-contained city with 350 floors, 12 hotels and a vast sub-basement 'Autoparc'. A fire threatens to engulf the entire building and International Rescue is called to save a family trapped inside. But Scott and Virgil have problems of their own...

In *City of Fire* Alan Fennell anticipated not only scale of the 1974 disaster movie *The Towering Inferno* but also its device of telling the story through a handful of characters desperate to escape. We never see the hordes evacuated from the Thompson Tower; here was a scenario that even miniaturisation couldn't make affordable. Instead the focus is on the beleaguered Carter family.

This is a cautionary tale of human fallibility – the shortcomings of the reckless driver who started the fire, the men monitoring the emergency from the Tower's control centre and even International Rescue itself. Brains' oxyhydnite gas can cut through steel faster than a laser beam, but has potentially lethal side-effects on Scott and Virgil when they use it.

The episode's predictions for our urban future are highly accurate, from the Goldfinger-inspired architecture to the surveillance cameras in the basement and car park. It's therefore surprising that some old-fashioned sexism was allowed to creep in at the end of the episode. On Tracy Island, Tin Tin reveals what she has discovered about the motorist ultimately responsible for the devastation. "You've guessed it," she says. "The driver was female."

vast horizontal bank of vehicles, each one nestling on its own shelf.

Nobody at AP Films could have foreseen the predominance of microprocessors, but the absence of computerised technology is just one of the factors that consigns *Thunderbirds'* vision of the 21st century to history. Nowadays, younger viewers of *The Cham-Cham* would doubtless be puzzled by Tin Tin's observation that the devious Olsen has secreted "some kind of electronic computer".

The series instead foresees a mechanised future of a rather different kind, with the sort of clunky labour-saving gadgets manufactured by Gazelle Automations Inc in *The Duchess Assignment*. Even the managing director's personal assistant is a machine. "The voice you are listening

to is the product of Gazelle Automated Secretaries" intones David Graham, in a variation of the grating delivery he employed in his portrayal of the Daleks in the early years of *Doctor Who*.

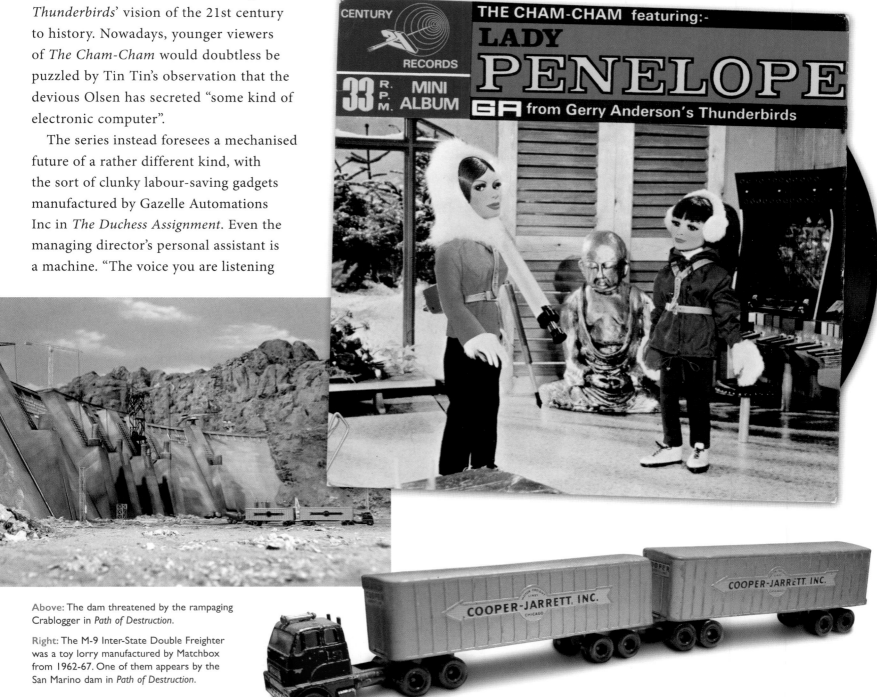

Below: This shot of Penelope and Tin Tin next to Olsen's computer never appeared on screen, but was used on the cover of the *Cham-Cham* mini album released in March 1967. Gerry Anderson devised the 'ski thrusts' Penelope and Tin Tin are wearing in this picture in order to limit any awkward puppet movements during the skiing sequences.

Above: The dam threatened by the rampaging Crablogger in *Path of Destruction*.

Right: The M-9 Inter-State Double Freighter was a toy lorry manufactured by Matchbox from 1962-67. One of them appears by the San Marino dam in *Path of Destruction*.

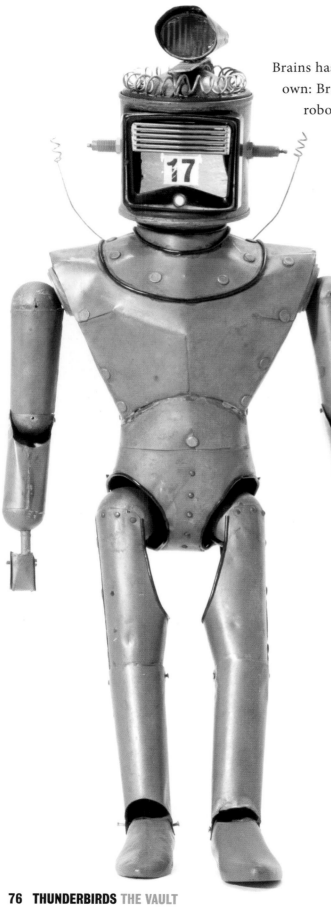

Brains has a mechanical assistant of his own: Braman is a copper-coloured robot that first appears in *Sun Probe*, going about his duties to the accompaniment of noises that make him sound like a walking telephone exchange. Braman is activated via a switch mounted on his illuminated face, and comes in handy as both a laboratory assistant and chess opponent. Brains relies on Braman's superior mathematical skill to calculate a formula that saves Thunderbird 3 from a collision course with the Sun. The resemblance is never explained on screen, but Braman's design is closely matched by that of the mechanical guards that defend a plutonium store in *30 Minutes After Noon*. The robots stand between the Erdman Gang and isotopes for all of Britain's nuclear power stations. They are, however, mostly nobbled by a 'ray machine' that is tuned to their frequencies.

Gimmicks such as the Erdmans' ray machine and mechanical men are used sparingly in a series that strives for

Above: Brains challenges the robotic Braman to a game of chess in *Sun Probe*.

Right: Jeff, Brains and Braman try to decode *The Cham-Cham* in this Somportex bubblegum card from 1966.

Left: The Braman puppet was adapted to play the mechanical guards in *30 Minutes After Noon*. Each robot was identified by a number on its face.

1.4 SUN PROBE

teleplay by **Alan Fennell**
directed by **David Lane**
first broadcast 9 December 1965

The solarnauts aboard the Sun Probe are on a mission to obtain a sample of the Sun, but when their radio-controlled retro-rockets fail they instead succumb to its gravitational pull. In an effort to save them, Thunderbird 3 launches into space and Thunderbird 2 heads for the freezing Mount Arkan...

The only episode to explore space travel in any detail reveals the full extent of Brains' engineering genius – the Sun Probe arrives at its destination in just one week, but Thunderbird 3 reaches the vicinity even quicker. Little wonder that International Rescue is known to the staff at Cape Kennedy, prompting Colonel Benson (Ray Barrett) to make a personal appeal to the organisation as part of a television broadcast.

This is a nerve-racking episode, skilfully extended from its original 25-minute running time and highlighting the sometimes neglected characters of Brains and Tin Tin. The trip aboard Thunderbird 3 represents Tin Tin's first mission, and Brains' relationship with his robot Braman is the subject of gentle humour, especially during their chess matches.

Dialogue and editing underline the contrast between the crew approaching the heat of the Sun and the simultaneous discomfort of Brains and Virgil as Thunderbird 2 endures the cold of Mount Arkan. The Sun itself is probably the series' weakest special effect, so it falls to Barry Gray to evoke its power with a score comprising both mysterious music and eerie electronic effects.

---

verisimilitude. The aliens and disintegrator weapons that appear in *Martian Invasion* would have been a familiar challenge for the crew of Fireball XL5, but here are satirised as B movie clichés. There are only a handful of instances where space-age technology is applied to anything like a functioning weapon, and in the most prominent examples neither device can actually be described as a gun. Scott and Virgil use a laser beam to break into the plutonium store in *30 Minutes After Noon*. (Voice artist David Holliday betrays his unfamiliarity with the word laser by mispronouncing it 'lazzer' during one scene.) In the second series episode *Path of Destruction*, Penelope needs to gain quick access to the personnel files of Robotics International Ltd. The jobsworth security guard refuses to comply with her request, so Parker activates something that resembles an elongated torch. This transfixes the guard as Penelope rifles through the filing cabinet. Once she has found what she needs she reassures him that "You'll suffer no after-effects of this beam."

Below left: Parker hypnotises the Robotics International security guard in *Path of Destruction*.

Below right: A visitor from outer space wields a disintegrator gun in *Martian Invasion*.

Such contrivances are divorced from recognisable extrapolations of current technology. They seem especially incongruous when employed as deus ex machina. In *Edge of Impact* the telecoms engineers stranded at the top of a collapsing tower float down to earth with the aid of International Rescue's low altitude escape harnesses. In *Path of Destruction*, Brains and Virgil fly away from the stricken Crablogger by activating jet packs.

The sort of advanced technology that is ubiquitous in the real world of the 21st century is the mobile phone. *Thunderbirds* didn't quite

Above: Telecoms engineers Jim and Stan are saved by low altitude escape harnesses in *Edge of Impact*.

Right: The booster mortar that fires the harnesses in *Edge of Impact* was renamed the Thunderizer in this 1966 bubblegum card.

No. 60 THE THUNDERIZER. THIS BLAST GUN CONTAINS A DYNAMIC UNIT PRODUCING IMMENSE ELECTRICAL DISCHARGES MORE POWERFUL THAN LIGHTNING.
© A.P. FILMS LTD ISSUED BY SOMPORTEX LONDON
A SERIES OF 72 PICTURES.

1.5 THE UNINVITED

teleplay by **Alan Fennell**
directed by **Desmond Saunders**
first broadcast 2 December 1965

Two archaeologists come to the rescue of the concussed Scott after Thunderbird 1 is shot down in the Sahara Desert. International Rescue returns the favour when the archaeologists become trapped inside the lost pyramid of Khamandides – the domain of an advanced but warlike civilisation...

The first script not to mention radiation seems out of step with the previous episodes in other, more significant ways. Archaeologists Wilson (Ray Barrett) and Lindsey (Matt Zimmerman) drive the plot, and their accidental discovery of a subterranean kingdom plays more like an episode of *Stingray*. The impression is emphasised by Barry Gray's recycling of a distinctive cue from that series when the pair are exploring the interior of the pyramid.

At Tracy Island, International Rescue responds to a personal plea for help ("One good turn deserves another," says Jeff) and Grandma, the matriarch of the family, makes her first appearance. On Thunderbird 2's second excursion to the Sahara Desert Gordon takes part

in his first mission, on this occasion accompanying Virgil.

The climactic battle is staged in the explosive style of the 1960s James Bond films, but cannot detract from some questions that linger after the closing credits. Lindsey's attempted murder of Scott seems very sudden and out of character. The warlike 'Z' people are named as 'Zombites' in the script, but why do they live under a pyramid? And what exactly are they trying to defend?

predict this communications revolution, instead portraying a two-tier future where videophone installations would be available to everyone, while personal devices would be reserved for International Rescue and its agents.

In the first episode, *Trapped in the Sky*, the Hood tells London airport about his sabotage of the Fireflash by calling the control tower from a circular screen that offers both sound and vision. These wall-mounted consoles are often installed in 'Phonavision' booths that operate in much the same way as public telephone kiosks of the 1960s. They are even accompanied by printed telephone directories. The facilities reappear in *The Mighty Atom*, and by the time Alan calls Grandma in *Move – And You're Dead* they have collectively gained a sign that reads

'Telecall Booth'. Alan dials Grandma using a combination of numbers and letters; her subsequent appearance on the screen in front of him anticipates the scene in *2001: A Space Odyssey* (1968) where Heywood Floyd (William Sylvester) calls his daughter (Vivian Kubrick). Jeff and Penelope have their own videophones of an identical design, although in *Vault of Death* Penelope's phone is compromised when Parker takes a pair of pliers to its power cable.

1.6 THE MIGHTY ATOM

teleplay by **Dennis Spooner**
directed by **David Lane**
first broadcast 30 December 1965

The Hood steals the Mighty Atom, an electronic espionage device disguised as a mouse, and uses it to photograph the machinery at an atomic irrigation plant in the Sahara Desert. He starts a fire that lures International Rescue to the scene, then sets the Mighty Atom an ambitious new task...

A plot involving two atomic irrigation plants constructed a year apart is further cluttered by the reintroduction of Lady Penelope and Parker, both making their first appearance in the series since *Trapped in the Sky*. Penelope has not visited Tracy Island since the International Rescue operation began. There is a further indication of the time that has elapsed when we learn that International Rescue was not in service when the original irrigation plant was destroyed a year earlier.

The demise of the first plant in Australia was an accident caused by the Hood, adding to our growing suspicion that he may not be quite the criminal mastermind his reputation suggests. His scheme at the new plant in the Sahara is rather more considered, but inevitably ends in failure. Someone else who seems rather diminished is Penelope, who has a screaming fit when she spots the mouse-like Mighty Atom in the control cabin of Thunderbird 2.

The greatest kudos in this episode goes to Barry Gray. The sinister score he composes to accompany the progress of the radioactive cloud makes these the most unsettling sequences in the entire series.

Right: Wall-mounted portraits of the Tracy brothers, as depicted in Barratt's first series of sweet cigarette cards.

Below: A 1960s ashtray identical to the one that was adapted for use on Jeff Tracy's desk.

At Tracy Island, Jeff communicates with Penelope and his sons using screens hidden behind wall-mounted portraits. When an incoming call is received, the eyes of the respective picture light up; alternately Penelope can contact Tracy Island using an emergency code that illuminates the necklace on her portrait. Visual contact is established via the picture frames, or a monitor next to Jeff's desk, and the sound is relayed through a speaker hidden in the underside of his ashtray. Mobile communication is essential during missions, and this is where the series comes closest to predicting the modern smartphone. Penelope's powder compact doubles as a visual transmitter/receiver. In *The Man from MI.5* Brains points out that its transistors are small but extremely robust. The compact lacks what we would now call a speakerphone facility, but it certainly has an impressive range – in *The Cham-Cham* Penelope uses it to call Jeff from Switzerland, and

in *Atlantic Inferno* she's in Australia when she asks him to join her. Brains has his own personal communicator in the form of a wristwatch that works in much the same way. Such technology is obviously highly unusual; in *Day of Disaster* a staff member at the Allington Suspension Bridge observes Brains talking to his watch. "I knew it all along," says the bridge controller. "The man's a nut."

As well as these remarkable inventions, the world of 2065 retains a number of traditional forms of communication that the series' original audience would have instantly recognised. In *Trapped in the Sky*, Jeff learns that Tin Tin is aboard the Fireflash when he receives a 'cable' she has sent from London. Towards the end of the series, Hiram K Hackenbacker (aka

Brains) sends Captain Ashton a telegram wishing him luck as he prepares to take off in the new Skythrust airliner. In the UK, the popularity of telegrams was already in steep decline by the 1960s, and the Post Office withdrew the service altogether in 1982.

Above left and right: Tell it to the hand – Brains tries to maintain discreet contact with Gordon in *Day of Disaster*.

Below: This 1966 intercom set, manufactured by J & L Randall, employed rather more traditional technology.

Top and above: The teleprinter and newspaper presses that spread the story about the radioactive cloud in *The Mighty Atom*.

Another relic of the age before consumer electronics is the teleprinter, an example of which can be seen in *The Mighty Atom*. Gerry Anderson clearly approved of the printer's chattering urgency as it updated Australian news rooms on the movement of a radioactive cloud; in 1969 he employed a similar machine to link various scenes in the title sequence of his live-action series *UFO*.

The teleprinter in *The Mighty Atom* gives way to stock footage of newspapers rolling off the presses. *Thunderbirds* is a reminder of an era when, despite the growing prevalence of television, printed media was still the means by which many people received news. The Tracy family is no exception: in *City of Fire* Tin Tin learns about the Thompson Tower enquiry by

reading the report in a newspaper, and in *The Imposters* it's a newspaper story that alerts International Rescue to the fact that they're being impersonated. The newspapers that feature in the series are usually fictitious (such as the *Astronaut Observer* in *Edge of Impact* or the *Spoke City Tribune* in *30 Minutes After Noon*), but *The Man from MI.5* is lent a touch of authenticity by the scene where the kidnappers discover Lady Penelope's intentions in Monte Carlo from an issue of *France-Soir*. One intriguing concession is made to the future in *Vault of Death*, where it can be seen that Parker's newspaper – *The Gazette* – has a cover price of five cents.

Magazines are another printed source of information. A November issue of

1.7 VAULT OF DEATH

teleplay by **Dennis Spooner**
directed by **David Elliott**
first broadcast 23 December 1965

An overzealous clerk is accidentally trapped inside an electronically sealed, airtight vault at the Bank of England. Parker is required to help Lady Penelope unlock the door, but feels similarly obliged to safeguard an unauthorised visit to the bank by his former cellmate Light-Fingered Fred...

Dennis Spooner's script is the first dedicated to Penelope and her crafty chauffeur. American misconceptions about English manners are once again reinforced, but this time we're invited to share the joke. At one point the condescending Lord Silton (Peter Dyneley) expresses his admiration for Parker. "A real treasure that man of yours," he tells Penelope. "Knows his place, dresses well. Sort of fellow you could take anywhere."

Silton's staff at the Bank of England are middle class clerics. Ray Barrett plays Lovegrove as John Gielgud, while David Graham voices many of the others with plummy accents.

Lord Silton enjoys a cigar while, at the other end of the social ladder, Parker, Penelope's cook Lil (Sylvia Anderson) and

Light-Fingered Fred (David Graham) look as if they prefer to roll their own. When Fred escapes from prison he manages to emerge from his hiding place inside a dustbin with his cigarette still in place.

However, the comedy highlight of this episode is Penelope's decision to take the wheel of FAB I when she rightly suspects Parker of procrastination. From the Bank of England to Parkmoor Scrubs, this take on the class struggle is an embarrassment of riches.

Above left: Jeff relaxes with an issue of *Kine* in *City of Fire* and (below left) an example of the original magazine.

Above right: Tin Tin's copy of *Chic* in *Alias Mr. Hackenbacker* and (below right) the *Thunderbirds* supplement of *Television Mail*.

Kine can be spotted on Tracy Island in numerous episodes, and in Maxie's office in *The Cham-Cham*. Made to look like a photography magazine, the title *Kine* was clipped from a recent issue of trade magazine *Kinematograph Weekly*. In *Alias Mr. Hackenbacker*, Tin Tin reads about Lady Penelope's modelling exploits in an issue of *Chic*, its glossy front cover an adaptation of another trade magazine, the December 1965 supplement of *Television Mail*.

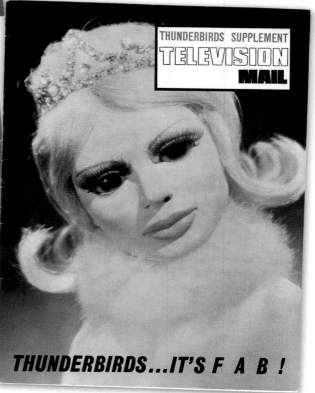

Clockwise from top: Somportex bubblegum cards showing three of *Thunderbirds'* most vulnerable vehicles – an RTL2 transporter plane from *The Cham-Cham*, the Ocean Pioneer II from *Danger at Ocean Deep* and the Crablogger from *Path of Destruction*.

The series' preoccupation with nuclear power is something else that betrays the era of its production. In episodes such as *The Mighty Atom*, *30 Minutes After Noon* and *The Man from MI.5*, the world comes perilously close to a major disaster. Elsewhere, mankind is shown to be dangerously over-reliant on atomic energy. The Fireflash airliner, the engines that move the Empire State Building in *Terror in New York City*, the giant tankers in *Danger at Ocean Deep*, the Crablogger in *Path of Destruction* and even Grandma's oven in *Give or Take a Million* are all nuclear-powered. In the 1960s it was hoped that the atomic age would bring a clean alternative to coal and other fossil fuels, but in *Thunderbirds*

1.8 OPERATION CRASH-DIVE

teleplay by **Martin Crump**
directed by **Desmond Saunders**
first broadcast 16 December 1965

A Fireflash airliner disappears on its way out of London, and Gordon rescues the crew of another that crashes into the sea. Scott joins the next test flight as co-pilot, while Virgil and Gordon follow in Thunderbird 2. History soon repeats itself as the Fireflash begins to dive towards the Atlantic...

It is acknowledged on screen that the latest crisis to hit the Fireflash occurs less than a year after the events of *Trapped in the Sky*. This is not the only reason that Martin Crump's story may seem mundane and repetitive, but it's worth contextualising his scenario with contemporary developments in civil aviation. Older members of the 1960s audience would almost certainly have remembered the fatal crashes that plagued the de Havilland DH 106 Comet, the world's first jet airliner, in the previous decade. The design flaw responsible was eventually fixed, but by the end of the 1950s a lack of confidence scuppered any hopes that Britain could lead the market as a manufacturer of commercial passenger aircraft.

Operation Crash-Dive evokes this uncertainty, offering sabotage as an explanation for the frequent system failures. But it also looks forward to a new era by casting the International Air Minister (Peter Dyneley) as a Frenchman. The first prototype of Concorde, the supersonic airliner designed under an Anglo-French agreement, began construction in February 1965, between the production and premiere of this highly topical episode.

the 21st century seems to teeter on the brink of a radioactive nightmare. *Thunderbirds* was conceived in 1963, the same year that brought us *Dr Strangelove*'s apocalypse and *Doctor Who*'s radiation-mutated Daleks; both symptoms of the widespread anxiety triggered by the Cuban Missile Crisis in 1962.

The world was united in its fear of nuclear destruction, but *Thunderbirds* confidently predicts a future unified as a formal global community. This was a theme of Anderson's work that had previously been explored in *Fireball XL5* and *Stingray*, but unlike the World Space Patrol or the World Aquanaut Security Patrol, International Rescue is an

independent, privately funded organisation with no military agenda. The Hood is happy to stoke Cold War-style tension in *Edge of Impact*, but elsewhere the consumer society seems to have settled into a vast common market. Journalists from World

Top: Buildings as well as vehicles hold the potential to trigger man-made disasters. This oil refinery in Ab-Ben-Dhu narrowly avoids a direct hit from a falling satellite in *Ricochet*.

Above: The plutonium store targeted by the Erdman Gang in *30 Minutes After Noon*. The gang aims to trigger an explosion that will destroy half of England.

Below left: A promotional shot of the World TV helijet from *The Imposters* appeared as a "hoverjet" on this Somportex bubblegum card from 1966.

Below right: World TV's Eddie Kerr (right) reports on what he believes to be a live rescue in the opening moments of *The Imposters*.

No. 72 WORLD T.V. HOVERJET PROJECTS HYPER-SPACE VIDEO PICTURES DIRECT TO I.R. HEADQUARTERS.
© A.P. FILMS LTD ISSUED BY SOMPORTEX LONDON A SERIES OF 72 PICTURES.

Television report on events in *City of Fire*, *Move – And You're Dead* and *The Imposters*, while both *Cry Wolf* and *Path of Destruction* feature bulletins from the newspaper *World News*. The presence of an International Air Minister in *Operation Crash-Dive* suggests some form of world government, and International Space Control in *Ricochet* has ultimate authority over satellite launches. According to *The Cham-Cham*, even the hit parade is now the international pop chart. The fast-talking DJ in *Ricochet* is actually a proto 'video jockey' with a worldwide audience, some 15 years before the advent of MTV.

This picture of global harmony must have seemed a logical development in a world that had divided into American, Soviet and now European super states after the Second World War. It's an essentially naïve prediction, common to much of the television science-fiction of the period.

Below: DJ Rick O'Shea broadcasts to the world from the unlicensed KLA satellite in *Ricochet*.

Far left and left: Gray & Houseman's colossal road-building machine transforms rough terrain into smooth Tarmac in *End of the Road*.

Below: A repainted version of the model appeared as a generic road-builder in *Atlantic Inferno*, as pictured on this Somportex bubblegum card.

It is actually *Thunderbirds*' underlying *pessimism* that has probably maintained its appeal to subsequent generations. International Rescue largely exists because of our increasing dependence on technology that places us, and the planet, in jeopardy. Modern machinery is fallible, and prone to sabotage. The world food shortage referred to in *Attack of the Alligators!* could be indicative of an unsustainable population boom (another preoccupation of contemporary science-fiction), while the tower blocks in *City of Fire* depict a soulless and slightly sinister model of high-rise living.

In *Vault of Death*, Parker is able to break into the Bank of England's new strong room using a hairpin. Once again, experience and ingenuity triumph over supposedly state-of-the-art equipment. This essentially sceptical view of progress set *Thunderbirds* apart from the optimism of its era, preserving its appeal in a 21st century more cautious and cynical than any scenario the series could have imagined.

Bottom: The cover of this January 1967 mini album recreates the scene in *Vault of Death* where Parker breaks into the Bank of England.

A CENTURY **21** PRODUCTION ▶

THE VAULT OF DEATH featuring

LADY

PENELOPE AND **P**ARKER

WITH ALL YOUR FAVOURITE CHARACTERS

33 R.P.M.

MINI ALBUM

CENTURY **21** Records

A GERRY ANDERSON CONCEPT

5
VIEWS FROM THE BRIDGE

After many months of preparation, production on *Thunderbirds* began in late summer 1964. By this time there were more than 100 employees at the Stirling Road studio, which was a crucible for diverse talents from the worlds of filmmaking and theatre puppetry. It was usually a happy collaboration, but on this occasion it would sometimes resemble a battle of wits. Things were further complicated by Lew Grade's insistence that each episode be doubled in length – a decision only made once scriptwriting and filming were well advanced.

AP Films quickly recovered, perfecting a workflow that generally allowed for the completion of a 52-minute episode in 13 to 14 days. The cost of each instalment was an estimated £38,000.

The first series of 26 episodes was nearing its conclusion when Gerry Anderson offered the *TV Times*' Anthony Davis a lift to the studio. "I should say the business is worth at least £2 million," said Anderson as his Jaguar Mark X arrived at the Slough Trading Estate. Davis was impressed by what he found. "In the puppet workshops, where the puppets are made at a cost of £300 each, modellers were sculpting impressively character-filled faces for new members of the cast. In the costume department women worked on uniforms for them. On the sets puppeteers on gantries were operating the tiny dollar-earners on wires 0.005 of an inch thick and in the props department the caps from toothpaste tubes and similar everyday objects were being turned into the controls of puppet-sized machines... The atmosphere is that of a factory devoted to the miniature."

Above: The credits for the *Thunderbirds* voice cast, as they appeared at the end of every episode in the first series.

Below left: David Graham, Sarah Brackett and John Bloomfield in *The Unkind Philanthropist*, a 1964 episode of *The Saint*.

Below right: Graham's most distinctive contribution to *Thunderbirds* was the voice of Parker. The character is seen here on a mid-1960s postcard published by CG Williams.

As with all of Anderson's puppet series, the process of recording the dialogue began before a single frame was shot. *Thunderbirds* had the largest repertory company of any Supermarionation series to date, but the casting requirements remained the same – most of the leading roles needed voice artists who could speak with convincing American accents, and who were versatile enough to also play guest characters in the series.

An English actor who had no problem with accents of any nationality was David Graham, and the strength of his track record meant that he was one of the first to be hired. Gerry Anderson's association with Graham went back to 1957, when Anderson had been a director-for-hire on a television series called *Martin Kane, Private Investigator* in which Graham had been one of the visiting cast members. Graham had mentioned that he "wasn't bad on accents and voices", so

when AP Films began pre-production of *Four Feather Falls* Anderson cast Graham as numerous characters, including an ageing pioneer, a Native American and a Mexican bandit. Graham also assumed an authentic-sounding Wild West twang for the series' opening narration. After *Four Feather Falls*, Graham appeared on screen in *Crossroads to Crime* before joining the cast of *Supercar* (where he was the voices of Dr Horatio Beaker and Mitch), *Fireball XL5* (Professor Matthew Matic and Zoony) and most recently *Stingray* (various guest characters and Oink the seal pup). In *Thunderbirds*, Graham would voice Gordon Tracy, Kyrano, Parker and the stuttering Brains.

The inspiration for Parker's distinctive cockney patois was a waiter called Arthur at The King's Arms in Cookham, a pub that was frequented by APF staff and was the

venue for their Christmas parties. Arthur had once been in the Queen's service at Windsor Castle, which was where Gerry presumed he had developed his curious way of addressing customers. "He had this warm patter, dropping his h's and putting them back in the wrong places, and this intrigued me," he remembered. "I thought Arthur's voice would be perfect so I sent David Graham down to the King's Arms to have lunch and pick up Arthur's style. When the series was on the air we wondered whether we should tell Arthur he was the inspiration for Parker's voice. The old boy was such a snob that we decided it would be kindest not to – he probably wouldn't have wanted to have been associated with a scurrilous safe-cracker."

Ray Barrett, an Australian actor whose craggy features were familiar to contemporary audiences, lived next door to David Graham in Hampstead and was cast at the same time. *Thunderbirds* made its debut in September 1965, the same month Barrett made the first of more than a hundred appearances as Peter Thornton in the BBC drama series *The Troubleshooters* (1965-72). Around six months after that he was back on cinema screens as the hero in Hammer's *The Reptile* (1966).

Barrett had already proved his impressive range to Anderson by voicing the gruff Commander Shore and his undersea nemesis Titan in *Stingray*. In *Thunderbirds* he would be stretched even further; Barrett's regular duties would comprise John Tracy and the Hood, but his numerous other contributions included the plummy Duchess of Royston in *The Duchess Assignment*.

Top: Ray Barrett in the 1965 television play *Come Into My Parlour*.

Above: *Trapped in the Sky* introduced the Hood, a character voiced by Barrett.

Left: John Tracy, another of Barrett's characters, was prominent on the display packaging for this *Thunderbirds*-themed nougat in 1965.

The voice of Jeff Tracy belonged to Peter Dyneley, an English actor whose commanding presence was a mainstay of television series produced by both the BBC and ITV from the mid-1950s until his death, aged 56, in 1977. Anderson recalled taking particular care recording the booming "5-4-3-2-1… Thunderbirds are go!" narration that opened every episode. Dyneley's countdown was considered so iconic that it was retained for the titles and launch sequences of the 2015 series *Thunderbirds Are Go*.

Virgil Tracy was voiced by David Holliday, the only American actor in the cast. Holliday was a prolific stage star who in the late 1950s had played

Tony in the first London production of *West Side Story*. *Thunderbirds* was a relatively rare television assignment for an actor whose career was dominated by international plays and musicals up until his death, aged 61, in

Above: Peter Dyneley in the 1967 *Saint* episode *To Kill a Saint*.

Right: Jeff Tracy, Dyneley's best-known character, pictured on a Dutch postcard published in 1965.

Top right: David Holliday, who voiced Virgil Tracy in the first series of *Thunderbirds*.

Far right: Virgil, Brains and Scott featured on this stencil set, issued by Berwick in the mid-1960s.

1999. Holliday was unavailable when the second series began production, so for these six episodes and the Andersons' *Thunderbirds* feature films Virgil was voiced by Jeremy Wilkin, an actor who was born in England but had subsequently emigrated to Toronto.

Episode one of *Thunderbirds* had already been recorded when Holliday recommended his friend and fellow stage actor Matt

Zimmerman to play Alan Tracy. Sylvia Anderson was delighted by the Ontario-born actor's facial similarity to the Alan puppet and cast him as soon as she heard his voice. Ray Barrett had voiced Alan's only line of dialogue in *Trapped in the Sky*, but Zimmerman took over from the second episode, *Pit of Peril*.

Tin Tin, Grandma and a handful of other roles were played by Christine Finn, an actress and voice-over artist who was raised in India and enjoyed a varied career in film, television, theatre and radio from the late 1940s. Following her death, aged 77, in 2007, tributes cited Tin Tin as her best-remembered role. It's worth noting, however, that writer and Quatermass creator Nigel Kneale highly rated her portrayal of Barbara Judd in the television version of *Quatermass and the Pit* (1958-59).

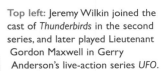

Top left: Jeremy Wilkin joined the cast of *Thunderbirds* in the second series, and later played Lieutenant Gordon Maxwell in Gerry Anderson's live-action series *UFO*.

Top centre: Matt Zimmerman was the voice of Alan Tracy in *Thunderbirds* and played a pilot in *Exposed*, a 1970 episode of *UFO*.

Above: Christine Finn as Barbara Judd in *Quatermass and the Pit* (1958-59). Christine voiced Tin Tin Kyrano in *Thunderbirds*.

Left: This cardboard figure of Tin Tin was given away with Dutch lollies in the mid-1960s.

Far left: Tin Tin and Alan share an intimate moment at the end of *Move – And You're Dead*.

The lead characters in *Thunderbirds* were predominantly American, fuelling a common criticism levelled at APF and Lew Grade that their pandering to the United States constituted some sort of cultural betrayal. In the December 1965 issue of *Television Mail* Rod Allen leapt to their defence. "It is a sad fact that the average American viewer finds it difficult to understand English as she is spoken in England; answer: the characters must speak American (and make no mistake about this: the characters' accents are real American and not mid-Atlantic pastiches of the dialect). In the previous films, virtually all the characters spoke in American, but *Thunderbirds*, with its essential internationality, has succeeded to introduce many English characters apart from Lady Penelope (who, it is thought, will wow them Stateside, as one might say)."

Sylvia Anderson had played a large part in developing Parker and Penelope – the only English members of the regular team and

Above: Gerry and Sylvia Anderson visit the set of Tracy Island during the filming of *Move – And You're Dead*. Sylvia is wearing a version of a Lady Penelope dress inspired by the grid-based abstracts of French artist Piet Mondrian.

Right: The dress also appeared in Roy Newly's illustrations for this book, published by World Distributors in 1966.

1.9 MOVE – AND YOU'RE DEAD

teleplay by **Alan Pattillo**
directed by **Alan Pattillo**
first broadcast 10 February 1966

Alan and Grandma are trapped on a suspension bridge high above the San Miguel River. Both are sweltering under the hot sun. Alan manages to contact his father at Tracy Island, and the anxious Jeff asks him to explain what has happened. How did they get there? And why can't they move?

This cleverly structured screenplay begins by placing Alan and Grandma in an intriguing predicament, tells most of their story in flashback and ends with International Rescue saving members of its own organisation.

Off-duty from Thunderbirds 3 and 5, Alan Tracy briefly revives his career as a racing driver. Wearing his director's hat, Alan Pattillo telegraphs the excitement of the Parola Sands Race in a dynamic montage comprising images from an oil painting. Elsewhere, he eschews the traditional painted backdrops to show aerial footage of real sky and clouds as Scott and Virgil fly to San Miguel.

It transpires that Alan's jealous rivals have left him and Grandma on the bridge, alongside a motion-activated bomb. The only unsolved mystery is a point of continuity that possibly indicates the series was never intended to be shown in its production order. After the race Alan collects Grandma so she can join International Rescue at Tracy Island... even though she has already featured in the four preceding episodes. ATV Midlands' original broadcasts of the show pushed *Move – And You're Dead* even further back, compounding the error.

arguably the most memorable characters in the series. The casting of Penelope had been the subject of a fierce debate behind closed doors. Gerry had wanted comic actress and voice-over artist Fenella Fielding to play the glamorous 'London Agent', but Sylvia felt she had a personal investment in the character and wanted the role for herself. Sylvia got her way, adopting a soft but aristocratic style that was not dissimilar to the voice she had given *Stingray*'s Marina on the rare occasions the character was required to speak.

"David and Sylvia enjoyed playing Parker and Penelope very much, and they gave a lot to those characters," says Alan Pattillo. "David was terribly, terribly good, which was why Gerry used him on everything we'd done up to then."

Right: Penelope modelled the original calfskin dress on the front cover of the 18 December 1966 issue of *The Observer* magazine.

Below: Another shot of Penelope in the Mondrian dress appeared on this bubblegum card published by Monty Gum in 1966.

27. Thunderbirds

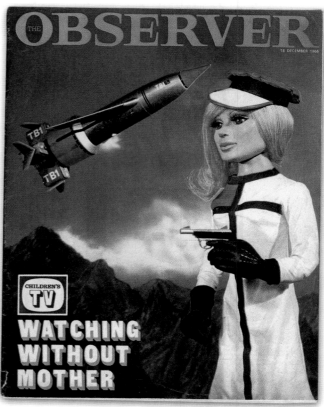

Scott Tracy was played by Shane Rimmer, an actor and singer who would become an Anderson stalwart as a voice artist and screenwriter. Like his fellow cast member Matt Zimmerman, Rimmer was born in Ontario. "I don't think I've ever played a Canadian in my life!" he says, reflecting on a career that includes such diverse landmarks as *Dr Strangelove* (1964), *Gandhi* (1982) and two stints in *Coronation Street*. "All the major American television networks come into Canada, so I was so used to the American accent and it's quite easily adaptable."

Rimmer has happy memories of the *Thunderbirds* recording sessions, beginning with a revelation about their venue. "We started recording them in a studio that was in a shopping centre in Slough. It was right beside the Mars Bar factory. In the summer, when we left the doors open, this incredibly strong smell of chocolate bars would waft across. After that we went to Anvil Studios in Denham, near Pinewood."

Rimmer is glad that the voice recording sessions took place before the filming. "This was a blessing for most of us," he says, "because it meant you didn't have to fit how

Above: Scott Tracy was the cover star of this Australian listings magazine in 1975.

Right: Shane Rimmer as Joe Donnelli, with Margot Bryant as Minnie Caldwell in a 1970 episode of *Coronation Street*.

you were voicing a particular part. That made it a lot easier for the actors, because you can get into all sorts of tanglements when you have to get the voice out and try to look as if you're the owner of that particular voice. I think it was good for the series as well, because there was no limitation on what you did, as long as you said the right words."

Rimmer recalls that Gerry Anderson would direct the voice recording sessions himself, accompanied by sound editor John Peverill. "John was the main force in the recording part of the operation. He was very experienced and Gerry relied on him a lot. We didn't have little sound booths or compartments – everything was recorded ensemble. Gerry insisted on this, because he said the series was an ensemble situation. There was a central suspended microphone. You said your bit, then you got out of the way for the next one to take your place. Sometimes it was a bit of a scrum and you had to be careful. But that's the way Gerry wanted it and I think he was right."

Only the actors playing lead characters were listed in *Thunderbirds*' end titles. Paul Maxwell, John Tate and Charles Tingwell were confined to guest roles, and although Tingwell in particular was a prominent character actor at the time, none of them received credit on the television series. Like Ray Barrett, Tate and Tingwell were Australian. "I think Gerry liked the verve that a lot of Australian actors have, that sparkle," says Rimmer. "They put a bit of lift into a lot of the situations. And he liked to have accents that were not entirely British. *Thunderbirds* was aimed at a global distribution."

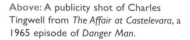

Above: A publicity shot of Charles Tingwell from *The Affair at Castelevara*, a 1965 episode of *Danger Man*.

Left: John Tate (right) with Patrick McGoohan in the 1961 television play *Sergeant Musgrave's Dance*.

Below: Tate's numerous uncredited *Thunderbirds* performances included Solarnaut Camp in *Sun Probe*.

Bottom: One of Charles Tingwell's most memorable characters was the fatalistic Bruno in *Lord Parker's 'Oliday*.

Bottom left: Slides depicting the Tracy brothers were included with this *Thunderbirds* viewer manufactured by Fairylite in the mid-1960s.

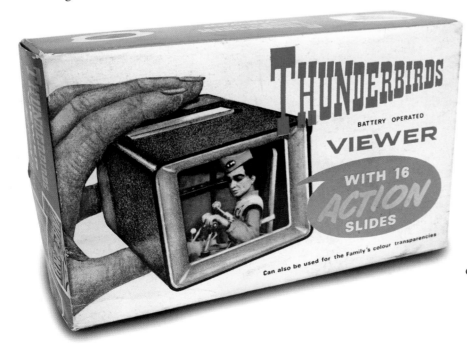

Top: John Read, Gerry and Sylvia at the head of the Stirling Road team in 1965.

Above: During the production of *Thunderbirds*, envelopes for stills negatives were stamped with the Stirling Road address.

These cosmopolitan aspirations were in sharp contrast to the series' unassuming origins. The Slough Trading Estate was a far cry from the popular conceptions of film studio glamour, although the location offered easy access to local engineering firms and retailers that were more useful to APF than most of the services on offer at more conventional facilities. In the history of the era's filmmaking, the reputation of Stirling Road is rivalled only by that of Hammer's Bray Studios – both operated outside the mainstream, both were renowned for their efficiency and both are still revered by many of those lucky enough to have worked there.

In 1965 Rod Allen was among the first to sing the praises of Stirling Road. "It's worth noting that APF is one of the happiest film studios I have ever come across from the staff point of view, that staff turnover is relatively low, and that there is a great deal of promotion from within on the studio floor; first names are the rule all the way up and down the shop, and in an operation that depends to such an extent on team work, the team seems to be really united."

Unlike Bray, and indeed almost every other film studio in the world, Stirling Road was not constructed around sound-stages designed to accommodate actors. "Stages are smaller and less costly than in live-action, but then everything is smaller, and that creates difficulties," Reg Hill told *Television Mail*'s Chauncey Jerome. "It is rather like producing a beautiful precision watch movement instead of a large, cheap alarm clock. Even in fundamentals such as camera tracking, what would be a nine- or ten-foot track at Pinewood or Shepperton is about a three-foot track for us."

The fundamentals of Supermarionation production remained the same for *Thunderbirds*, although the process had been fine-tuned in recent years. Front projection had now been abandoned, as the delays in perfecting each shot exacted a heavy toll on the schedule. Other changes saw a reduced dependency on the booths in the two puppet stages. "The director and the lip-sync operator would sit in a little hutch, a control room above the rest of the studio where you could overlook the whole scene," remembers Alan Pattillo. "You could stay in there all day and just speak through a microphone, telling the cameramen and the puppeteers

what they had to do. I didn't really like that very much. I preferred to have more contact with everyone, so I stayed out of there."

By the time production of *Thunderbirds* began, the Four-channel Natterers had been moved out of the soundproofed booths they previously occupied. Pattillo and the other directors followed the machines onto the studio floor, getting closer to the sets and watching each shot on monitors that were often positioned alongside their respective cameras.

Below: The issue of *Weekend and Today* magazine dated 12-18 January 1966 included this article on a visit to Stirling Road. The picture at the top was taken during the making of *Security Hazard* and shows a Four-channel Natterer on the studio floor.

Things aren't what they seem in 'Thunderbirds.'

Lady Penelope even wears curlers every night

JUST A LOT OF THREE-FACED DOLLS

PUNCH AND JUDY certainly started something. *Thunderbirds*, for instance, the £38,000-per-episode television super-puppet series which has millions of viewers gripped with suspense every week.

Of course, we have come a long way since the striped-awning box on the beach and its drama of domestic disharmony. For one thing, each *Thunderbirds* character has three heads—one with a serious expression, one "normal" and one smiling—to allow for changes of mood, and each head is fitted with an electronic device for lifelike synchronisation of mouth and dialogue. And the production of 55 minutes of film a week is a full-time job for 95 people at Slough, Buckinghamshire. They range from husband-and-wife studio chiefs, Gerry and Sylvia Anderson, to the girl who puts curlers in the blonde nylon hair of glamorous, 22-inch-tall Lady Penelope after each day's filming.

The series reveals the secret activities of a world peace-keeping organisation called International Rescue, run by handsome Jeff Tracy, whose five sons pilot the Thunderbirds.

Illusions of fast movement in this one-third-size world are created mainly by moving the scenery rather than the vehicles. The undersea Thunderbird IV is filmed through a fish tank, and the action is made realistically smooth by filming at nearly five times normal speed.

Dials and dolls . . . The 'lip-sync' machine keeps their mouths moving at the right speed

Launching bay count-down for Thunderbird III piloted by the 'romantic' Alan Tracy

Lady Penelope's pink Rolls has six wheels and plenty of Bond style gadgets

Baby alligators joined the act—as fully-grown man-eaters

Although the super - puppets owe a lot to electronics, humans pull the strings

Thunderbird I has a careful check before being launched on the next International Rescue mission

Realism depends on tricks — like running the cameras fast, then screening at normal speed

Thunderbird I flies at 7,000 m.p.h. — in the story

Right: A 1966 publicity shot of Brains, perched on top of a camera equipped with Add-a-Vision.

Below left: Inside a control booth, Alan Perry (foreground) watches a live feed from a camera on the studio floor.

Below right: The *Thunderbirds* periscope produced by Bell in the mid-1960s was rather less sophisticated than the CCTV systems developed by AP Films.

The construction of the Arriflex 35mm cameras that were used on the puppet stages was crucial to the way APF had developed its CCTV requirements since the system had been introduced on *Four Feather Falls*. Each specially adapted Arriflex head now incorporated a mirror reflex optical system which didn't split the incoming light beam but intermittently made all of it available to both the focusing-tube eyepieces (to which the CCTV was linked) and to the film.

"Use of CCTV monitoring has proved essential," Reg Hill told *Television Mail*'s Kenneth Ullyett. "Advantages to the director and lighting cameraman are obvious. The lighting cameraman can see what part of the set is being shot without needing to get down and monopolise the viewfinder. (On small stages our cameras have to be placed inconveniently low anyway). Further, he can light without the need to look through the camera. Apart from mirror work, the puppeteers can see only the tops of characters' heads, but for CCTV. Now the eye movements are so important, viewing on a 23-inch monitor helps to produce a sympathetic and artistic result."

Camera operator Alan Perry wasn't alone in considering this an ideal way to work. In 1966 he collaborated on a further refinement. "We pioneered what was called Add-a-Vision with [film service company] Livingston," he says. "They created a zoom lens and put

1.10 MARTIAN INVASION

teleplay by **Alan Fennell**
directed by **David Elliott**
first broadcast 17 March 1966

The Hood adds his own camera to the filming of a movie in the Nevada Desert. Using telepathy, he forces Kyrano to disable Thunderbird 1's Automatic Camera Detector, then engineers an explosion that prompts International Rescue to save two actors stranded at the location...

Alan Fennell's script parodies the previous decade's science-fiction B movies and the crass Hollywood culture in which they thrived. Every level of the business is lampooned, beginning with an uninterested make-up girl (Sylvia Anderson) and an egotistical actor (Ray Barrett) who claims he has better things to do than playing a Martian zombie. Higher up the chain is the corrupt, cigar-smoking producer Bletcher (David Graham). The pint of milk he keeps on his desk is presumably relief from an anxiety-induced stomach ulcer. In the middle of this hierarchy is Goldheimer (Barrett), a fawning, has-been director. Goldheimer employs a special effects man called Brian (Barrett) and is able to immediately play Scott a video recording of the day's rushes, all of which

suggests that Fennell was also taking his inspiration from the AP Films studio.

The final act is dominated by Scott and Virgil's efforts to prevent the Hood delivering his film of the rescue operation to the Blofeld-like General X (Matt Zimmerman). There is little here to match the wit and ingenuity of the earlier action, although the Hood's accidental demolition of the General's mansion wraps things up in satisfyingly style.

a prism in at an angle. Part of the light that came down the lens hit the prism, and was then channelled to a monitor. This meant everyone who looked at the monitor was seeing exactly what I was shooting. I worked from the monitor – I didn't often look down the camera eyepiece."

While director David Lane approved of the CCTV system, he found shortcomings in its latest application. "Add-a-Vision used an Angenieux 10:1 zoom lens," he remembers. "The CCTV camera was now in front of the gate, rather than looking through the shutter, which was what they had before. This gave a much clearer, more accurate picture of what was being shot, and this was the image that Gerry had piped into his office. I hated the Angenieux zoom, because you couldn't get it where I wanted to get it on the puppet

sets – it didn't have the depth of field. I'd tell Alan Perry that I really wanted him to shoot a scene on the Arriflex, but we both knew that Gerry would be watching from his office. Alan suggested we put the Angenieux on the dolly, while we actually shot the scene with the Arri alongside it. So in those instances Gerry was looking at a picture that we weren't actually shooting."

Lane is quick to point out that such deceptions were purely pragmatic and only ever employed in the production's best interests. "I've never been so happy as I was working in that studio," he says. "Apart from the company directors at AP Films, it didn't feel as though there was an inner circle there because it was such a wonderful place to work. I've never known anything like it since – it was a really magic era."

Top and above: Christine Glanville, Mary Turner and Wanda Webb study monitors showing the puppets beneath their bridge.

The miniature sets that presented such a unique challenge to the camera crews were designed by supervising art director Bob Bell. "It was a fascinating period, and I learned a hell of a lot," he said in 1991. "I adjusted myself to time schedules, I learned how to design for films, I learned about scale and its use in films and I learned how not to get too het up. Later on, when I became a designer for feature films, I enjoyed it even more because I found it easy in comparison."

One of Bell's greatest innovations was a method to make it appear that puppets could walk through door frames. Bell created the illusion by constructing a tiny door lintel and hanging it between the top of the door frame and the camera lens. "The puppet would walk though the doorway that had no top, to allow for the wires, but with the foreground miniature of the lintel it would look as if it walked through a complete door frame. I was quite excited to see how it would look, and it was perfect, but I only did it on one or two occasions. It took a long time to line everything up and the camera had to be locked down, so it was a bit of a pain. And when you're working to a tight schedule you can't afford that sort of pain."

Production at Stirling Road was divided between the puppet and special effects stages. Puppet filming was supervised by each episode's director, while special effects were the responsibility of Derek Meddings. Each half of

Top: Supervising art director Bob Bell makes some careful adjustments on the set of Wilbur Dandridge III's office.

Above: The set as it appeared in *The Duchess Assignment*.

Right: Bell's designs included the Tracy Island lounge, seen here in *Operation Crash-Dive*.

the process had its own dedicated team. "My sets were primarily concerned with the puppet department," said Bell. "Anything a puppet appeared in or in front of, I designed and made. If, for example, the interior of a power station was required, then I would design it. If a puppet was then to press a button labelled 'Danger' and the shot cut to the outside of the station, this scene would have then been the responsibility of the special effects crew. The power station would probably have been designed by Derek Meddings. He'd create the outside and then blow it up!"

The APF art department had a dedicated office elsewhere on the Slough Trading Estate, in the nearby Edinburgh Avenue. Bell delegated to two assistants, Grenville Nott and Keith Wilson, who worked on alternate episodes of *Thunderbirds*. A team of specialist miniature prop-makers included Arthur Cripps, Tony Dunsterville, Eddie Hunter and Stewart Osborn. Together, they helped to realise Bell's vision of the future – designs that encompassed the Georgian trappings of Creighton-Ward Mansion, the luxurious modernity of Tracy Island, and a staggering array of international settings in between the two.

Above left: The *Thunderbirds* prop store at Stirling Road.

Above right: A publicity portrait of the International Rescue team, gathered on the set of Creighton-Ward Mansion.

Right: One of the prop statues that decorated the Hood's temple.

Below: This sweet cigarette card, issued by Barratt & Co in 1966, was entitled 'Inside the Asian Temple'.

Above left to right: Toothpaste tube caps (*30 Minutes After Noon*), a doorbell (*Sun Probe*), pieces of Lego (*City of Fire*) and a reel-to-reel tape recorder (*The Uninvited*) were just some of the items that Bob Bell, Grenville Nott and Keith Wilson used to embellish their props.

Below left: These cutaway illustrations from the first *Thunderbirds* annual recreated Bell's designs for the interior of Thunderbird 5.

Below right: The tape recorder fixed to the Thunderbird 5 set was a battery-operated Homey HR-408A. This portable device featured a built-in speaker and a microphone.

Although there was no time for Bell's foreground miniatures on *Thunderbirds*, he continued to find ingenious solutions to on-set problems. "Most of the sets in the science-fiction series were very practical," he remembered. "They might have tables and chairs and some books tucked on a shelf, but they'd also have a console with a screen where they'd talk to people out on a mission. One of our problems in those days was dressing up the panels of the consoles, which were full of knobs and lights. I used to ask the crew, in fact

everyone working for AP Films, to save their toothpaste tube caps which we painted and stuck in a row to form knobs on a control unit.

"I used to go to Lisle Street, just behind Leicester Square. Before the war I went there with my mates to look at the prostitutes, but after the war it had a shop that sold second-hand wireless parts. It was a sort of fairyland as I could buy all kinds of dials and grilles from loudspeakers which were probably overspills from factories. Each lunchtime the

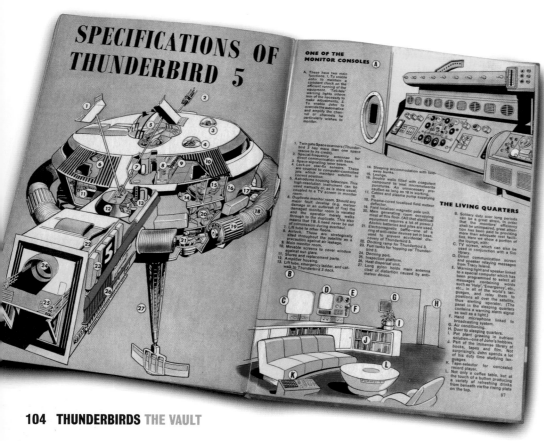

street became filled with radio enthusiasts in search of vital replacement parts. I would take several large bags, fill them up and stagger back to my car."

Bell's professional association and friendship with Gerry Anderson continued until his death in 2009. One of the few souvenirs Anderson retained from the Supermarionation years was a framed illustration by Bell, depicting the frenzy of activity at Stirling Road.

"At the time I didn't realise how big the puppet films would become, and how important they were to children of that era," Bell remarked. "If I meet someone aged between 30 and 50 and I tell them I worked on *Thunderbirds* they'll often tell me it was their favourite programme. It's so thrilling to meet people who appreciate work that one did so long ago. I get a great kick out of that."

Above: The control room from the runaway monotrain in *Brink of Disaster* was another set that incorporated a doorbell.

Left: This Barratt sweet cigarette card featured an illustration of Thunderbird 5's communications console.

1.11 BRINK OF DISASTER

teleplay by **Alan Fennell**
directed by **David Lane**
first broadcast 24 February 1966

Warren Grafton visits Creighton-Ward Mansion to secure investment for his new monotrain, but a suspicious Penelope nominates Jeff Tracy. Damage to automated signals spells doom for the train, with Jeff, Tin Tin and Brains on board. Back in England, two of Grafton's associates burgle Penelope's house...

The subplot extending the 25-minute version of this story asks us to believe that Warren Grafton (David Graham), the head of the syndicate behind the Pacific Atlantic Monorail Company, is also a New York gangster who masterminds the theft of Lady Penelope's jewellery collection. These thinly connected ideas strain credulity, but *Brink of Disaster* succeeds because both plot strands would have been worthy of an episode in their own right.

As their monotrain hurtles towards a shattered bridge, Jeff, Tin Tin and Brains become increasingly desperate, but at Creighton-Ward Mansion things remain perfectly calm from the moment that Parker surreptitiously informs his mistress that he recognises Grafton's chauffeur, Harry Molloy (David Graham), as an American mobster.

The visit by Grafton confuses Penelope, but she seems to regard the ensuing mayhem as a minor irritation. "I hope they don't scratch the paintwork," she tells Parker as the burglars steal FAB 1. "I'm off to Ascot in the morning."

This episode places three of Tracy Island's leading characters in extreme jeopardy, but elsewhere reminds us that *Thunderbirds* can be just as entertaining when it breaks from its rescue format.

Top and above: John Blundall creates a wig for a puppet at Stirling Road. On the workshop wall are various *Thunderbirds* heads and Tin Tin's Air Terrainean bag.

Right: Sculptor Terry Curtis used close-up photographs of human eyes to create a lifelike appearance for the puppets' eyes in *Thunderbirds*.

While Bell was designing the sets in Edinburgh Avenue, members of the puppet workshop in Stirling Road were sculpting the heads of *Thunderbirds*' 13 major cast members. "Creating the puppet characters in the first place is a long and difficult task," Anderson told *Television Mail*'s John Dickson. "Heads are sculpted in clay, then roughly painted so that the final results can be judged. With luck the head goes to the next process, but more often than not it is scrapped and the whole procedure starts again. Heads which are accepted as sympathetic character visualisation are copied in the form of a fibreglass shell. Puppet bodies are now produced in plastic, and

these can be produced in quantity at very short notice, because a library of male and female bodies has been built at Slough, so that a character can be made up from interchangeable components. The balance of a puppet is of great importance. The weight has to be just right, for if the figure is too heavy it will require heavy control wires which will be easily visible, and a strain on the operators, while a light puppet does not respond to control."

When Dickson wanted to find out more about the new fibreglass process known as Bondaglass he turned to Mrs P Smith, "wife of the creator of one of the techniques used." Mrs Smith explained: "For the creation of *Thunderbirds* characters we supply AP Films with special glass-fibre cloth and a polyester resin, similar to that used in the automobile industry for glass-fibre car bodies. However a matt is used for coach work, whereas the glass-fibre cloth is smooth and suitable for modelling. A plaster mould is made, as described by Mr Anderson, and then the constructor of the figure starts to laminate, putting on various layers of cloth, each of which is soaked in the resin. It becomes touch dry in 30 minutes, completely dry in an hour. The final colour is a natural beige; the resin itself is merely translucent... *Thunderbirds* figures also involve the use of a material known as Bondapaste, a putty-like filling compound which is used to fill cracks and contours, although it is not intended to be a moulding medium."

Someone who was less than enthusiastic about these innovations was puppet sculptor John Blundall. Something of a traditionalist, Blundall had been part of APF since Christine

Glanville asked him to join the crew of *Supercar* as both a sculptor and operator. The introduction of Bondaglass on *Thunderbirds* was simply the latest in his list of grievances with the Andersons.

"Making marionettes is more a science than an art," he argued in 2008. "I was always trying to improve the technology. I designed and made a whole series of bodies in highly polished wood, with ball-and-socket joints. When you relaxed the strings they would actually stand in attitudes. The ball-and-socket joints were there to prevent the clothes getting trapped, but the clothes were generally very tight anyway, and that's why the figures never walked properly. Later on all the bodies were cast and moulded out of materials that were totally unsuitable. The puppets had very heavy bodies and very light arms and legs, which create problems with balance."

Before each series began, Blundall and his colleagues – who included puppetry supervisors Christine Glanville and Mary Turner – created the stock characters. "When Christine, Mary and the others went on the bridge to operate figures that left me to

continue running the workshop, creating the other characters," said Blundall. "To my mind they were often more interesting, and in the early series in particular we would also make creatures, monsters and all sorts of things. It was Lew Grade who said the audience didn't like that sort of thing, but I don't know if that was actually the case. "Mary was steeped in puppetry; her mother was a very good puppeteer and made very fine puppets too. Mary was a very good sculptor as well, but for me a little bit bland. Different artists use different techniques, and I remember she used to work with a mirror sometimes; do one side then turn it over so the puppet's face was perfectly symmetrical. When you do that you can sometimes lose the character, but she was very methodical and completely dedicated.

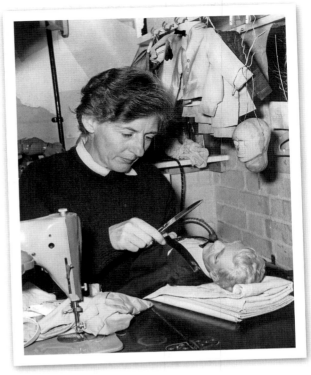

Above: Wardrobe mistress Elizabeth Coleman dresses Olsen, one of the characters from *The Cham-Cham*.

Below left: An APF sculptor seeks inspiration from the actors' directory *Spotlight*.

Below right: Mary Turner (centre) and her assistant Judith Shutt (left) create new characters in the Stirling Road workshop.

"Christine was brilliant. She was a very good designer, creator and maker of heads. And like me, she was very interested in dance and opera, so the influence of theatre became very strong."

Mary Turner and her assistant Judith Shutt also sculpted Brains, John, Gordon and Penelope. John Brown, another puppeteer, was the sculpting supervisor and made Virgil, Jeff and the Hood. Other sculptors in the workshop included Tim Cooksey, Terry Curtis, Peter Hayward and Mike Richardson. The hands and head mechanisms were made by outside companies, as were the puppets' teeth – supplied by a dental technician in Maidenhead.

Mary Turner's sculpt of Lady Penelope was closely scrutinised by Sylvia Anderson. As each new version was rejected, it seemed that Turner would be subjected to the same pressure suffered by Christine Glanville while making Venus for *Fireball XL5*.

"Mary and I worked and worked at it, but we had a lot of trouble getting Penelope right," says Sylvia. "I asked her to take it home for the weekend to see if she could do anything with it. When she came back she showed me what she'd done and I thought we were nearly there. When some reporters came to the studio they asked me who the Penelope puppet was based on. I didn't know, so I asked them to speak to Mary. She came in and I let them loose with her. They asked her who Penelope was based on and she said, 'Oh, Sylvia.' I said 'What?!' They looked and me and said, 'You knew all the time!' But I didn't. I would have been embarrassed if I'd recognised anything."

Below left: Sylvia Anderson was a frequent visitor to the wardrobe department at Stirling Road.

Below right: Of all the Supermarionation puppets, Penelope was the one that most closely resembled Sylvia.

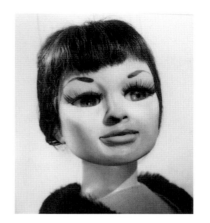

Left: Publicity portraits of Alan, Virgil and Tin Tin.

Below: The puppets' heads were sometimes used to portray more than one character. The head in the centre of this picture appeared as Professor Heinz Bodman in *Sun Probe* and Dr RG Korda in *Day of Disaster*.

Bottom: *Thunderbirds'* puppetry supervisors Christine Glanville and Mary Turner with some of their cast members. A picture of Sean Connery is pinned to the wall behind them.

While Mary Turner struggled with Penelope, Christine Glanville and her assistant, puppeteer Wanda Webb, sculpted Alan, Scott and Tin Tin. In 1991 Glanville fondly recalled the inspiration for Scott. "It was very difficult to create a face from someone else's description. Reg was an artist, so he could draw his ideas, but none of the others were. The only other way was to look at the actors' directory, *Spotlight*, and this is what we did. We didn't copy the faces we saw there, but rather used them as types. Sean Connery was the handsome hero of the time. He was young and modern, so happily I was given the job of modelling his face. He did actually turn out to be more of a copy than a type."

On instructions from Sylvia, Glanville modelled Alan on Robert Reed, a fresh-faced actor from the American legal drama *The Defenders* (1961-65). When Sylvia tried the same approach with John Blundall she got short shrift. "She'd often come into the workshop with a copy of *Spotlight* that had tags in various pages," he remembered. "She'd show you a page

and say that so-and-so should look like him or her. I had to say to her, 'I'm sorry, that isn't the way I work.' I didn't want to make the puppets look like exactly like actors; I worked to create a character. So to be quite honest I was being bloody-minded when I made Parker."

Right: Publicity portraits of Parker, Kyrano and Grandma, the three main characters sculpted by John Blundall.

Below left: An advertisement from the *Thunderbirds* supplement that appeared in the December 1965 issue of *Television Mail*.

Below right: Blundall at work on a character from *Fireball XL5* in 1962.

A TEAM PROUD TO
BE ENGAGED ON

THUNDERBIRDS

PUPPETEERS
CHRISTINE
GLANVILLE
MARY TURNER
MEL CROSS
PLUG SHUTT
WANDA WEBB

✳ ★ ✳

WARDROBE
ELIZABETH
COLEMAN

✳ ★ ✳

PROPS
TONY
DUNSTERVILLE
STEWART OSBORN

✳ ★ ✳

SCULPTORS
JOHN F. BROWN
TIM COOKSEY
TERRY CURTIS
PETER HAYWARD
MIKE
RICHARDSON

ALL GO PEOPLE
FOR AN ALL GO
PROGRAMME

Blundall admitted that Penelope's chauffeur was in fact inspired by a couple of film stars, but stressed that this was only part of his creative process. "I was thinking of small-time crooks, barrow-boy types who wanted to better themselves, and the sort of characters played by Ronald Shiner and Miles Malleson in old movies. If you look you can see aspects of both of them in Parker's face, but I also applied some of the technical aspects of Japanese Noh masks. David Graham was wonderful, and we understood each other very well. The voice he came up with reinforced the stylisation. I think we proved the point, because Parker is a character that's recognised all over the world. Particularly in Japan, where he's a superstar."

Along with Parker, Blundall also sculpted Kyrano and Grandma – it's no coincidence that all three have more exaggerated features than any other puppet in the series. "I didn't like the idea of creating naturalistic little human figures," said Blundall. "With puppets you should try to create what an actor can't do, not try to duplicate it. If you look at the puppet faces I created throughout the programmes you'll see they're not caricatured, they're stylised. The art of creating puppets is to give the character

teleplay by **Alan Pattillo**
directed by **Alan Pattillo, Desmond Saunders**
first broadcast 14 October 1965

Professor Borender, one of the pioneers of a new process to create rocket fuel from sea water, goes missing on a journey from Paris to Anderbad. Aboard the Anderbad Express monotrain, Lady Penelope and Borender's colleague Sir Jeremy Hodge discover the terrible truth about his fate...

In *Brink of Disaster*, FAB 1 deployed some special features worthy of James Bond's Aston Martin in the 1964 film *Goldfinger*, and uncannily like that car's gadgets in *Thunderball* (1965). In *The Perils of Penelope*, Lady P's mission takes her to the French Heraldry Archives (in 'Rue Desmonde') for a sequence that could have been inspired by Bond's visit to the College of Arms in the 1963 novel *On Her Majesty's Secret Service*.

The title of this episode never appears on screen, but Alan Pattillo's script was named after *The Perils of Pauline*, pre-war cinema serials that regularly placed their heroine in cliffhanger jeopardy. Rather than having Penelope bound to railway tracks, Pattillo updates a famous old sequence by tying her to a ladder that's placed in the path of a monotrain.

Despite these homages, the most obvious model for this idiosyncratic episode is neither James Bond nor silent cinema. Lady Penelope's collaboration with International Rescue associate Sir Jeremy Hodge (Peter Dyneley) has much more in common with *The Avengers*, a contemporaneous hit that thrived on pairing the stylish Cathy Gale (Honor Blackman) with the traditional John Steed (Patrick Macnee).

a life and soul and spirit of its own. You should be able to register the puppet's character before it even moves."

Although Gerry Anderson adored Parker – which was ultimately the only puppet he kept from the series – it took him many years to appreciate Blundall's point of view. Anderson had little interest in the art of puppetry, and Blundall found it impossible to tolerate his inexorable drive towards realism. Feeling increasingly sidelined, Blundall quit APF in March 1965 to take a lower-paid job at a Welsh puppet theatre. He harboured a private resentment towards Anderson for the rest of his life, but escaped the shadow of *Thunderbirds* to become one of the world's foremost scholars and historians of puppetry. He died in 2014.

Right: This string puppet was part of a *Thunderbirds* range produced by the Cecil Coleman company in 1965.

To Sylvia, the puppets' attire was almost as important as their facial features. "I think Gerry always had the final say, but Sylvia was really in charge of the characters," says Lane. "When it came to *Thunderbirds*, she designed the puppets' costumes and dressed them. When you were making an episode she would always be talking to you about Lady Penelope, checking that her hair was right, her eyes were right and so on. She

had an obsession with that, and it's quite understandable – she built the character and brought it to life with her voice."

Out of all the *Thunderbirds* cast, Penelope had the most expansive wardrobe – in *The Imposters* she packs light for what she describes an "emergency mission" to the United States, but even this entails more suitcases than Parker can squeeze into the boot of FAB 1. On the way to London Airport she seeks inspiration for

further purchases by perusing a copy of fashion magazine *What's New*.

It was the job of wardrobe mistress Elizabeth Coleman to realise Sylvia's ideas. Coleman literally had her work cut out on *The Duchess Assignment*, where Penelope goes through eight different costumes and numerous accessories. Sylvia also commissioned life-size versions of Penelope's outfits, including that episode's Mondrian dress and the frock she

wore to a Television Society awards ceremony in May 1966. For the launch of the *Lady Penelope* comic in November 1965 she and a Penelope puppet wore matching dresses that had been hand-painted by Keith Wilson. Sylvia promoted the perception that she was somehow invisible from International Rescue's London agent, at the same time adding to her own wardrobe. "That was my way of getting some nice clothes!" she now jokes.

Above left to right: More highlights from Penelope's seemingly endless collection – the Mondrian dress from *The Duchess Assignment*, two of the frocks Penelope wears while posing as cabaret artiste Wanda Lamour in *The Cham-Cham* and lounge wear from *Atlantic Inferno*.

The approvals process on *Thunderbirds* was particularly fraught, but once a major puppet was accepted the workshop was then commissioned to create a duplicate – the two puppet stages worked on different episodes, but each required the leading characters simultaneously. In addition, four or five heads were created for each version of every leading character. Different heads had different facial expressions or the capability to blink, as opposed to the usual mechanism for moving eyes left to right. "We call them 'smilers', 'scowlers' and so on," said Reg Hill, telling John Dickson about the extraordinary lengths APF went to in an effort to make their essentially static puppets appear animated. "And of course for the special effects shots there are duplicates of many of the characters in quite different scales.

1.13 TERROR IN NEW YORK CITY

teleplay by **Alan Fennell**
directed by **David Elliott, David Lane**
first broadcast 21 October 1965

Scott can deal with an irritating journalist who attempts to film Thunderbird 1, but Virgil is less fortunate when a misjudged attack by the US Navy cripples Thunderbird 2. The incident leaves International Rescue ill-prepared to deal with the collapse of the Empire State Building...

After mocking Hollywood filmmakers in *Martian Invasion*, Alan Fennell turns his satirical gaze to the American television networks. Reporter Ned Cook (Matt Zimmerman) of the NTBS Newservice Division is a man who, as Jeff Tracy observes, would "do anything for a story". This extends to flagrantly disregarding the rules surrounding the coverage of International Rescue's operations; Ned instructs his cameraman Joe (David Graham) to shoot Thunderbird 1 in action, only for their videotape to be subsequently wiped by Scott.

The Hood has previously tried to steal International Rescue's secrets, but this scenario tackles the threat posed by opportunists such as Ned and the mistaken act of aggression launched by the *USN Sentinel*. Like many previous episodes, *Terror in New York City*

features two major plot strands – in this instance the maintenance of IR's security and the consequences of moving the Empire State Building – but unlike some of the scripts originally written for the 25-minute format it dovetails them perfectly.

Fennell's final act is quintessential *Thunderbirds*, with one jeopardy piled on another, a last-minute rescue and the sentimental redemption of the wheelchair-bound Ned.

"Main characters, such as Jeff Tracy, his five handsome sons, Kyrano, Tin Tin, Hood, Brains, Lady Penelope and Parker are mostly built up of fibreglass," continued Hill. "But the 'revamp' puppets (those playing bit parts!) are constructed from plastic shells. During the making of a series like this, characters change. Parker, the impassive chauffeur and perfect butler, was not originally envisaged as a main character but the critics liked him... Well, the same thing happens with live-action!"

The official term 'Supermarionators' was rarely used – and even then only in the pages of the trade press. To everyone else, the characters in *Thunderbirds* were operated by puppeteers. Christine Glanville supervised the puppetry on one of the stages, and Mary Turner supervised the other.

"My association with Christine lasted many years," said Anderson, "and she was an absolute darling. I used to drive her up the wall, however, as I was always striving to make our shows more and more life-like, which was the antithesis of Christine's approach. She was a 'pure' puppeteer, but she eventually came round to my way of thinking and we learned from each other."

Glanville remained loyal to Anderson from her first assignment for him, *The Adventures of Twizzle*, through to the end of her life in 1999. "Gerry would present a challenge and we simply had to solve it," she said. "He was never interested in a negative comment like 'A puppet can't do this or that.' We just had to find a way, and using all the film techniques we usually did."

One technique Glanville and her colleagues found especially useful was the CCTV system. The puppeteers worked from 25-foot wide steel gantries, positioned high above the sets. The images displayed on their monitor screens were reversed. "On the Gerry Anderson shows we always had the monitors switched, so they showed a mirror image of what we were doing," said Glanville. "I would have found it very difficult to do it any other way – imagine looking at an image and turning your head one way, only for the picture to turn in the opposite direction. It made it much easier to find eyelines. You had to have one puppet looking at another puppet in the eyes, and sometimes things that actually looked correct on the stage wouldn't appear that way on camera. But if you judged it from looking at the monitor then you could get it right."

Opposite page: *The Imposters*' Jeremiah Tuttle is in the centre of these off-duty puppets.

Below left: Wanda Webb and Christine Glanville, operating from a bridge above one of Stirling Road's puppet stages.

Below right: Gordon Tracy was based on a design by Mary Turner and her assistant Judith Shutt.

Glanville's style was more instinctual than that of her fellow supervisor Mary Turner. "Mary was a very accurate puppeteer," she remembered. "What she did in rehearsal was matched during each take. She was a very neat, precise worker. The director always knew what he was getting, which was not the case with me. If I did something that was good and we had to do a re-take, I could never repeat it as I didn't know what I had done to get it right!"

The other puppeteers on *Thunderbirds* included Yvonne Hunter, Ernest Shutt, Judith Shutt, Carolyn Turner and Wanda Webb. The team's skill was conspicuous in the scenes where puppets were called upon to do things that many actors would have found demanding, such as when Penelepe is tied to a chair in *The Man from MI.5* and attempts to shuffle her way across the room. But even things most actors would have considered effortless demanded highly precise operating from the puppeteers. At the beginning of *The Duchess Assignment*, for example, Parker lights the tip of Lady Penelope's cigarette, and at the end of *Move – And You're Dead*, Alan shoots a knowing glance at the audience before appearing to lean towards Tin Tin for a kiss. For more complex shots, close-ups of real hands and feet – or in the case of *Vault of Death*, Judith Shutt's left eye – were intercut with the puppets.

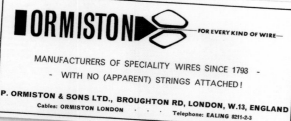
Top: Christine Glanville and Wanda Webb are among the puppeteers on a bridge in this picture taken during the production of *Thunderbirds* in 1965.

Above: A 1965 advertisement for the Ealing-based company that supplied APF with steel wire to suspend the puppets.

Right: Another of the Cecil Coleman string puppets produced in 1965.

Below: Judith Shutt uses a Murrayprodder to pass a puppet up to a bridge.

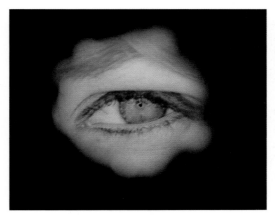

By the second series this practise had reached epic proportions – *Alias Mr. Hackenbacker* features almost 30 inserts of human hands.

Puppets were generally controlled by nine long wires attached to a conventional X-shaped control bar. The length of the wires (another of John Blundall's grievances) meant that a special system had to be devised to get tangle-free control bars up to the bridge. Puppets would be brought across using devices that were nicknamed 'Murrayprodders' – these were essentially long wooden sticks with crossbars at the top. Hooks embedded in each crossbar would go under the controllers and the puppets would hang beneath. The name Murrayprodder came from Murray Clark, a puppeteer on some of Anderson's earliest productions. Reportedly prone to bouts of laziness, Clark would be prodded into action by one of these sticks.

The use of Murrayprodders meant that wires remained taut, minimising the risk that they would kink and break. There remained, however, the problem of meeting Anderson's insistence that the wires should be invisible on screen. "A puppet weighs seven or eight pounds, and has to be moved, and although

it is possible to use steel wire only 0.003-inch diameter for arms, the main wires which take the weight need to be at least 0.005-inch diameter," Reg Hill told John Dickson. "Now this is much thicker than a human hair (around 0.002), and of course on a good domestic TV receiver it is frequently possible to distinguish a hair standing out. So you will see the problem we have in concealing wires. It has to be steel, and although there are alloys of greater tensile strength than we customarily use, at present these cannot be drawn finer than 12 thou or so. Copper can be drawn incredibly fine, but unfortunately this stretches and – worse – *stays* stretched. Our special steel wire is drawn by Ormiston's of Ealing, who also have developed special treatments for non-reflection. We initiated a technique of blackening by a photographic process, but this has now been improved, and the process is confidential."

Above left: A pair of real feet help to depict Penelope's gruelling journey in *The Imposters*.

Above centre: Judith Shutt doubles for an inquisitive Penelope in *Vault of Death*.

Above right: More human intervention as a London Airport officer detonates the Skythrust's ejectable fuel pod in *Alias Mr. Hackenbacker*.

Below: Christine Glanville and Mary Turner demonstrate the Murrayprodder on the set of *Four Feather Falls* in 1959.

1.14 END OF THE ROAD

teleplay by **Dennis Spooner**
directed by **David Lane**
first broadcast 25 November 1965

The successful completion of a major road-building contract means everything to civil engineer Eddie Houseman. When the project's deadline is threatened by treacherous terrain and a monsoon, Eddie decides to neglect the lovestruck Tin Tin and ignore his safety-conscious business partner...

While far from being a soap opera, *End of the Road* introduces an element of domestic tension between the residents of Tracy Island, and relatively sophisticated emotional dilemmas elsewhere.

Alan has fallen in love with Tin Tin, but is forced to watch from the sidelines as Eddie Houseman (Ray Barrett) sweeps her off her feet during a surprise visit. Eddie makes a hasty departure to safeguard the future of his construction company, and then argues with his partner Bob Gray (David Graham) about whether or not they should continue. This tense scene is arguably *Thunderbirds'* first adoption of the boardroom-drama style that Gerry Anderson so admired in the television series *The Plane Makers* (1963-65).

Eddie's one-man attempt to blast a path through a mountain almost gets him killed, and Bob contacts International Rescue. Alan is clearly reluctant to rescue Eddie for personal reasons, and the others wonder whether they should try to save someone who could identify them.

Despite this anguish there is ultimately no place for moral ambiguity or unhappy endings. Jeff points out that "We don't turn down *any* call", and by the time Alan heads back to the base Tin Tin has come to her senses.

Below: APF had been disguising puppet wires against backdrops painted with vertical lines since *The Adventures of Twizzle*. This technique continued with *Thunderbirds*.

Bob Bell's sets would often include design motifs featuring vertical lines, but this would only go part of the way towards disguising the wires. "I was quite good at blending them into the background using Anti-Flare No 1 spray and various colours of powder paints," remembered Christine Glanville. "The puppeteers hated the powder paint, because sometimes it would come off the wires and drop onto the puppets' hair. This was all right if the puppet had black hair, but it wasn't good if the puppet was blonde."

More than 50 years after the production of *Thunderbirds*, Alan Perry is still bemused that so much time was spent trying to create the illusion of live-action. "Gerry was trying to get away from the fact that they were puppets, even though they were what made him famous," he says. "Full-length shots of them walking were one of his pet hates. One way round that was going in close while someone held their legs out of shot and bobbed them up and down a bit so they looked like they were walking."

With each new Supermarionation series it seemed the puppets increasingly relied on vehicles and other machinery to move them from one place to another. "Gerry didn't like the walks and he was always trying to improve them," said Glanville in 1991. "Seeing *Thunderbirds* again, I'm surprised there are as many walking scenes as there are, or at least the beginnings of walking scenes."

Although the characters often comprised numerous duplicated elements, the value and delicacy of the puppets meant they were carefully stored in a designated area when not being used. Some of them would, however, find their way to other parts of the studio. Anderson in particular took a dim view of opening up in the morning to find Parker and Penelope *in flagrante* on the studio floor. The culprit was never discovered, but Christine Glanville suspected mischievous director Desmond Saunders.

Above: When not required for filming, puppets were suspended in a specially designated area of the Stirling Road studio.

Left: Preparing to film the final sequence in *30 Minutes After Noon*, as Southern and Penelope conclude their dinner at Creighton-Ward Mansion.

Below: *Vault of Death*'s Lambert, in one of the few *Thunderbirds* scenes that showed a character walking.

Above: Lighting cameraman Paddy Seale takes a reading on the set of *The Imposters*. The Jenkins puppet (right) had previously appeared as a policeman in *Terror in New York City* – the hat it wore in that episode is still suspended on the wires above its head.

Top right: This publicity photo was taken on the set of Brains' laboratory. The two puppets are guest characters from *Pit of Peril*.

Right: Scott confers with the controller of the Thompson Tower in this shot from *City of Fire*.

Shooting scenes with puppets on miniature sets had long been a challenge for the studio's supervising lighting cameraman (ie director of photography) John Read. On *Thunderbirds*, each puppet stage had its own lighting cameraman – Paddy Seale was in charge of lighting on Christine Glanville's stage and Julien Lugrin was in charge on Mary Turner's. Lugrin had survived polio, and walked with the aid of aluminium crutches. "Alan Perry's got a wicked sense of humour," says David Lane. "He always used to say about Julien, 'May he rust in peace!'"

Perry was Seale's camera operator, and he distinctly remembers the additional challenge posed by shooting in colour. "In black and white you had to build contrast ratios to get sharper, more dramatic pictures, but *Stingray* was the first time anyone in England had filmed a whole series in colour for television. About a month before we started shooting,

Reg Hill went out to America to look at colour television and find out how it should be done. When he came back he spoke to the directors of photography – John Read, Julien Lugrin and Paddy Seale – and told them that the colour would take care of itself as long as we didn't have any high contrast ratios. This meant that we couldn't have hard or heavy shadows, so we would diffuse the light to make it soft."

The studio's Mole-Richardson lamps would be strategically aimed at all corners of the sets to create as 'flat' a lighting scheme as possible. David Lane was one of the directors who felt that the rules of lighting for colour were too restrictive. "You were always, always arguing with the lighting cameraman about the contrast ratio," he says. "I would always say, 'Can't we make this scene a bit darker?' and he'd say, 'No, the contrast ratio for television has to stay at this level.' Nowadays you can virtually shoot in the dark, but the technology wasn't as receptive in those days."

Another problem that plagued lighting cameramen and camera operators on all four stages was depth of field. "Our biggest sets are no more than ten foot deep, and with standard lenses that brings depth of focus troubles, so the only solution is to stop down and illuminate at high level," John Read told Chauncey Jerome. "As is well-known in camera work, the closer in one has to get, the greater the depth of focus you need to hold for a given distance. Our cameras are usually worked close to the floor for these small stages, and the average point of focus is around five feet six inches."

Above: Filming John on the set of Thunderbird 5.

Below right: This picture, taken during the filming of *The Duchess Assignment*, shows how many lights were required on the puppet stages.

Below left: Scott and Virgil watch the filming of a science-fiction movie at the end of *Martian Invasion*.

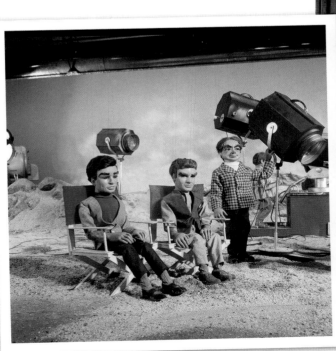

Below: Belgian cigar bands decorated with pictures of Penelope and Parker from *The Duchess Assignment*.

Bottom left: Mary Turner and director David Elliott (pointing) prepare to film Penelope's visit to the recovering Deborah in *The Duchess Assignment*.

Bottom right: The scene as it appeared in the finished episode.

The Arriflex cameras on the puppet stages and the Mitchell R35s on the special effects stages were running from Monday morning to Saturday lunchtime, and sometimes even longer. Over a million feet of 35mm film was consumed by APF from 1964 to '65. At the end of 1965 it was estimated that the company was Britain's largest consumer of colour stock.

Alan Perry remembers that each puppet stage was expected to produce between four and four-and-a-quarter minutes of usable footage per day. This would be considered a high turnover on most film sets, and is approximately four times what could be achieved on the special effects stages, which had even more technically demanding set-ups.

"Four minutes was a hell of a lot," says Perry, "but we knew exactly how long each scene should be because the dialogue came from pre-recorded tapes. While we were shooting, it was my job to get the composition the director wanted. I would make suggestions, depending on the length of the scene. If it was 25 or 30 seconds I might suggest a move, such as a tracking shot, but that was always done in consultation with the director. I had to help him make the compositions and the close-ups as interesting as possible."

The directors of the puppet units took overall credit for each episode. The 32 episodes of *Thunderbirds* were directed by just five people: Brian Burgess, David Elliott, David Lane, Alan Pattillo and Desmond Saunders.

"David Elliott was a good director," says Perry. "He had been an editor, and editors are storytellers – they know where a wide-angle is supposed to be, and where to use a close-up."

There is a common consensus, however, that Alan Pattillo was one of the production's greatest talents. "He was very good," says Perry. "He really worked hard to make those puppets look interesting. I learned a lot from him."

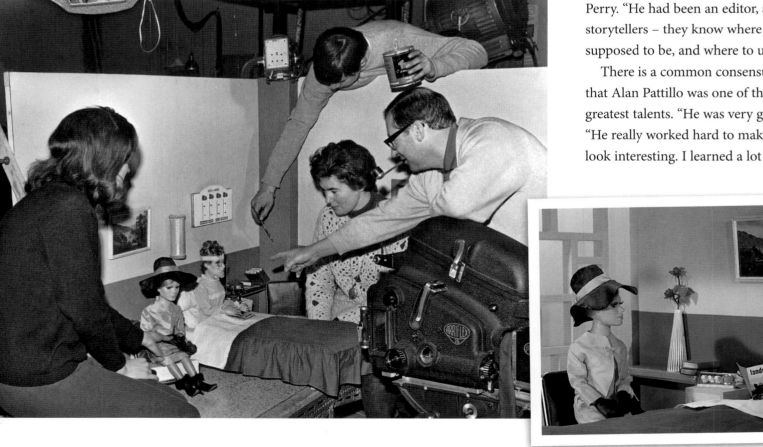

Pattillo also earned the respect of fellow director David Lane, who considers him "The best, without question. Emotionally, he got things right. There were a lot of nice little touches in his directing. He would write some of them as well, and I felt his shows really had the Alan Pattillo stamp."

Pattillo's sensitivity even impressed John Blundall. "Alan had a very strong feeling for the theatre, and he really did seem to enjoy working with the figures. I thought his direction was much stronger than the others, more organic. And he was a nice, thoughtful guy. He would talk to you about the characters. He was an interesting guy to work with."

Right: Director Desmond Saunders and Bob Bell on the set of the Tracy Island lounge in 1966. Jeff is holding a novel based on the film *Thunderbirds Are Go*.

1.15 DAY OF DISASTER

teleplay by **Dennis Spooner**
directed by **David Elliott**
first broadcast 4 November 1965

The Martian Space Probe rocket and two of its engineers are travelling over Allington Bridge when its suspension cables snap and the rocket plunges into the river. The automated launch countdown begins and Gordon must save the engineers before the rocket explodes...

If one can accept that Cape Kennedy would construct a Martian Space Probe and then take the trouble to bring it to England for its launch, then this story presents a refreshing picture of Anglo-American relations.

The Englishmen in charge of the doomed bridge are rather more believable than some of their toffee-nosed predecessors, but elsewhere it's business as usual. "In my home, *everything* stops for tea," Penelope tells the visiting Brains. Rocket scientist Professor Wingrove (Peter Dyneley) is German, just like Professor Borender in *The Perils of Penelope* – recognition, no doubt, of the contribution German expertise made to the Space Race after the Second World War. And the psychiatrist Dr RG Korda (Ray Barrett) who treats Brains at the end is, of course, Austrian.

These stereotypes are presented in typically good humour by Dennis Spooner, who padded out his script with a comedy interlude about Jeff accidentally eating a raspberry-flavoured transmitter belonging to Grandma. Jeff blames three of his sons in turn, before realising he must have swallowed the device himself. Entirely unconnected to anything else in the episode, this is probably the most baffling sequence in the whole series.

Pattillo had joined APF when David Elliott suggested to Gerry Anderson that he should be hired as an editor on *Four Feather Falls*. The western remains Pattillo's favourite out of all the puppet series. "Subsequent to *Four Feather Falls* they felt very like live-action stories performed by puppets," he says, with a hint of regret. "The search was always for more and more realism."

Anderson entrusted Pattillo with *Trapped in the Sky*, aware that – even in its original 25-minute form – *Thunderbirds*' first episode was APF's most ambitious production to date. "Making it was awful," says Pattillo. "We had all sorts of technical problems that took ages to shoot. It took a long time to do and we all got very weary."

As the series' first director it was Pattillo's responsibility to shoot much of the launch sequence footage that would be recycled in later episodes. "There's one bit [in *Trapped in the Sky*] where Scott rings up the base, tells his father there's trouble at London Airport and he needs help. Jeff says to Virgil, 'All right Virgil, off you go,' and goes out of shot. Then we see what I call one of the library shots of him going down the chute. We had to film the scenes in any kind of order, as soon as the sets were ready. We'd already done the scenes where

Above: Desmond Saunders, Lily and Reg Hill, Christine Glanville and Alan Pattillo at the Dorchester Hotel on 13 May 1966. That evening APF was awarded the Television Society's silver medal for "work of outstanding artistic merit" on *Thunderbirds*.

Right: Fairylite produced a range of 12" *Thunderbirds* dolls in the mid-1960s, including Lady Penelope. The doll could be dressed in six additional outfits, which were available separately.

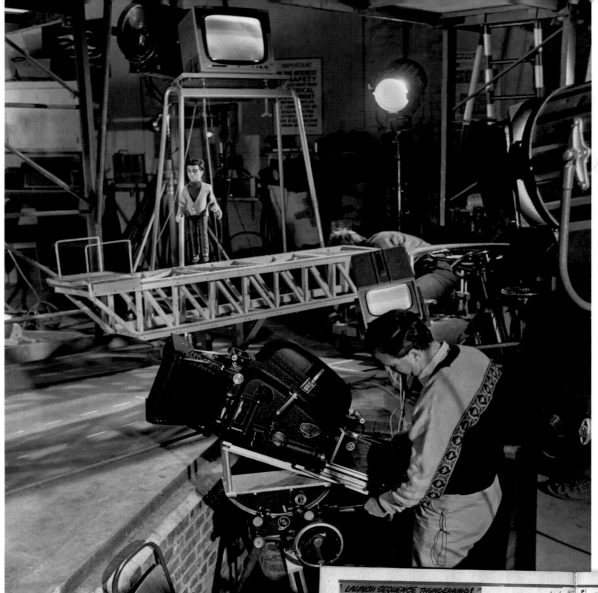

Top: Scott boards Thunderbird 1, in a sequence familiar from numerous episodes of *Thunderbirds*.

Above: The shot of Virgil's uniform that Alan Pattillo had to hastily insert for continuity reasons.

Left: Filming Scott's entrance to Thunderbird 1 during the making of *Trapped in the Sky*. Camera operators in both the puppet and special effects stages often worked from pits dug in the studio floor.

Below: How some of the launch sequences were described in the first *Thunderbirds* annual, published in 1966.

Virgil was in the cockpit of Thunderbird 2, getting ready to take off with his uniform on. But in the scenes where he was saying goodbye to his father and going down the chute he was in his civilian clothes. Now, we didn't notice this until the picture was cut together. So at the last minute we had to get a shot of his uniform, on something that looked like a cake-stand, coming out of a hole in the ground. I remember we stayed behind one night to get that little shot."

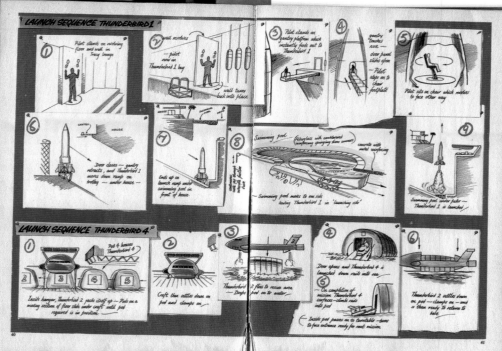

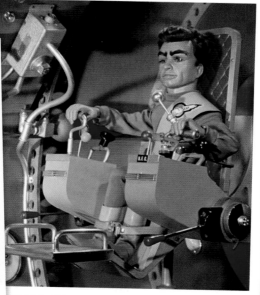

Left and above: Two pictures of Scott that indicate which scenes belong to the 25-minute version of *The Uninvited* and which scenes were shot for the ultimate, 50-minute version. The HFC (horizontal flight control) marker was added to the cockpit of Thunderbird 1 for *Martian Invasion*, and was still there when the crew returned to the set to extend *The Uninvited*.

Having worked with puppets on previous shows, it seems Anderson was aware of his directors' burden. "Gerry would leave you alone," says Pattillo. "While the filming was going on he very rarely interfered. He would sit in his office, watching what was going on with the camera on his monitor. If something worried him, such as the puppets' strings showing up, then he'd let you know. But with things like schedules he very rarely interfered. If we went over schedule he was very good about it. He'd just tactfully say something like, 'I hope you're going to finish soon.'"

The first nine episodes had either been shot or were shooting by December 1964, when Anderson screened a dubbed and edited version of *Trapped in the Sky* for Lew Grade at ATV's preview theatre in London. "This is not a television series," exclaimed Grade when the

1.16 EDGE OF IMPACT

teleplay by **Donald Robertson**
directed by **Desmond Saunders**
first broadcast 28 October 1965

The Hood is hired to sabotage the test flights of a new jet fighter. After the first flight crashes, the colonel in charge of the project visits Jeff at Tracy Island. This makes it difficult for International Rescue to launch when the second flight is diverted by the Hood's homing device...

A line from *End of the Road* provides a clue about the direction of this episode. When Eddie Houseman pays a surprise visit to Tracy Island, Virgil tells his father: "Lucky we didn't have a call while he was here."

This is exactly the situation Jeff finds himself in when Colonel Tim Casey (David Graham) visits him after being dismissed from supervising tests for the Red Arrow fighter. Casey is an old friend "from the early days of the space programme" but Jeff still won't tell him about International Rescue. When the next Red Arrow test flight crashes into a television relay tower, International Rescue receives a call for help and it's Tin Tin's job to divert Casey while Thunderbirds 1 and 2 take off. She takes him on a tour of more than

20 underground caves, looking for the mythical water mamba.

Donald Robertson's story is a disappointingly familiar routine of sabotaged test flights, but there is novelty in Brains' latest inventions. These range from the innovative (low altitude escape harnesses) to the frankly ridiculous – discreet security updates are provided by tiny flashing lights on Jeff's cocktail stick and Tin Tin's swimming cap.

lights went up. "This is a feature film!" He then told Anderson that he wanted each episode expanded to fill an hour's broadcast slot.

As a consequence, in early 1965 Alan Pattillo was appointed script editor and writer Tony Barwick was hired to help expand some of the scenarios. There was no time to immediately adapt episode ten, *Martian Invasion*, and episode 11, *Brink of Disaster*, so these were filmed as half-hour shows in January. From episode 12, *The Perils of Penelope*, each instalment was both scripted and shot in the series' ultimate format.

The New York branch of ITC required a new episode to be delivered every two weeks, and while Anderson was daunted by this demand he welcomed the dramatic possibilities of the new format. "The extended shows gave us more time for character development," he said. "For example, if you have a character that is put in jeopardy, the audience will either sit on the edge of their seat filled with concern

or they won't be the least bit interested, depending on how well the character has been set up in the first place. Suddenly, we were able to take a bunch of new characters, make them likeable and interesting and, at a point where we felt the kids knew enough about them and had got to like them, that was when disaster would strike. Part of the success of *Thunderbirds* was because it ran for an hour and enabled the character development that we were unable to feature in previous shows."

Top left: The restaurant kitchen is the root of the trouble in *Path of Destruction*. David Elliott bravely examines the meal that the owner cryptically refers to as "the special".

Top right: Pages from the episode's shooting script. The front cover features a prototype *Thunderbirds* logo that never reached the screen.

Right: An original negative can, returned to the archive by the Rank laboratory in Denham.

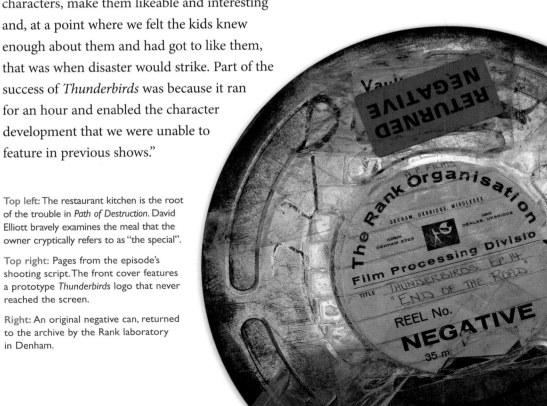

Above: Filming Culp and Blackmer's treacherous journey along the Ambro River in *Attack of the Alligators!*

Top right: A publicity shot from *Attack of the Alligators!* Moments later, the alligator went for Penelope. "We had terrible trouble trying to retrieve her leg," remembered Christine Glanville.

Below: "High society keeps me pretty busy." Penelope dances with Olsen in *The Cham-Cham.*

Writer Alan Fennell was similarly enthused. "The good thing about *Thunderbirds* was that we had time to run parallel plots," he said. "They started off as half-hours, but when they went to an hour it was wonderful to be able to develop that. At one point there were three separate productions going on at the same time: one was the new hour-long scripts that we were writing, two was changing the half-hours into hours, and three was they were still shooting half-hour scripts. We knew that eventually the half-hours that they were shooting would have to be extended, and it was a bit of a nightmare logistically."

The staff at Stirling Road soon adapted to the new way of working but, as had often been the case with previous series, the schedule began to suffer as production wore on. *The Cham-Cham* – written and directed by Alan Pattillo – was one of Anderson's personal favourites. Unfortunately, as Pattillo recalls, it went way over-schedule. "Gerry was very good about it," he says. "I was about three or four days over before he said anything. The next day he saw some rushes, and called me in to say they looked fabulous. We were perhaps over-ambitious on that one, trying to do things we hadn't done before, like Penelope dancing a slow foxtrot."

Attack of the Alligators! – written by Pattillo and directed by David Lane – proved to be one of the most memorable episodes. Its use of live animals caused significant problems for Derek Meddings' special effects department as well as the puppeteers. "On that one I remember Gerry said we had 48 hours to complete the episode – we'd have to make the film from whatever we'd shot in that time," says Lane. "So we went for 48 hours non-stop, simultaneously shooting and editing. Derek was filming the last special effects and I was putting them in as we were shooting. We got the film to the labs for processing at six o'clock in the morning."

Top: The Cass Carnaby Five back Wanda Lamour's performance of *Dangerous Game* in *The Cham-Cham*.

Right: An original stage costume worn by one of The Cass Carnaby Five at the Paradise Peaks Hotel.

Below: Christine Glanville and Wanda Webb prepare some of the audience members at Paradise Peaks.

Left: Operators from both puppet stages gather on a bridge for this crowd scene. Alan Pattillo, writer and director of *The Cham-Cham*, is bottom left.

1.17 DESPERATE INTRUDER

teleplay by **Donald Robertson**
directed by **David Lane**
first broadcast 18 November 1965

Brains and Tin Tin spend their holiday diving for sunken treasure at Lake Anasta, under the guidance of archaeologist Professor Blakely. Their underwater activities are being watched, however, and soon they come face to face with International Rescue's greatest enemy...

Aside from featuring only two guest characters – Professor Blakely (Peter Dyneley) and his taxi driver Hassan Ali (David Graham) – Donald Robertson's second script for the series is unusual because it chooses to ignore many of the themes that characterise *Thunderbirds*. Once Virgil takes Brains and Tin Tin to the Middle East the story remains centred in and around a single location. The emphasis on technology and engineering that is predominant in other episodes is almost entirely missing here.

This is a straightforward yarn about a struggle to possess a horde of jewels – Brains' and Tin Tin's archaeological curiosity verses the Hood's avarice. The extensive scenes beneath the surface of the lake give the AP Films team the chance to use the techniques they perfected on *Stingray*, as well as recycling a music cue and sound effects from that series.

The sight of Brains buried up to his neck in sand is a memorable image, and the Hood's encounter with Tin Tin brings her tantalisingly close to guessing the secret of his inside knowledge. Ultimately, however, we have to agree with Jeff when he says "International Rescue was not set up to go joyriding round on treasure trails."

Below: The Sidewinder is rescued in *Pit of Peril*. Gerry Anderson found editing the episode similarly challenging.

APF had six cutting rooms to deal with not only the high volume of footage on *Thunderbirds* but a style of editing that was unusually rapid by the standards of 1960s' filmed television series. "We must do three or four times the amount of cutting as in live-action," Reg Hill told John Dickson. "This is made necessary, for instance, by the fact that you cannot hold the interest of a scene for more than a few seconds since a puppet's facial expression cannot be altered... except by cutting, of course, to a different strip, shot when the puppet is fitted with a different head. In live-action you can hold a scene for an appreciable time, getting continuity of dramatic effect by an actor's changing expression, or perhaps by moving up from a mid-shot to a close-up of the actor's hand. With puppets this can be done, but it involves cutting – cutting, in many cases, from a close-up of the puppet's head to a live-action shot of a gloved hand."

Gerry Anderson brought his own technical expertise to bear in the cutting rooms, where he would ensure each episode bore the unique pace and rhythm of his shows. In the case of the second episode, *Pit of Peril*, the imposition of the longer format made this an insurmountable challenge. "It was an absolute pig of a film," he remembered. "For three weeks I kept cutting and recutting because we couldn't get it right. One night I said to the editor, 'Let it go. Cut the negative and dub it – we can't do anything more with this.'"

It was with some trepidation that Anderson later received a phone call from Abe Mandell, who ran ITC's New York office. "Gerry, I've just seen *Pit of Peril*," he said. "What a wonderful show. If only you could make them all like that!"

Thunderbirds' signature style included a penchant for including consecutive lines of identical, or near-identical, dialogue. This arresting trick was first used in *Trapped in the Sky*: Fireflash pilot Captain Hanson says "We don't stand a chance," before we cut to Commander Norman in the control tower, who mutters, "They haven't got a chance..."

When it came to film editing, the series wasn't above stealing from the best. In *Brink of Disaster*, overlapping the sound from a subsequent scene briefly creates the impression that a speeding monotrain has crashed, and in *The Perils of Penelope* the sound of an exploding firework suggests that her ladyship's Pernod has once again been shot from her hand.

Both are sequences that would have prompted amused recognition from Alfred Hitchcock.

Thunderbirds' groundbreaking opening titles were another creation of the APF cutting rooms. The montages of highlights that open each episode inherit their pace from *Stingray*'s similarly breathless title sequence. *Thunderbirds'* opening titles proper introduce each of the leading characters and their vehicles in the style of contemporary, scene-setting cinema trailers. In this way, each instalment begins with a trailer for the episode, followed by a trailer for the series itself – any episode could work as an introduction to *Thunderbirds* for an unfamiliar viewer.

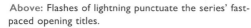

Above: Flashes of lightning punctuate the series' fast-paced opening titles.

Left: Fans could screen relatively simple stories using the *Thunderbirds* Give-a-Show Projector. In 1966 Chad Valley reported sales of nearly two million sets across its entire Give-a-Show range, which included projectors devoted to *Stingray* as well as *Thunderbirds*.

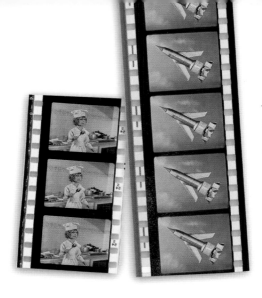

When each episode was completed, APF delivered the original cut negative to ITC, alongside a finegrain insurance print and often a 16mm 'reduction dupe'. Although the series was shot and processed in colour, black-and-white prints were specially prepared for British transmission. ATV requested these prints because it was felt that reds may appear too dark and blues may disappear entirely on the 405-line monochrome screens that were standard at the time.

Having been asked to reconfigure the series in 52-minute episodes, Anderson must have been exasperated that hour-long transmission slots weren't immediately available in all of the ITV affiliates screening the show. The masters went back to the cutting rooms, where each episode was edited down into two 25-minute instalments and a reprise narration was added

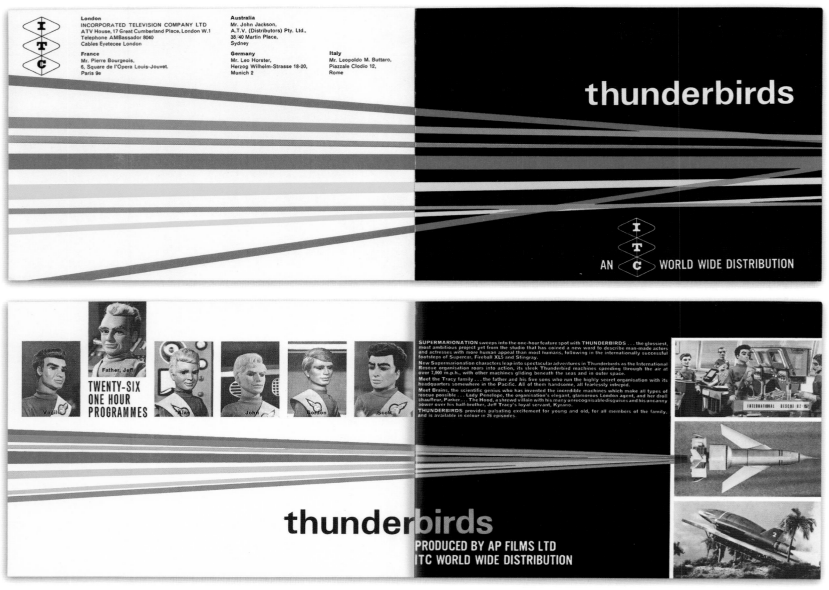

by Shane Rimmer. This version of the show, now largely forgotten and unseen for decades, was how viewers in the Granada region first saw series one, and how viewers in ATV Midlands first saw series two.

Production of *Thunderbirds'* second series came to an end in summer 1966, by which time 32 episodes had been completed. David Lane looks back on this busy period with a mixture of nostalgia and disbelief. "We were young," he says. "We could work all day, all night, go to the pub, get drunk, and still come back at seven o'clock the following morning. We never stopped. We would have four stages shooting, I would be preparing one episode, directing one and editing another. And we would work on storyboards in the lunch hour."

It was a punishing schedule, but Lane maintains it didn't breed resentment.

"No," he says emphatically. "I loved it. I loved every single minute of it."

6
DANGEROUS GAME

AP Films invested significant time and resources into puppet technology, but it was the quality of the company's special effects that earned the greatest acclaim.

In the 1960s supervising special effects director Derek Meddings and his team were denied much of the publicity attracted by the creators of *Thunderbirds*. Speaking in the December 1965 issue of *Television Mail*, Gerry Anderson was quick to praise Meddings' input to the series but reluctant to discuss his techniques. "This department... turns out daily the most remarkable model shots which, I think, are the finest example of special effects shooting anywhere in the world," he said. "The staff are the 'back-room boys' of AP Films and we do not like to discuss details of the work, since the ingenuity that enables us to obtain such wonderful screen value is something we wish to retain."

Meddings wasn't quoted in the article, but in subsequent years he went into great detail about *Thunderbirds* in particular. "I was being given the chance to do what I always believed I could do: to make convincing miniature shots for films," he said in 1992. "Nobody had a clue what I was doing except the people working with me, and even some of them didn't know because they'd never been in the film industry. So I was leading them by the hand."

Meddings raised his colleagues to a standard that matched and usually surpassed anything created by the feature film industry up to the advent of computer-generated imagery in the 1990s. This pioneering work helped to distinguish *Thunderbirds* at the time of its original broadcast and is still a major factor in its enduring appeal.

In 1979 Derek Meddings' craftsmanship was finally recognised with an Academy Award and a BAFTA for his work on *Superman* (1978). Since his death in 1995 his reputation has grown to the degree that he is probably the most fondly remembered and certainly the most admired member of the *Thunderbirds* crew.

"Derek *was* bloody *Thunderbirds*," says camera operator Alan Perry. "The puppets were great, but the special effects were superb. Derek Meddings designed the Thunderbird craft and he pioneered model special effects. He was also one of the nicest guys I ever met. He had a brilliant sense of humour.

"Derek was his own man. Gerry briefed him, of course, but I think there were times when Gerry might have cramped Derek's style a bit. And there were problems later on... I could be speaking out of turn, but I think part of the problem could have been that Derek was getting more famous than Gerry."

Above: Derek Meddings with a model of the Fireflash airliner he designed for *Thunderbirds'* first episode, *Trapped in the Sky*. Creating convincing miniatures for film was a passion that dominated his career. "I had a lot of great people working there," he said of his team at AP Films. "They put their hearts and souls into it, and they'd do anything I asked. The following day we'd see the result in the rushes, and that would inspire me to go onto even better things. People would look at it and say, 'I believe it — it looks so real!'"

Right: Meddings designed this vehicle for *The Uninvited* (below), when that episode was known as *Desert of Danger*. It subsequently appeared in *Desperate Intruder*.

SAND JEEP FOR DESERT OF DANGER

THUNDERBIRD 1

One of Meddings' chief collaborators was Brian Johnson, who directed the special effects second unit for 21 episodes of *Thunderbirds* under his original name Brian Johncock. He recalls that Meddings ran the special effects at AP Films as a relatively autonomous unit. "Gerry and Reg Hill had nothing to do with it; Derek was the person who decided what's what."

Johnson had joined APF as Meddings' first full-time assistant during *Fireball XL5* and stayed with the growing special effects department following the move to Stirling Road. Meddings remarked on this expansion in an article for the April 1969 issue of *Film & Television Technician*, noting that *Fireball* had required an average of 20 special effects set-ups per episode. That number doubled for *Stingray*. "Soon filming became increasingly complicated," he wrote. "Every picture now contained exciting sequences which could only be achieved by using processes such as painted foreground glass shots, matte shots, back projection, travelling matte and the use of pyrotechnics – all these things, combined with miniatures, were introduced into *Stingray*."

Top left: The craft designed by Meddings inspired *Thunderbirds* collectables all over the world. Rotterdam-based company Vita Nova published a set of 14 postcards in 1965, including this example showing Thunderbird 1 and its pilot, Scott.

Above: Meddings suspends a Fireball model over a set at APF's Ipswich Road studio. Meddings and his assistants were first given a dedicated special effects stage during the making of *Fireball XL5* in 1962.

Left: The shape of Thunderbird 1 lent itself to this pencil case, which was produced in Hong Kong in 1967. The case was opened using the zip beneath its nose cone.

Meddings was clearly one of APF's visionaries, but he had come along several years after the organisation was established – a little too late to be considered as a partner or company director. As an employee, he was obliged to wait alongside the other staff for Gerry to return from Great Cumberland Place with details of the next production. "We'd always wait with baited breath for Gerry to come back and tell us what had happened," he said. "And it was always good news."

Although Meddings wasn't present at Gerry's meetings with Lew Grade, the ATV boss identified special effects as one of the key selling points of the

Supermarionation series. "When we started *Thunderbirds*, Lew saw a few of them and said he wanted more and more effects," said Meddings. "So they were written to include every conceivable effect. I ended up having to do a hundred special effects shots for each hour programme. That varied from craft in the air, on the water, underwater, against a night sky, day sky, a storm sky and in the desert."

The increasing demands of each series, and the requirement to keep pace with the turnover on the neighbouring puppet stages, had led Meddings to assemble a large team by the time of *Thunderbirds*. Many of these recruits were young art school graduates and all were dedicated to special effects. On Meddings' principal stage Michael Wilson was his lighting cameraman and Jimmy Elliott became one of his directors. Joining Brian Johnson as a

1.18 30 MINUTES AFTER NOON

teleplay by **Alan Fennell**
directed by **David Elliott**
first broadcast 11 November 1965

The British Security Service infiltrates a criminal gang attempting to blow up a plutonium store, but the agent is discovered and the gang abandons him after the fuses are set. If International Rescue can't reach him in time the result will be the biggest explosion the world has ever known...

The stakes have never been higher than in this densely plotted episode, the title of which was almost certainly borrowed from the Oscar-winning thriller *Seven Days to Noon* (1950).

Alan Fennell's story begins with Tom Prescott (Matt Zimmerman) being forced to wear a steel bracelet that will explode on his wrist unless he returns to his office to use the hidden key. Prescott manages to unlock the bracelet, but the ensuing blast sends his elevator car crashing into the basement, necessitating a daring rescue by Virgil and Alan.

The Erdman Gang's next target for the exploding bracelets is more ambitious. Their unseen leader directs them to a plutonium store patrolled by powerful mechanical guards (each one played by the puppet of

Brains' robot Braman). When the British agent Southern (Ray Barrett) is captured by the last surviving robot, director David Elliott frames them in the face of a clock counting down to the detonation at 12.30. Elliott's most distinctive flourish, however, occurs in the headquarters of the British Security Service, where a conversation between Southern and his superiors is accompanied only by shots of their respective hats on a hatstand.

director of the second unit were Ian Scoones and Shaun Whittacker-Cook (credited as Shaun Cook on *Thunderbirds*). Both had been recommended to Meddings by his former mentor Les Bowie, as they had been part of his collective of apprentices known informally as 'Bowie's Boy Scouts'. The second unit lighting cameraman was Harry Oakes who, like Scoones, migrated to APF from Hammer Film Productions when that company mothballed its production base at Bray Studios.

Johnson enjoyed working with Oakes, whom he had met at Hammer while assisting Les Bowie on horror special effects. "Harry was a great character," he says. "You could never get into a serious situation, because if everybody got tense then Harry was there to cheer you up. We used to call him 'Oakes for jokes'. Such a dry wit."

Below: Meddings uses an oxyacetylene torch to prepare for a scene.

Above right: Derek Meddings (far left) and Brian Johnson (left) film the launch of Thunderbird 1. The sequence was originally shot for *Trapped in the Sky* (top) but was reused in many subsequent episodes.

Right: Thunderbird 1 featured prominently on this Instant Pictures set manufactured by the John Waddington company in 1966.

Above and right: Mike Trim studied graphic design at the London School of Printing before joining APF's model workshop in 1964. Meddings soon recognised Trim's potential, offering him design duties from *Thunderbirds*' second episode, *Pit of Peril*.

For the series two episode *Lord Parker's 'Oliday*, Trim designed the power station and solar reflector dish that overlook the Mediterranean town of Monte Bianco. The resulting model was built to several scales and was the centrepiece of a dramatic rescue sequence.

Below left: In June 1964 Trim received this letter inviting him to join AP Films.

Below right: Mike Trim (right) with fellow APF model-maker Roger Dicken.

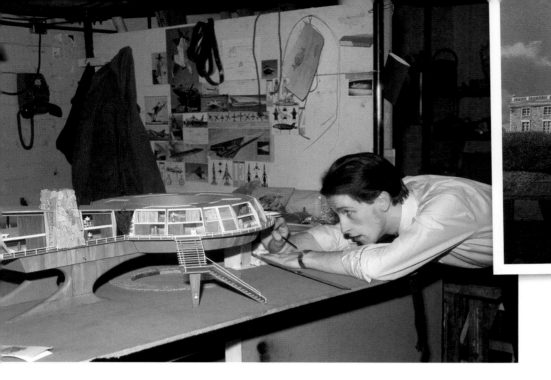

During pre-production of *Thunderbirds* in 1964 Meddings placed an advertisement in a London evening newspaper that resulted in the recruitment of three young model-makers: James Channing, Roger Dicken and Mike Trim. Channing would create the exterior of Creighton-Ward Mansion before leaving APF, but Dicken and Trim would stay with the company longer. Trim in particular would become something of a protégé, as Meddings entrusted him with storyboards and even the design of certain minor vehicles on *Thunderbirds*.

Just as Les Bowie had been an inspiration to Meddings, so Meddings proved an inspiration to his closest colleagues and their small army of uncredited technicians and model-makers.

"Les Bowie taught me everything," said Meddings in 1992. "I learned from him, and I was then able to go off and do *Thunderbirds* full of confidence. I gathered a lot of people around me who didn't have a clue about effects. They had to be led by me, but they learned

very quickly and they became indispensable. Most of them are still in the film industry and are highly respected technicians."

The December 1965 issue of *Television Mail* estimated that over 200 models and sections had been constructed for the five Thunderbird vehicles. Some of these were created by the Stirling Road model workshop, but many of the major vehicles were built by outside contractor Mastermodels and its offshoot Space Models. Arthur 'Wag' Evans was an employee of both companies at various times, and had been associated with APF since he built a model of Fireball XL5. In 1964 Evans was commissioned to make the original model of Thunderbird 2.

"I made the big version, all from balsa, starting with the main frame and then half a dozen different pods from a vac-form moulding," he recalled in 1991. "I'd say it was at least

Top left: Mike Trim 'dirties down' the Tracy Island Round House for the feature film *Thunderbirds Are Go* in 1966. On the wall behind him are extracts from the series' Character Merchandise Specification Sheet.

Top right: FAB 1 is parked outside James Channing's model of Creighton-Ward Mansion.

Above: A postcard of Stourhead House in Wiltshire, the 18th-century Palladian mansion that inspired the design of Lady Penelope's residence.

Below: A December 1965 advertisement for Mastermodels, the Feltham-based company that APF contracted for much of the model work on *Thunderbirds*.

Mastermodels Limited, Spur Road, Feltham Trading Estate, Middlesex

We are proud to be associated with A.P. Films and Merchandising Limited as master model builders of the

THUNDERBIRDS

SPACE CRAFT

DISPLAY AND EXHIBITION MODEL MAKERS, FILM AND TV COMMERCIAL WORK, PROTOTYPES FOR TOY MANUFACTURE ETC.

TELEPHONE: FELTHAM 7191-2-3

To the design of A.P. Films Limited

Evans enjoyed Meddings' occasional visits to Mastermodels on the Feltham Trading Estate, and the two built up a rapport. "He would give us a rough sketch of what he wanted, and the size, and then we would make it. I used to call him Derek 'Air Intake' Meddings, because everything had to have lots of air intakes on it."

Evans later helped to build FAB 1, by which time he had joined some of his former Mastermodels colleagues at the nearby Space Models. "We built the puppet-sized car, which was about seven foot and largely made out of plywood," he said. "It had to be split behind the windscreen so they could film the front or the back for interior shots. There were steel tubes built into the front and back half and the different pieces would slide along them. Each side also had to come apart, and the two sides of the canopy were removable so they could shoot across from one side or the other. The car had to steer and roll along, and the lights had to work. They were battery-driven bicycle headlamps. That was a feat of engineering that was, but it was a goddam awful design. I don't know

Above: One of the craftsmen at Space Models attaches the canopy to the puppet-sized version of FAB 1.

Below left and right: Filming FAB 1's radiator cannon for a scene in *The Man from MI.5*. Buying and then modifying a Rolls-Royce radiator shell and shutters cost APF more than £100, but this was considered more economical than building a miniature, and easier to light.

four foot. It was balsa wood, because the brief was always the same – the models had to be light enough to fly on thin wires. The difficulty was getting the ship's legs, which were made of telescopic brass tubing, to retract into the given depth. We never achieved it, in fact. They must have added the legs especially for the lifting shots because you couldn't animate them."

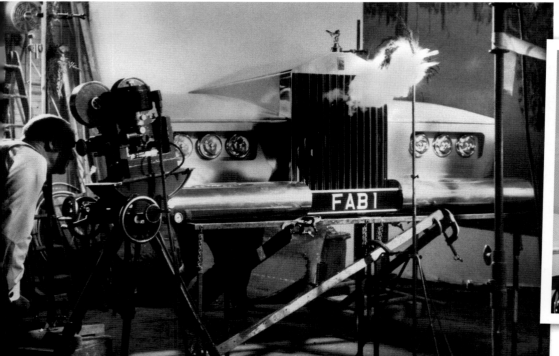

how they got permission from Rolls-Royce. You don't get straight lines on motor cars, and the bottom line on that car was straight. That's what upset me. But I must admit it looked magnificent on screen."

Just as Bob Bell customised sets with wireless components, Meddings would visit the Slough branch of Woolworths to buy salt shakers and plastic containers for similar adaptation. The launch bay of Thunderbird 1 is notorious for the most prominent example of this – a thinly disguised lemon squeezer attached to the wall.

"If we needed extra craft we'd get plastic kits and bastardise them," says Brian Johnson. "There was a big model shop on Bath Road. And there was a shop that sold Letraset, which we used on the sides of the models."

1.19 THE IMPOSTERS

teleplay by **Dennis Spooner**
directed by **Desmond Saunders**
first broadcast 13 January 1966

International Rescue faces an unprecedented challenge – the organisation's name and copies of its uniforms have been used as a decoy for the theft of some top secret plans. With the Tracy brothers now wanted criminals, Jeff decides to suspend operations until the culprits are found...

The plans for the AL4 – a strategic fighter that can fly at the speed of "accelerated light" – are a MacGuffin in this multi-layered story by Dennis Spooner. Far more interesting is the moral dilemma faced by Jeff and his sons when, as subjects of a global manhunt, they agonise over breaking cover to rescue a stranded astronaut with just hours to live.

Along the way we discover, by way of a casual announcement from Jeff, that International Rescue has a network of agents all around the world. The hillbilly branch is represented by Jeremiah Tuttle (Peter Dyneley), aka Agent 47. Jeff recruited him to the cause many years ago, when Jeremiah guessed his ambition to establish International Rescue.

Jeremiah provides the vital clue that leads Penelope and Parker to the imposters. Penelope's slingbacks are less than suitable for a journey through a swamp, and by the time she arrives at the disused mine where the villains are hiding she's in no fit state to tackle them. Fortunately Jeremiah is on hand, and the villains are flushed out the old-fashioned way – with a few cans of Ma's highly explosive beans.

Above: A special effects technician decorates the large model of the world that appears in the final screen of *Thunderbirds*' end titles. In the foreground is the partly constructed Sidewinder from *Pit of Peril*.

Below right: Parts from Airfix's girder bridge construction kit were ubiquitous in *Thunderbirds*' sets and models. They can be seen in the bridge from *Brink of Disaster* (below) and these cranes from *Day of Disaster* (bottom).

used to rob them of all the bits. We'd call it 'jazzing it up' – finding an object like a plastic container and spraying it grey to use it as part of a spaceship. Brian Johnson was very good at this. We'd then get these kits, take out all the bits, and use them as air intakes or whatever. I could see how it was going to look, but it seemed no-one could imagine how this could be used to turn something into a space vehicle. When it was given a spray of paint, all of a sudden it became something that would have taken weeks if you were making it from scratch. A lot of the detail came from adding these pieces."

While inventive and economical, this customisation caused problems for Wag Evans. "We would make a large model, and then they'd come back and say they wanted a small one for long shots," he recalled. "We'd refer to the original drawings and remake the model at a smaller scale, but by this time it wouldn't always match the large model because they'd added lots of extra bits to that one. We'd have to find out which bits of plastic kit they'd used and make all those little bits to a smaller scale. On the other hand, if we had to make something that was seen alongside one of the puppets we'd have to take these bits of model kits and make enlarged versions. You couldn't use plastic kits for those jobs, because there wouldn't be a kit that was four times larger than the one they'd used."

"We were given the red carpet treatment in the local toy shops because we would buy all their Airfix, Monogram and Revell kits," said Meddings. "They were quite expensive, but we'd buy hundreds of pounds' worth. We never actually made up any of the kits – we

As far as Meddings was concerned, the process was not complete until the painted model had been suitably distressed. "I got that from Les," he said. "We used to do miniatures together and he was a stickler for detail. I see, as Les did, that an aeroplane isn't just silver and white with a name on the side – I see that the panels that make up the fuselage are a slightly different shade. The white might have a slightly dirty mark on it, and there might be some discolouration at the back of the engines, where the jets have blasted out. Les and I used to do that on feature films, and that's why I insisted that we did the same thing on every model we ever shot."

In addition to what Meddings called 'dirtying down', aircraft and other vehicles had their panels drawn in with a thick 2B pencil which was then smudged. Johnson had a particular knack for this meticulous task, as did Mike Trim. When Trim was promoted from the model workshop to design duties, his place dirtying down models was taken by Brian Smithies.

Above right: Two different-scale models of the Ocean Pioneer ships from *Danger at Ocean Deep*. The larger one (at the top) was used for close shots, while the smaller one (below) was made to create the impression that the ship was in the distance.

Left: The yellow road-builder vehicle from *Atlantic Inferno* was a repainted version of a model first seen in *End of the Road*.

Above left: The *Atlantic Inferno* road-builder is customised by Brian Smithies, one of Meddings' most talented 'dirtying-down' artists.

Below: Model-makers Mike Trim and Charlie Bryant adapt vehicles for use in *The Imposters*.

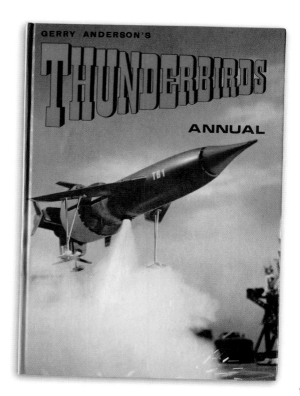

Above: The second *Thunderbirds* annual was published in 1967. The cover featured a picture by APF photographer Doug Luke showing Thunderbird 1's Schermuly rocket in action.

"As far as special effects were concerned this was one of the most important stages and this is what made many of the shots totally believable," said Meddings. "People are not aware of what they're looking at, but if a car doesn't have mud splashed up the side, the audience is aware that something isn't quite right.

"After a vehicle had been dirtied down the model-makers would always show it to me to see if they'd done enough. Sometimes they'd work hours on something, and I'd say it still wasn't strong enough. I came up with the idea that if they did it very hard to start with, so it was really over the top, then we could spray it lightly with the base colour just to take it down in places. So it wouldn't be a case of

going over the whole lot again – we'd just be taking it down."

Additional authenticity was provided by fitting Thunderbirds 1, 2, 3 and other craft with jet exhausts supplied by the Schermuly Pistol Rocket Apparatus company. Schermuly's usual business was providing the Royal Navy and other large institutions with life-saving devices, but its research division came up with special compressed gunpowder rockets for *Thunderbirds*. The rockets were triggered by an electrical pulse from the wires suspending the models.

"Thunderbird 2 had four rockets underneath and two in the tail," said Meddings. "It was sod's law that if a rocket failed to fire it would always be the one that was nearest the camera. Or sometimes they wouldn't all ignite together. You'd keep the

1.20 THE MAN FROM MI.5

teleplay by **Alan Fennell**
directed by **David Lane**
first broadcast 20 January 1966

A British Secret Service agent asks International Rescue to help him recover some stolen plans that, in the wrong hands, could mean the end of the world. Lady Penelope and Parker pick up the trail at the French Riviera, where Penelope initiates a scheme that will lure the villains to her yacht....

This entertaining espionage mission has little to do with International Rescue's brief, and the story's callous disregard for human life further distances it from the *Thunderbirds* format.

When Southern threw his fedora onto the hat-stand in *30 Minutes After Noon* it was clear that the series' tributes to James Bond were becoming increasingly obvious. *The Man from MI.5* is the most brazen homage of all, yet seems to have escaped the attention of the Bond filmmakers, who in 1964 had threatened the producers of *Carry On Spying*.

The Man from MI.5 takes its inspiration from other sources as well. Barry Gray's incidental music is more Henry Mancini than John Barry, and the title is surely a

nod to *The Man from UNCLE*. The American spy series began in September 1964 and subsequently featured in the Anderson comics *TV Century 21* and *Solo*.

The most accomplished secret agent here is not Bondson (Ray Barrett) but Penelope. Her typically cool remark "Are you going to tie me up? ... Oh I don't mind really," was cheekily sampled for the 1990 hit *Thunderbirds Are Go!* by 'FAB featuring MC Parker'.

power running and the wire would get red hot, glow and break. The person firing the rockets would have to see they were all firing and then switch off. Sometimes he didn't throw the switch quick enough."

Meddings admitted that model-makers spent much of their time fixing damage incurred during filming. "We had terrible accidents with things. The craft had to be as light as possible, but the wires holding them up also had to be as thin as possible. Once one wire broke then they would all break, because the weight would then go on to three wires. We never caught anything – they always seemed to hit the set, and bits broke off. Originally we had someone sitting at a workbench in the corner, putting all the bits back on, but by the time we did *Thunderbirds* we had a workshop. If a craft was damaged it went straight into the workshop. I would reschedule what we were doing until the craft was repaired."

Wag Evans was often asked to rescue damaged models. He remembered that Thunderbird 2 was a particularly frequent patient. "When the pod was lowered, the craft wasn't left with much strength. It kept breaking in the same place and was a bit of a job to repair."

Above left: This out-take from a publicity session photographed by Doug Luke illustrates what happened if the Schermuly gunpowder rockets were left on for too long.

Above right: The second postcard in the 1965 set issued by CG Williams. The corresponding view of Thunderbird 2 and Virgil in the show's title sequence was cropped and selectively blurred.

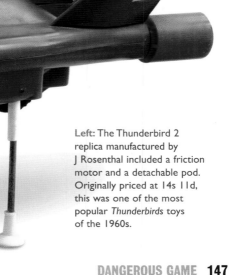

Left: The Thunderbird 2 replica manufactured by J Rosenthal included a friction motor and a detachable pod. Originally priced at 14s 11d, this was one of the most popular *Thunderbirds* toys of the 1960s.

As well as independent model-makers and Slough retailers, Meddings also built good relationships with local engineering firms. He maintained his closest liaison, however, with the units working on the puppet stages to ensure that his footage dovetailed with theirs. "At lunchtimes I would see the director," he said. "He'd be doing his prep for the afternoon's filming, and I'd sit with him and do a storyboard. We'd get some sandwiches and a cup of coffee, and he'd explain what he wanted to see – for example he'd ask to see the rocket coming in from right to left, because he was then going to show the characters getting out in a particular place.

I would try to build up my part by asking, 'Do you want to see the rocket coming through the clouds first?' and things like that.

"Each director wanted to do something individual. At the beginning of the series we filmed a lot of library shots of Thunderbirds 1, 2 and 3 taking off. After a while we used up all these angles – we'd seen them in every episode. The director would come to me and say, 'Do you think you could shoot Thunderbird 2 taking off from a different angle, just for my film?' If Gerry found out he'd get a little uptight and say, 'We won't finish on time if you do that,' but I used to do it."

The complex process of filming special effects sequences relied on the storyboards that Meddings, and later Mike Trim, prepared from scripts. Gerry and Sylvia Anderson's shooting script for *Trapped in the Sky* had already presented Meddings with more complex challenges than he had faced on the previous Supermarionation series. The launch of Thunderbird 2 was just one of the sequences he had to realise:

Thunderbird 2 taxis out... Once in position it stops, and an enormous concealed ramp structure raises it to an angle of 60 degrees. We hear the motors wind up as though building up pressure. The rockets in the tail fire, and in a fury of smoke and flames the giant machine streaks into the air...

The build-up to Thunderbird 2's take-off was ultimately enhanced by the palm trees that fell back from its taxiway. "A lever on each side operated a row of palm trees, activated from under the set," said Meddings, describing Thunderbird 2's slow journey from its hangar to its launch ramp. "There was always a problem getting it in sync with the person doing the other row of palm trees. Another problem was the rock face coming down in front of Thunderbird 2. You could never show Thunderbird 2 coming out immediately after that because when the rock face came down it left a great big gap in the set. When the rock face came down I'd have to cut to another angle, and then we'd put a piece of wood across so Thunderbird 2 would come out over the wood."

Above: Thunderbird 2's original launch sequence, as seen in *Trapped in the Sky*, and a Barratt sweet cigarette card from 1966 (inset).

Below left: Derek Meddings (foreground) supervises the filming of Thunderbird 2 emerging from Tracy Island.

Below right: Part of the finished sequence, as it appeared on screen.

20. Thunderbirds

In order to make Thunderbird 2 and the other craft look convincing in airborne scenarios, Meddings called on a simple method he had been employing since the days of *Supercar*.

"We didn't have CGI then, so all the models had to be suspended on very thin titanium wires," says Brian Johnson. "At the top we had a bit of wood, like a T-piece. The same parallel of wires went down to the model and were tied off. I would get up on the top of this stand, which was a scaffold pole suspended out over the set. This meant I could stand in front of the camera, but above where it could see. I would get hold of the model and swing

Above: Special effects floor technician Ian Wingrove (far left) and special effects second unit lighting cameraman Harry Oakes (centre) prepare a scene for *Martian Invasion*. Floor technician Peter Wragg balances on planks overhanging the set, ready to fly Thunderbird 1.

Top right: A different view of the same scene, showing special effects director Derek Meddings. This image appeared on a Dutch bubblegum card published by the Monty Gum company in 1966.

Right: A box for J Rosenthal's replica of Thunderbird 1. The toy had a friction motor in its base and originally retailed for 8s 11d.

A JR 21 TOY

THUNDERBIRD 1

Scale Model Friction Motor

TB1

WITH VARIABLE WING MOVEMENT

1.21 CRY WOLF

teleplay by **Dennis Spooner**
directed by **David Elliott**
first broadcast 27 January 1966

Following a misunderstanding over a distress call, two Australian children are invited to Tracy Island and shown why such signals are reserved for actual emergencies. Soon afterwards, the Hood begins a relentless pursuit of the boys' secretive father. The boys' next call for help is genuine...

Gerry Anderson was never afraid to cast younger characters in his Supermarionation shows. One of the heroes of *Supercar* was ten-year-old Jimmy Gibson, and towards the end of the 1960s Anderson built a whole series around the nine-year-old Joe McClaine, better known as *Joe 90*.

Scriptwriter Dennis Spooner had already created something of a template for *Cry Wolf* with *A Christmas to Remember*, a 1964 episode of *Stingray* in which the young orphan Barry Byrne is invited to spend Christmas at Marineville. Highlights of Barry's stay include a trip in *Stingray* alongside Captain Troy Tempest, and at bedtime he wears *Supercar* pyjamas.

Like Jimmy Gibson and Barry Byrne before him, *Cry Wolf*'s Tom Williams is voiced by Sylvia Anderson. Bob is voiced by Christine Finn, in a rare instance of a child character being played by anyone else.

This sentimental tale only becomes uncomfortable – at least for a modern audience – during the sequence where the Hood questions the boys and traps them in the mine. Fortunately it ends on a lighter note, as the children's latest game leaves Scott jammed in a dustbin with a banana skin on his head.

---

it through the frame or land it. That was part of my job. I spent a lot of time keeping my hand very still and making very small moves to get it right. If you look at Fireball XL5 taking off you'll see how badly I succeeded – when it takes off it wobbles up the ramp!"

Meddings occasionally flew Thunderbird 2 himself, but he preferred to leave the task to his more adept technicians. He was particularly impressed by Peter Wragg's graceful ability to fly models, a skill he attributed to Wragg's penchant for ballroom dancing. "Some of my lads were really steady-handed and they had a feel for it," said Meddings. "You couldn't just lift the thing off and push it forward. You had to pretend you were flying it. I'd say 'Action!' and they'd make engine noises when they were flying the models. We were just big kids."

Right: Peter Wragg was so adept at flying models that by the late 1960s Meddings had put him in charge of a special effects stage dedicated to such shots.

Below: In 1965 Meddings explained that his biggest challenge in special effects was "anything that flies". In these pictures Thunderbird 2 is filmed coming in to land in *Cry Wolf*.

1.22 DANGER AT OCEAN DEEP

teleplay by **Donald Robertson**
directed by **Desmond Saunders**
first broadcast 3 February 1966

The atomic-powered Ocean Pioneer I is enveloped in a strange sea mist before exploding. Its replacement ship, with an identical cargo of liquid alsterene, gets into similar trouble on its maiden voyage. By the time the crew radios for help, John, Scott and Virgil are already on their way...

For a series seemingly aimed at the *Look and Learn* generation, *Thunderbirds* was surprisingly creative when it came to scientific accuracy. In this story, liquid alsterene joins a list of mysterious innovations that in recent episodes has included hydrochromatised steel (*30 Minutes After Noon*) and nutomic charges (*End of the Road*), the latter an old favourite from the days of *Fireball XL5*.

This futuristic verisimilitude wasn't achieved without a sense of humour. The combustible combination of alsterene and the sea fungus OD60 could have been considered a serious threat to the environment, until it's revealed that OD60 is a key ingredient in a type of dog food endorsed by Lady Penelope.

The launch of the Ocean Pioneer II by Penelope is one of several sequences enlivened by the addition of uncredited voice artist John Tate. He proves his versatility by playing both a Scottish dock-worker and Stevens, the chauffeur who joins Parker in getting drunk on a stolen bottle of Champagne. Series regular Ray Barrett provides another refreshing change by casting his English television reporter from the Richard Dimbleby school of broadcasting – quite a relief after the breathless Ned Cook.

Below: Filming the launch of the Ocean Pioneer II in *Danger at Ocean Deep*. The special effects department saved time by only adding fine details and dirtying-down to the side of the model that faced the camera.

Johnson enjoyed operating International Rescue's space vehicle for its spectacular launch through the centre of Tracy Island's round house. "Thunderbird 3 was easy, because it went up on a wire over a pulley.

I used to just walk away with the bit of string in my hand and it would go up with the rockets firing beneath it. So that was a piece of cake. Thunderbird 1 was tricky to fly and Thunderbird 4 just bobbed around in the water, so that wasn't a problem. The big Thunderbird 2 was heavy, but it was the right shape and it was easy to control."

Johnson recalls that there were three Thunderbird 2 models built to different sizes, the smaller models being used to create the impression the craft was in the distance.

"We very rarely pulled a model on a straight wire across the set," he says. "Usually I would swing it out over the set in an arc. That always seemed to look better when we saw the rushes."

Meddings wholeheartedly endorsed Gerry Anderson's insistence that wires should be invisible, and this caused the same headaches as those experienced on the puppet stages. "We used to black the wires out with iodine," says Johnson, "and we used little puffers with different colours of paint. If the model was suspended in a particular space we could make parts of the wire disappear against the clouds or whatever. But on DVD or Blu-ray you'll see all that. Momentarily."

If a prominent wire was spotted while reviewing the rushes of the previous day's filming Meddings would be just as likely as Anderson to order a reshoot. "Losing the wires was always a great problem," he said. "I used to have to paint them, spray them, or get Harry [Oakes] to back-light them. Because if you saw the wires you gave the game away. We all took pride in doing a shot that didn't show how the models were held up."

Above: Director of photography Harry Oakes uses a puffer bottle to disguise the wires suspending Thunderbird 3 during its launch sequence in *Thunderbirds Are Go*.

Below right: One of the puffer bottles used by special effects second unit director Ian Scoones during the making of *Thunderbirds*.

Below left: The Thunderbird 3 construction kit introduced by Lincoln International in 1967. The assembly instructions inside each box were presented by Brains.

Above: Thunderbird 2, pictured against the roller sky during the filming of *Alias Mr. Hackenbacker*.

Below: The roller road was used to depict FAB 1's journey to intercept the Erdman Gang in *30 Minutes After Noon*.

The hand-operated method of flying models could only be convincingly sustained for brief scenes. When land or air-based vehicles needed to be seen on longer journeys Meddings came up with an ingenious twist on the age-old trick of keeping the model stationary while the background moved.

"I could see that there were going to be a lot of flying shots," he said. "To track with an aircraft, or Thunderbird 1, you'd be up the other end of the stage before you'd had the chance to show the audience what was happening. And on the way you'd probably hit some bump, so the camera would judder or the model would jump. Then I remembered that in the film industry they had these enormous drums, which they sometimes put outside train carriage windows. I thought we needed an enormous drum to create a background for the

aircraft to fly against, but where the hell were we going to put it? Every corner of the stage was cluttered with bits of equipment that we'd built and needed. Then I thought – a roll of *sky*. So I had that designed and made, and then we got to the first episode, which was the one with the Fireflash coming in to London Airport. I read the script and sketched it all out, but once I'd done the storyboard I thought, 'How the hell am I going to do this?' That's when I came up with the idea for the roller road."

In simple terms, Meddings took the concept of the moving sky backdrop and turned it on its side to become a horizontal representation of a road or, in the case of *Trapped in the Sky*, a runway. "It had three moving surfaces," he explained. "Each one could run at a different speed, to give a sense of perspective. The foreground band moved very fast. Then there was the mid-distance band, which was the road or the runway, and then there was the band in the far distance which travelled just a little slower. The sky background moved slower still. And that's how we created that effect of tracking."

The roller sky in the background was a huge loop of painted canvas wrapped around tubes at either end. Early tests showed that once the tubes started spinning, the canvas would slide down until the lower edge snagged. Adjusters were fitted and the rollers were set at an angle, but it still took considerable effort to achieve smooth and consistent running. Another problem was disguising where the two ends of the canvas met. "I had a diagonal join put in it," said Meddings. "But it didn't matter what you did, you couldn't lose that join. The clouds painted on it couldn't cover it up. So I used to have somebody standing on the edge of the backing. He used to watch the back of it, and when he saw the join coming round he'd give a squirt of smoke through a fan. This would appear in front of the backing like a puff of cloud, covering up the join. The timing had to be just right."

The roller road and roller sky combine to impressive effect in the climax of *Trapped in the Sky*, when the sabotaged Fireflash lands on International Rescue elevator cars that are trying to match its air speed and position while racing along Runway 29 at London Airport.

"Those vehicles had to be held by a wire, front and back," said Meddings. "The person holding the wire at the back had to always ease off when I was shouting commands to the person who was pulling one of the little trucks. I would shout, 'Faster! Faster! Go forward a bit more!' Meanwhile he would be shouting at his partner to ease off a bit and let him have some

more slack because he couldn't pull it. I don't know how anything ever got done, really."

A broken wire sent one of the elevator cars careering off the roller road, but rather than abandon this shot the incident was written into the story. An additional scene showing the errant car crashing into a parked plane helped create the suggestion that a radio fault in its control system had sent it off course.

As well as designing new gadgets, Meddings customised the corner of the Stirling Road building that housed his two special effects stages. "We had a lot of rostrums made of Dexion," he said. "We used to wheel them out and put hardboard or chipboard on the top. We'd dress them with sand, and then cover the sand with various paints, powders, dust or cement. We used to get in a terrible state. I don't know why half of us

Below and bottom: Shaun Whittacker-Cook oversees filming of the Pacific Atlantic Monorail in *Brink of Disaster*.

didn't die with blocked-up lungs. It used to get in your hair and all over your clothes. If you arrived in a clean shirt and pair of jeans, by lunchtime you were filthy. By the evening you looked like a coalman. Eventually they put a shower in, which made things better.

"We found that the rostrums were never big enough. We used to add pieces to them, or prop them up, but someone would end up kicking them and they'd fall over, destroying part of the set. And if we did explosions, we had to make sure they didn't shake. One day I decided to start building sets on the floor and

CRABLOGGER FOR "PATH OF DESTRUCTION"

CRABLOGGER PROCESSING UNIT TO BE TOWED BY CRABLOGGER

we got rid of the rostrums. With everything on the floor we could do any sort of explosion without the set shaking. After a while I got so fed up with lying on my stomach, having my face pressed against the concrete while I was trying to look through the camera, that I talked Gerry into letting us have pits dug in the floor. One weekend the contractors came and dug holes to the size I wanted them. When we came in on Monday morning there they were, cemented and ready to use. It meant that we could put a camera on legs, stand in the pit and look at the set on the floor."

The camera pits were approximately four feet deep, and Alan Perry recalls that they proved to be a hazard for the unwary. "For one scene we had to have all the lights out, and the only thing that was lit was the set. Derek came wandering in, said 'How's it going lads?' and then disappeared. He'd fallen down one of these holes! I remember he climbed out and said, 'I've just been in the Pit of Peril!'"

Above left and right: Derek Meddings' original sketches of the Crablogger and its processing unit from *Path of Destruction*.

Right: Meddings operates one of the Crablogger's claws on a floor-mounted set. The scene is filmed from inside one of the camera pits.

Below right: The Crablogger's powerful claws uproot a South American forest.

Below left: The Crablogger, as it appeared in *Path of Destruction*.

Above left: The special effects department shot models behind fish tanks for other productions as well as *Stingray* and *Thunderbirds*. This picture was taken during the filming of *Renegade Rocket*, an episode of *Captain Scarlet and the Mysterons*, in 1967.

Below: J Rosenthal's Thunderbird 4 was a battery-powered replica that included a figure of Gordon Tracy. The toy cost 32s 11d when it was released in 1965.

Above right: Thunderbird 4 negotiates an underground river to rescue television reporter Ned Cook and his cameraman Joe in *Terror in New York City*.

Underwater scenes, such as those featuring Thunderbird 4, were shot using the same method most recently employed on *Stingray*. *Television Mail* reported that models stayed dry behind tanks constructed of half-inch armoured plate glass, double-walled with water contained in a six-inch sandwich. "Special effects shots involving the water tanks have to be completed quickly," observed Elizabeth Millar Gow, "for if repeat shots are needed a day or two later it is found that algae in the water have

Left: The fourth postcard in the CG Williams set featured International Rescue's submarine and its pilot, Gordon.

Below left: This scene from *Terror in New York City* illustrates how the puppet-sized Thunderbird 4 differed from the model built to Meddings' specifications.

Below: The original plans used by Wag Evans to build the 18" model of Thunderbird 4. Evans inserted halogen light bulbs in the trough at the front. "At the time I couldn't understand how the model would work underwater; the batteries would short-out straight away," he said. "Of course, it was then that I realised that the model never came near water and that it was filmed through a tank!"

multiplied, causing a noticeably different shade of green. This had been detected in *Stingray*, for the first time, but the new tanks are nearly eight feet wide and hold so much water that the algae growth within a reasonable time is not so troublesome."

On the other side of the glass from the models, Alan Perry and fellow members of the camera crew struggled with a predictable challenge. "A lot of the stuff was shot through tanks, so straight away you've got a reflection problem," he says. "You couldn't shoot the tank at an angle or you'd get flares, so you had to be square on to the glass in the tank. The camera had to be blacked out and I had to be blacked out as well. We were behind black boards, and there was a hole cut in each board for the camera lens to poke through."

Experience had already taught Perry and his colleagues to be careful with the types of fish that populated the tanks. "They had to be small," he says. "If you got fish that were too big they looked like sharks!"

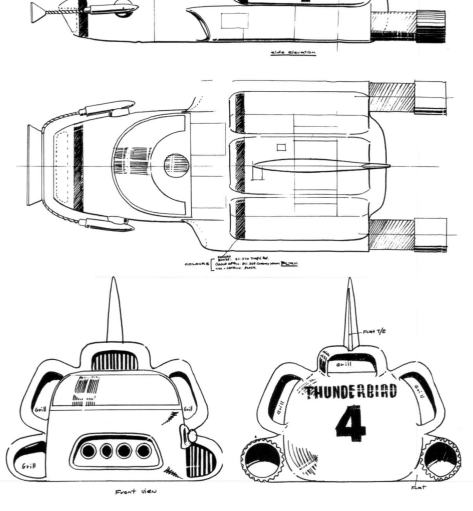

Shots showing the water's surface were achieved using one of the tanks designed for *Stingray*. Meddings considered that it was too large to be left as a permanent fixture during the production of *Thunderbirds*, so had it cut in half and wheeled outside. Clamps were fitted to each segment, so the tank could be reassembled when necessary.

"Reg Hill was a lovely man," says Brian Johnson, before explaining how Hill's intervention compromised the efficiency of the whole operation. "We should have had a nice six-inch plughole. That

would have drained the water in about five minutes, but Reg had an engineering firm on the Slough Trading Estate make a pump which had a bath plug-sized hole. It ended up taking about four hours to pump the water out."

Filming surface water or anything involving fire or explosions introduced elements that were beyond the control of the special effects crew. It was impossible to miniaturise waves or flames, so the effect of greater scale was achieved by setting cameras to shoot at high speed. Robin McDonald worked alongside Alan Perry as a clapper/loader and became used to shooting at speeds of anything up to 120 frames per

1.23 THE DUCHESS ASSIGNMENT

teleplay by **Martin Crump**
directed by **David Elliott**
first broadcast 17 February 1966

Lady Penelope suggests that the destitute Duchess of Royston hires her valuable Braquasso painting, 'Portrait of a Gazelle', to wealthy American businessman Wilbur Dandridge III. The Duchess agrees, but when she takes the painting to New York she doesn't get the reception she expected...

The first episode of *Thunderbirds* hinted at hard times for the aristocracy when Lady Penelope mentioned that she was expecting three coachloads of visitors. The subject is explored in more detail here when the Duchess of Royston (Ray Barrett) is forced to sell her own stately home to property developers.

The Duchess has lost her fortune through her addiction to gambling, which is another of the adult vices that makes a surprise appearance in a series ostensibly aimed at children. We are further reminded that *Thunderbirds* is the product of a very different era when Jeff visits the office of Wilbur Dandridge III (David Graham), the head of Gazelle Automations Inc. A mechanical dispenser offers Jeff a freshly lit cigarette, and another machine pours him a Scotch on the rocks from an authentic-looking bottle of Johnnie Walker.

Another noteworthy aspect of this engaging episode is Ray Barrett's performance as the Duchess, which was based on Dame Edith Evans' defining portrayal of Lady Bracknell in *The Importance of Being Earnest*. It's never fruitier than when the warbling Duchess gleefully recalls being saved by "those romantic young men from International Rescue..."

---

second. "You would still project at 24 or 25 frames per second," he says, "but if you shot faster and projected it at the usual frame rate it slowed the whole thing down so it looked more realistic."

"We needed that speed to create convincing explosions, and to give vehicles travelling down roads the impression of real weight," said Meddings. "I had the vehicles made with independent suspension – only foam rubber trapped between two metal shims. A vehicle was pulled down the road on wires under the set, and it ran along a slot. It was pulled at quite a speed, and when shot at 120 frames per second that vehicle bounced, rather than juddering down the road."

Left: Pod 4 deposits Gordon Tracy into the hazardous water around the Seascape in *Atlantic Inferno*.

Below: This inflatable Thunderbird 4 toy was produced by the Cecil Coleman company in 1965.

Right: Members of the press visit Stirling Road's special effects department in 1964, during production of *Trapped in the Sky*. The London Airport set on display featured two circular buildings that had previously been used as radar tracking stations in *Stingray* (below).

Bottom: The first of four *Thunderbirds* jigsaws issued by John Waddington in 1965 featured a cover photograph of Thunderbird 1 in front of London Airport.

The action-packed nature of the *Thunderbirds* stories meant that members of the special effects crew frequently handled potentially dangerous substances. One electrician was dismissed for detonating an explosive charge he'd buried in the ground outside the studio, but a more responsible attitude prevailed elsewhere. "We were sensible about things like explosives, which we kept in a safe," says Johnson. "The safe was tucked out of the way, but was on wheels so we could get it out of the building in a hurry if there was a fire. Fortunately we never had to do that, and we had fire extinguishers everywhere."

"It wasn't dangerous because it was always under control," says Perry. "But yes, the ceiling did catch light sometimes..."

One of the great legends of Supermarionation concerns a visit made to the Stirling Road studio by Lew Grade and other members of the ATV board who gathered to view a special effects sequence being directed by Shaun Whittacker-Cook. There are as many variations on this story as there are people who claim to have been there, but the version recalled by Derek Meddings in 1992 is one of the most plausible. "Because they were so excited by all the special effects we felt we had to show them something dramatic, and we happened to be doing this explosion," he said. "They all lined up behind the camera crew, and I said that if they stood there they'd be okay. But Reg, who was flapping around like a mother hen, insisted on moving them somewhere else. He stood them underneath some boards, which we'd put in the rafters to get them out of the way. So I thought, 'Okay, they're safe there too, really.' All my lads couldn't really care one way or the other, but Reg and everyone else who was in a high position wanted to impress them.

"So I got the camera rolling, called for action and let the explosion go. To get this sort of pluming effect I used to put cement or paint powder into paper bags, so that when the charge went off it would leave a trail of powder. One of these paper bags didn't burst. It didn't really matter for the shot, but it went straight up, over the heads of Lew Grade and all his friends. It hit one of the boards above them and burst. It was full of cement powder which rained all over them. Reg got in a real panic. He started running around, brushing Lew Grade down with his hands, just making it worse! Lew just stood there with his big cigar, smiling away. He thought it was very funny. If Reg had left them where I'd put them they'd have been all right!"

Above: The cinemagazine *Parade* was distributed by the Foreign and Commonwealth Office from 1963-73. In 1965 the series visited APF's special effects department where, as the narrator explained, "skilful science deceives the eye and nothing is what it seems to be". For the benefit of the *Parade* cameras, Derek Meddings staged some explosions on a model gunboat built for the *Stingray* episode *Star of the East*.

Below left: This colourful Thunderbird 1 was a disguised pencil sharpener issued by Pressflag in 1966.

Below right: Explosions in the special effects department could sometimes lead to a toxic atmosphere.

1.24 ATTACK OF THE ALLIGATORS!

teleplay by **Alan Pattillo**
directed by **David Lane**
first broadcast 10 March 1966

Two scientists develop theramine, an additive that could end the world's food shortage by increasing the size of animals. A clumsy thief drops some of the potion, which finds its way into the nearby Ambro River. Only International Rescue can save them from the terrible consequences...

The exclamation mark at the end of this episode's title is an early clue that we are once more entering the territory of science-fiction B movies. However this is a story that appropriates the genre, rather than satirising it.

Attack of the Alligators! draws upon HG Wells' 1904 novel *The Food of the Gods* and the 1939 film *The Cat and the Canary* for inspiration. Housekeeper Mrs Files (Sylvia Anderson) even evokes *Psycho* (1960) when she appears at the top of the stairs during a storm.

The reputation this episode enjoys is based more on the quality of its special effects than its rather thin scenario, specifically the impressive way baby alligators interacted with the miniature sets and puppets. The treatment of the unco-operative reptiles by the special effects crew caused dissent in the ranks at AP Films, leading to a visit from an RSPCA inspector.

The team's painstaking approach paid dividends in the scenes where an angry alligator thrashes the side of a house with its tail, and Culp (David Graham) is hoist with his own petard. But the effect on the schedule was rather less positive, and the experiment was never repeated.

Below: *Attack of the Alligators!* was the first of five 8mm *Thunderbirds* episodes released by Arrow Films in the mid-1960s.

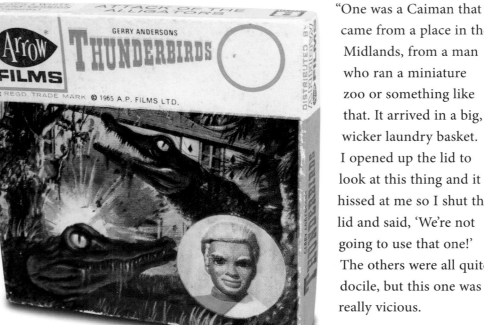

Another perilous situation was narrowly averted during the special effects shoot for *Attack of the Alligators!* "We had two five-foot alligators," remembered Meddings. "One was a Caiman that came from a place in the Midlands, from a man who ran a miniature zoo or something like that. It arrived in a big, wicker laundry basket. I opened up the lid to look at this thing and it hissed at me so I shut the lid and said, 'We're not going to use that one!' The others were all quite docile, but this one was really vicious.

"We had a shot where there had to be a point of view from whoever was in the boat. They look out and see this enormous alligator coming towards them. We used the big tank, the one that could be split down the middle. We had the camera very low and I was pulling a rope that was around the alligator's neck and front legs. The rope was beneath the camera and under the water, going through a screw eye. I was in the corner of the tank, wearing a big pair of thigh waders, pulling the crocodile at an angle.

"The crocodile would surface because I was pulling it so fast, but it would never open its mouth, which was what we wanted it to do. When it came right up to the camera I said 'Cut' and wondered how we could get the thing to look frightening. I think we did about six takes but it still wouldn't open its mouth.

Left and below: Baby alligators are released onto the set and into one of the tanks during the filming of *Attack of the Alligators!*

Bottom: Designer Keith Wilson (standing) and puppet sculptor John Brown (in the white coat) at work on one of the series' most unusual props. "For the shots where the big alligator is whacking the house we made up a massive tail," remembers Alan Perry. "We tried to do it with a real alligator but it didn't understand English!"

We decided to have one more go. I pulled the rope to feel the tension, I pulled the rope, and I pulled the rope, and suddenly there was no tension. The crocodile had come off and was now swimming around the tank. We'd put dye in the water to make it look like a swamp, and it was so murky and green that I couldn't see it. As soon as I realised it was free, I leapt over the high edge of the tank, clearing it very quickly and landing on the concrete floor in my boots. Afterwards, the crew told me that I had staged a vertical take-off! Then we had to go around, prodding the tank with a stick, trying to find the alligator."

Below left: Alligators are poised on the banks of the Ambro River as Derek Meddings (bottom left) wafts dry ice onto the surface of the water.

Below right: A baby alligator is gingerly removed from its box and placed on the set.

The heat of the studio lamps had made the reptiles sluggish, so it was decided to subject them to mild electric shocks just before each take. An anonymous but understandably concerned crew member reported the unit to the RSPCA and Gerry Anderson was alarmed to find an inspector in his office. "My first thought was for the welfare of the animals," he said, "and then I thought, 'What if the papers get hold of this?' To pre-empt any accusations of a cover-up I said I'd take the inspector to the special effects stage right away so we could both see if anything untoward was happening."

Along the way, the inspector spotted the Lady Penelope and Parker puppets hanging up and realised with some excitement that he was at the studio where *Thunderbirds* was made. When they arrived at the special effects department the alligators were being given 12-volt electric shocks. To Anderson and Meddings' surprise, the inspector recommended upping the voltage. "He said we could give them 36 volts or more," said Meddings, "but we didn't have the means to up the voltage on the batteries we were using, so I asked the electrician what we had that worked off DC. He said we had 110 volts DC, so why didn't we try that? I knew it wasn't going to kill them, so when the RSPCA man was on the other stage watching the puppets we gave this poor old alligator 110 DC. He opened his mouth, and when we

switched off he shut his mouth again. And that's how we got the shot."

For both the special effects and puppet crews, *Attack of the Alligators!* was probably the most arduous shoot in an already punishing schedule. Meddings put in particularly long hours, sometimes staying at the studio until three o'clock in the morning, and his marriage suffered. "I was never at home," he said in 1992. "I look back on it now and think I must have been crazy but, like a lot of people, I was only doing it because there was this chance to be part of a new era."

Above left: In *The Cham-Cham*, the intrepid Parker attempts to halt a speeding cable car with the help of Thunderbird 2.

Above right: The Paradise Peaks Hotel was another memorable contribution to *The Cham-Cham* by Meddings and his model-makers.

1.25 THE CHAM-CHAM

teleplay by **Alan Pattillo**
directed by **Alan Pattillo**
first broadcast 24 March 1966

On three occasions, US Air Force transporters are shot down by mysterious assailants while The Cass Carnaby Five perform a live radio broadcast of their hit Dangerous Game. *Posing as torch singer Wanda Lamour, Lady Penelope visits the group at the highest hotel in Europe to see if there's a link...*

"What sort of business will it be this time?" asks Parker. "Showbusiness," replies Lady Penelope.

Alan Pattillo and Barry Gray may have had some quaint ideas about the hit parade, but this episode rates as one of the most entertaining thanks to the novelty of its central conceit, the winning investigative team of Penelope and Tin Tin, and one of the most exotic locations in the series.

Pattillo exploits the opportunities presented by the Swiss Alps when Penelope and Tin Tin ski their way to and from the chalet occupied by shady music arranger Olsen (David Graham). Aside from being a charming sequence, it's the most inventive use yet of Derek Meddings' roller road technology.

In the opening episode of *Thunderbirds* nobody at London Airport had heard of International Rescue. Now, as the first series draws to a close, the organisation's success can be measured by its notoriety. The commander at the Matthew Field control tower ignores the valuable advice he receives, telling his colleague: "If we paid attention to every nut who claimed he was International Rescue we'd never get any work done!"

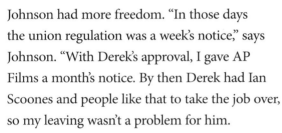

Above left: Members of the special effects team, including Harry Oakes (left), Ian Scoones (second from left) and Brian Johnson (second from right), recreate the French Riviera for *The Man from MI.5.*

Above right: The corresponding sequence in the finished programme – Carl sails past Lady Penelope's yacht, FAB 2, on the way to a secret rendezvous with the other criminals in his gang.

Below: Only the bow of FAB 2 was built for the scene where Carl passes the yacht.

Although they were undoubtedly committed, both Meddings and Johnson had ambitions beyond Supermarionation. "There was an undercurrent of frustration," says Johnson. "We'd go to see a feature film and wish we were working on something like that." Towards the end of *Thunderbirds* an opportunity arose that one of them found impossible to resist.

Stanley Kubrick's daughters were *Thunderbirds* fans, and Kubrick had been impressed by the quality of the series' special effects. During pre-production of *2001: A Space Odyssey* he called APF and asked Sylvia Anderson whether her company undertook special effects for other productions. When she said it didn't, he changed tack and asked Meddings to join him at MGM's Borehamwood studio on *2001.* Meddings' contract with ATV prevented him from leaving at that time, but

Johnson had more freedom. "In those days the union regulation was a week's notice," says Johnson. "With Derek's approval, I gave AP Films a month's notice. By then Derek had Ian Scoones and people like that to take the job over, so my leaving wasn't a problem for him.

"About a week before I was due to leave I was called into the main office, and there were all the directors of AP Films, looking rather uncomfortable. At that time I was getting 30 quid a week. Gerry said he'd been to see Lew Grade, and that Lew said I could be paid three times as much if I stayed. I said I'd given a month's notice, and it was agreed that I was going to leave. Gerry said, 'Is that your final word?' And when I said yes, he stubbed his huge cigar into his ashtray. All the sparks went up into the air. He said, 'F**k you! You'll never work in the film industry again!'"

Johnson would spend three years with Kubrick on *2001.* Despite Anderson's threat, they were reunited for several television series in the 1970s, and at the end of the decade Johnson won Academy Awards for his contributions to *Alien* (1979) and *The Empire Strikes Back* (1980). Meddings, Johnson, and many of their colleagues may have outgrown the small studio

1.26 SECURITY HAZARD

teleplay by **Alan Pattillo**
directed by **Desmond Saunders**
first broadcast 31 March 1966

Thunderbird 2 returns from a rescue operation in England with a frightened stowaway in Pod 1. Jeff is initially furious at the breach of security, but Virgil, Alan, Scott and Gordon can't resist showing young Chip around Tracy Island. One by one, they regale him with stories of their adventures...

Chip Morrison (Christine Finn) is one of the curiously large number of *Thunderbirds* characters who have fathers but no mothers. The Tracy brothers, Tin Tin and the boys from *Cry Wolf* are all in the same position. It's a theme that dates back to *Stingray*'s Atlanta Shore and would continue in future series. Like International Rescue, the Spectrum organisation in *Captain Scarlet and the Mysterons* is run on paternalistic lines, and *Joe 90*'s Joe McLaine is an orphan who has an adoptive father in Professor McLaine and no mother figure at all.

Jeff's paranoia about Chip's presence on Tracy Island is entirely inconsistent with his attitude towards the junior

visitors in *Cry Wolf* and the later episode, *Give or Take a Million*, but does at least add some intriguing tension between him and his more relaxed sons.

Chip is treated to highlights from *End of the Road*, *Sun Probe*, *Trapped in the Sky* and *Day of Disaster*. Closing a series in this way was a tried and tested means of balancing the books and recovering the schedule; the final episode of *Stingray* had employed a similar ruse.

on the Slough Trading Estate, but the experience they had gained was invaluable.

Towards the end of his life, Meddings was asked whether another series of *Thunderbirds* could be produced using the same painstaking techniques. "I don't think so," he replied. "I don't know if you could get anybody to work the way we worked. We were like maniacs."

Below left: Some of the special effects department's greatest contributions to *Thunderbirds*, Thunderbird 2 and Creighton-Ward Mansion, were recreated inside snow globes by the Linda company in the mid-1960s.

Below right: Derek Meddings and some of his fellow technicians, including Bill Camp (left), attend to the Pacific Atlantic Monorail from *Brink of Disaster*.

7

SHOOTING STARS

Thunderbirds had barely had time to prove itself a success before the decision was taken to adapt the series for the big screen. Gerry and Sylvia Anderson's first film screenplay borrowed Jeff Tracy's catchphrase for its title, *Thunderbirds Are Go*, and was drafted by December 1965, just a few months after *Trapped in the Sky* made its television debut.

Thunderbirds Are Go was a joint venture between AP Films, its parent company ATV and United Artists. The American distributor was responsible for the James Bond films that had fast become a cultural phenomenon; in 1966 one of the company's executives encouraged Gerry Anderson to believe that *Thunderbirds* could be just as big.

Thunderbirds was by no means the first television hit to make the transition to cinema, but the challenge it posed to British filmmakers was unprecedented. Series as diverse as the *Six-Five Special* and *Doctor Who* appeared more lavish in their cinematic incarnations, but unlike those programmes *Thunderbirds* was already being shot on 35mm film, with production values that exceeded those of most movies.

Thunderbirds Are Go would offer fans the chance to watch International Rescue in colour, with the added benefits of Techniscope widescreen and spectacular on-screen pyrotechnics. A follow-up, *Thunderbird 6*, was released in 1968.

But United Artists' optimism proved to be short-lived. Rather than providing a new lease of life, the two feature films produced by the Andersons and their team would actually bring the original run of *Thunderbirds* to an end.

Above left: Sylvia Anderson, the producer and co-writer of *Thunderbirds Are Go*, with the film's director David Lane (left) and visual effects director Derek Meddings.

Above right: An advertisement from the 31 March 1966 issue of *Kinematograph Weekly*.

Below: A frame of Techniscope occupied only two perforations of a negative, but prints were converted to a four-frame, anamorphic format for projection in CinemaScope.

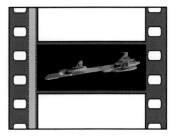

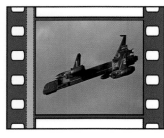

The title sequence of *Stingray* had begun in black and white, before giving way to vibrant 'Videcolor'. Gerry and Sylvia Anderson's shooting script for the first *Thunderbirds* film proposed another gimmick to unveil the next advance in Supermarionation. After the opening titles, the film would reveal the space exploration vehicle Zero X as it made the lengthy preparations for take-off:

> VARIVISION shutters open
> to Academy Frame. We are
> looking at the letters ZERO X,
> which are painted on sheet
> metal, music strikes dramatic
> chord, as VARIVISION shutters
> slowly open to scope width...

The Andersons' script adds an exclamation mark to the title *Thunderbirds Are Go* and

opens with a brief list of specifications, including 'Varivision' aspect ratios, stereophonic sound and a 100-minute duration. Only the first two requirements on the list – Technicolor and Techniscope – would be realised in the finished film.

The decision to shoot in a widescreen scope format was the most obvious way to distinguish the film from its television counterpart, which was shot in a 4:3 'Academy' ratio tailored for television screens of the era. *Thunderbirds Are Go* had a relatively generous budget of £250,000, sufficient under most circumstances to employ the CinemaScope process developed by Twentieth Century-Fox in the early 1950s. CinemaScope relied on the use of an anamorphic lens that captured a vertically stretched frame occupying four perforations of a 35mm negative. When a print came to be projected, another anamorphic lens stretched the image horizontally, restoring the correct aspect ratio and creating a much wider picture.

When AP Films investigated the possibility of shooting *Thunderbirds Are Go* in CinemaScope, Derek Meddings advised that the lenses wouldn't allow the depth of field dictated by the unusually shallow puppet and model stages. Meddings instead requested that the film was shot using Techniscope.

Regarded by some in the industry as a poor man's CinemaScope, Techniscope had been devised by Technicolor's Italian division in 1960. Techniscope created its widescreen effect not by distorting the original image, but by using a specially adapted camera to shoot each frame in a widescreen ratio that only occupied two perforations of the negative. The image was 'flat', and the use of a spherical lens avoided the areas of 'fish-eye' distortion that were sometimes noticeable in the corners of a CinemaScope frame during panning shots.

The system did, however, have conspicuous disadvantages. Creating a widescreen image in half the negative space occupied by a CinemaScope frame inevitably led to a softer, grainier picture. The narrow proximity between frames increased the risk of hairs and other minute debris creeping into the picture, as well as strong sources of light bleeding from one frame to another.

The process was largely sold on its economy; Techniscope saved money in the shooting, if

not necessarily the processing, because it used half the negative stock of CinemaScope and Academy ratio filming. This meant that takes could last twice as long before a magazine of film needed changing – a luxury that increased Meddings' options for the lengthy shots of Zero X at the beginning of *Thunderbirds Are Go*.

Above: Meddings' design for the Zero X space exploration vehicle.

Below left: The Zero X was built by Mastermodels. This picture, taken in the company's Feltham workshop in 1966, shows a model that preserved the tail numbers 'ZX-26' from Meddings' original sketch.

Below right: The model had been renamed 'Zero X' by the time Meddings (top) filmed its take-off on the roller road.

THUNDERBIRDS ARE GO

screenplay by **Gerry and Sylvia Anderson**
directed by **David Lane**
first screened 12 December 1966 (London Pavilion)

The first manned mission to Mars is aborted when the Hood triggers a mechanical failure in the space exploration vehicle Zero X. Two years later, a new Zero X leaves the Earth's atmosphere under the protection of International Rescue. The surface of Mars proves terrifying, but the journey back to Earth is just as dangerous...

Feature film spin-offs traditionally expand on their television forebears, and *Thunderbirds Are Go* is no exception. This is the first *Thunderbirds* story to visit another planet and encounter alien life, although neither of those events is witnessed by anyone familiar from the series. Indeed, it's puzzling that Gerry and Sylvia's story largely relegates the Tracy family to the status of supporting characters.

There are compensations in the production team evidently seizing the opportunity to work in a Techniscope aspect ratio. Director David Lane opens the sequence set in the Space Exploration Center with an overhead shot that pulls back from its rectangular table. Derek Meddings is just as inventive, filling the entire screen with a looming Thunderbird 2 as the vehicle prepares to launch from Tracy Island. Elsewhere, Bob Bell's designs for the Swinging Star nightclub are gloriously kitsch, even if the dream sequence they appear in is too anachronistic a homage to pre-war Hollywood.

No amount of window dressing can paper over the shortcomings in the screenplay. Gerry and Sylvia's concept for *Thunderbirds* was brilliant, but by 1966 their creation was better served by other writers.

After surmounting the first of the film's technical challenges, Gerry Anderson faced another problem when his first choice of director turned him down. "I'd had enough," says Alan Pattillo. "Working with puppets is so limiting and I found that it was not creative enough. Everything was a compromise. I also wondered whether it would really work on a big screen because it was such a cosy show, with nice little characters appearing on the small screen. I felt that the intimacy would be gone, and it wouldn't stand up. It was the intimacy that helped you to overlook the blemishes and the strings. But on the big screen I felt you wouldn't tolerate those things."

Anderson instead turned to his protégé David Lane, who had directed eight episodes of *Thunderbirds'* first series. Lane

felt the demands justified a £10 increase in his salary, and only accepted the job after Anderson agreed to pay him £60 a week.

"It had to be the new Rolls-Royce," says Lane, recalling the pressure of trying to improve on the television series' impressive production values. "The major difference was detail. You knew more detail would be seen, so you paid even more attention to the lighting and the quality of shooting. There's a huge difference between putting something on a 70-foot screen and what was then a 17-inch television screen."

The film would be made in parallel with *Thunderbirds*' second series and retained the voice cast from those episodes. Additional actors included Alexander Davion as Space Captain Greg Martin and comedian Bob Monkhouse in several roles, notably Space Navigator Brad Newman. Monkhouse was a late replacement for comic actor Alfred Marks, who had withdrawn from the production following a disagreement over his fee. Monkhouse had met the Andersons when he visited Stirling Road in 1964 to request permission to use some of the *Stingray* characters and vehicles in a sketch he was writing for *The Des O'Connor Show*. Monkhouse was such a fan of *Thunderbirds* that when he heard about Marks' departure he offered to take his place for free. "The price is right," responded Gerry Anderson enthusiastically.

Opposite page: The comic *TV Century 21* began a four-part adaptation of *Thunderbirds Are Go* in the issue dated 24 December 2066.

Above left: Sylvia asked supervising art director Bob Bell to decorate the Space Exploration Center in an orange-and-black colour scheme so the committee's blue uniforms would stand out.

Above right: The cover of the 20 March 1971 issue of *Countdown* comic featured a picture of David Lane on the set of the Space Exploration Center.

Left: Captain Paul Travers, commander of the Zero X missions. The character was voiced by Paul Maxwell, who had played Steve Zodiac in *Fireball XL5*.

Above left: Meddings applies the finishing touches to one of the Martian Rock Snakes.

Above right: Elements of Meddings' design for the snakes were adopted by Gerry and Sylvia Anderson's script.

Below: A Martian Rock Snake featured in this German lobby card promoting the film.

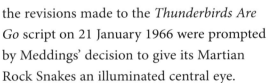

FEUERVÖGEL *Startbereit*

As pre-production continued, Lane recruited Alan Perry as his camera operator. "Dave was, and still is, a very talented director," says Perry. "He sees things through a different light. He's also a red hot editor, and I think this was something else Gerry recognised in him. Dave knew how to pace the films – when to keep a scene brief or when to prolong it to make it better."

Lane's apprenticeship with Gerry Anderson had begun in the AP Films cutting rooms, where Lane became so proficient that he worked alongside Anderson creating the benchmark title sequence for *Stingray*. Derek Meddings had also made a key contribution to the *Stingray* title sequence, storyboarding it with Lane before filming and editing began. Meddings' input to *Thunderbirds Are Go* was just as influential – some of

the revisions made to the *Thunderbirds Are Go* script on 21 January 1966 were prompted by Meddings' decision to give its Martian Rock Snakes an illuminated central eye.

The edition of *News Trade Weekly* cover-dated the 22nd predicted that "sales of anything connected with Lady Penelope and *Thunderbirds* will go soaring, as, for the first time ever, the puppets are coming to the big cinema screen in colour... Can this be the James Bond success all over again in miniature, and just how long will it be before a full length book is written about these popular little characters?"

Filming began on 3 March and continued for the next five months. For the first time there was the luxury of a foreign location,

2.1 ATLANTIC INFERNO

teleplay by **Alan Fennell**
directed by **Desmond Saunders**
first broadcast 2 October 1966

Penelope persuades the overworked Jeff to join her on vacation in Australia. In his father's absence, Scott sends Gordon to cap a fire at an Atlantic gas field. Jeff tells Scott the decision was misjudged, but decides to stay in Australia. The disaster soon escalates, and Scott is no longer sure how to act...

When the World Navy proclaims "We are about to commence target practice – there could be a number of nuclear explosions", that should warn anyone in the vicinity that International Rescue will soon be required. Sure enough, a maverick gyropedo ultimately results in the explosive demolition of a nearby drilling rig.

The opening episode of the second series begins by efficiently reminding the audience about the Tracy family, their associates and the various Thunderbird machines. Penelope has a trendy new hairdo for 1966, and there are numerous other, relatively inconspicuous changes. The foremost sign of the series' growing maturity, however, is the focus of Fennell's story. For a large part of *Atlantic Inferno*, the

encroaching flames serve as the backdrop for a revealing study of Jeff's personality and his sometimes tangled relationship with his sons.

The emphasis switches to the rescue in the final act. Director Desmond Saunders keeps his camera low to shoot the imposing Seascape rig, while Derek Meddings' special effects team confidently tackles both fire and water, the two most difficult elements to tame on their miniature sets.

---

although Lane's second unit was only given a weekend in Portugal in between other duties in Slough. "I was shooting on the stage until four or five o'clock," he remembers. "Then they put me in a taxi and took me to the airport. I flew to Portugal on a Comet, filmed for a whole weekend, flew back Monday morning and went straight back to work on the stage."

The second unit – comprising Lane, Derek Meddings, Alan Perry and director of photography Paddy Seale – was on a mission to film a rapid descent towards Tracy Island for the end of a dream sequence, and footage of a lush landscape to be back-projected beneath the Zero X as it completed its return journey to Earth. Lane now describes the expedition, which was fraught with technical problems, as "a disaster".

Right: This *TV Century 21* special was published in late 1966 and explored the making of the film.

Below: One of eight front of house cards issued to British cinema managers in December 1966.

The dream sequence footage required Lane, Meddings and Perry to board an Alouette helicopter that hovered over a Portuguese island. "In the bottom of the Alouette there was a trap door that the pilot took out," remembers Perry. "I was holding an Arriflex camera and looking through the eyepiece, giving Derek a running commentary on what I could see. Because the pilot didn't speak French, Derek communicated what we wanted through drawings. The idea was that we would get above the island, and then spiral down until Derek told the pilot that we had what we needed. So there I was, on my knees on the floor of this helicopter with the camera in my hand. Derek had taken his seatbelt off, looped it through my belt and grabbed hold of the other end, to keep me safe."

When Meddings gave the signal, the pilot cut the engine and the helicopter started to plummet. "It went deathly quiet," says Perry. "I was wetting myself. I said, 'Derek, I think you've got it mate, it's really great... Honestly Derek, you've definitely got it now...' But we were still going. I was still looking though the camera, and by this time I could see the bloody detail of the rocks. Finally the rotors started up again. All right, we were probably 50 or 60 feet above the island, but when you're looking through a viewfinder it looks a lot closer!"

Lane considers that it had been a mistake not taking Seale in the helicopter. "Derek knew more about cameras than I did, so he would set the apertures himself, from what he'd gleaned from Paddy. Unfortunately he got it wrong." The footage looked even worse when it was sped up, and was entirely abandoned. In the finished film it was replaced by a briefly seen model shot.

THUNDERBIRDS ARE GO

by Gerry and Sylvia Anderson

2/6

ARMADA PAPERBACKS for Boys & Girls

The high-altitude shots of the landscape beneath the Zero X were compromised when the juddering of the helicopter altered the exposure on the camera. When the rushes were evaluated back at Slough, Reg Hill instead suggested creating a painting of the ground below on large pieces of cardboard. These paintings were slowly moved from top to bottom for the back projection filming and proved surprisingly effective in the finished sequence.

The only part of the Portuguese shoot that did make it into the film was the low-altitude footage of the ground rushing by, which can be seen in the Zero X sequence prior to its crash-landing. "We were able to use some of the low-flying stuff because Paddy was on board for that," says Lane, "and the juddering actually looks authentic."

2.2 PATH OF DESTRUCTION

teleplay by **Donald Robertson**
directed by **David Elliott**
first broadcast 9 October 1966

The Crablogger is an atomic-powered behemoth that ingests the trees in its path and discharges wood pulp in convenient barrels. When the Crablogger's drivers succumb to food poisoning it veers dangerously off course. International Rescue must intercept the vehicle before it reaches a dam...

A story extolling a machine's tree-felling capabilities in the South American jungle would probably not be commissioned in the 21st century, but there's no denying that the gigantic Crablogger is as awe-inspiring as anything in the International Rescue arsenal.

Barry Gray's reuse of cues from *Pit of Peril* underlines the fact that this is a very similar tale. But almost everything about *Path of Destruction* is an improvement on that series one misfire; Donald Robertson's heady cocktail of food poisoning, nuclear contamination and flooding makes this one of the most compelling *Thunderbirds* episodes.

When the Crablogger finally ground to a halt, David Elliott's long and prolific collaboration with Gerry Anderson also came to an abrupt end. Elliott was one of AP Films'

most competent directors, and he went out on a high.

In a tense scenario full of daring deeds, special mention must go to the fearless Jim Lucas (David Graham). The engineer reveals the procedure to shut down the Crablogger's reactor shortly before Lady Penelope administers a tranquiliser. As the drug takes effect Lucas starts flirting with her, regardless of the fact that his wife lies sleeping in the neighbouring bed...

Right: Cliff Richard Jr and The Shadows perform *Shooting Star* on top of a giant guitar in Alan's dream.

Below: Bob Bell examines the guitar prop at APF's art department in Edinburgh Avenue.

At Stirling Road, the puppet stages made a rather more successful contribution to the dream sequence. Alan Tracy's fantasy of visiting the Swinging Star nightclub with Lady Penelope was given a psychedelic twist by supervising art director Bob Bell and a modern beat by 'Cliff Richard Jr' and his backing group The Shadows. The Andersons had written *Trapped in the Sky* while staying in a Portuguese villa owned by Cliff and the Shadows' manager Peter Gormley. "One day he asked why we didn't use any of his people for our characters," says Sylvia. "I thought it was a good idea, and that's how Cliff Richard and The Shadows came to be in *Thunderbirds Are Go*."

The Shadows wrote two songs for the film's soundtrack: *Shooting Star* and the instrumental *Lady Penelope*. Gerry Anderson even went to the trouble of filming Cliff and the group performing both numbers so his puppeteers would have accurate reference for their dance steps and hand movements.

Considered by some to be the best part of the film, and by others as a bizarre interruption to the narrative, the sequence is fondly remembered by The Shadows' Brian Bennett, who was given his puppet's miniature drum kit as a souvenir.

2.3 ALIAS MR. HACKENBACKER

teleplay by **Alan Pattillo**
directed by **Desmond Saunders**
first broadcast 16 October 1966

Revolutions in the worlds of aeronautics and haute couture combine when Lady Penelope models a new fabric on the inaugural flight of Skythrust, a jet airliner partly designed by Brains under his pseudonym Hiram K Hackenbacker. The fashion show is a great success – until the plane is hijacked...

This ambitious episode could have been designed for readers of both the Gerry Anderson comics available in 1966. *TV Century 21*'s technologically minded boys would have appreciated Brains' innovative take on air safety, while for readers of the style-conscious *Lady Penelope* there was Penelon, a versatile synthetic fabric that enabled a dress to be folded into a tiny space. Penelope is delighted when fashionista François Lemaire (Ray Barrett) produces a frock from a container no bigger than a cigarette packet.

The successful integration of such diverse storylines is a testament to the second series' increased sophistication. This is further exemplified by Bob Bell's opulent production design; the purple furnishings and Art Deco styling of Monsieur Lemaire's office resemble

the trendsetting signatures of Biba, the Kensington boutique that had popularised the mini-skirt.

This episode also benefits from the expansion of the voice cast in the second series, with former *Fireball XL5* star Paul Maxwell joining as the Skythrust's Captain Ashton. Female roles remained limited to Sylvia Anderson and Christine Finn, an obvious shortcoming in the scenes where Sylvia's characters were required to talk to each other.

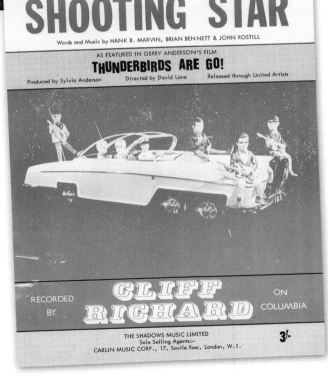

Above left: A poster advertising the 7" *Thunderbirds Are Go!* EP released by Columbia Records in November 1966.

Above right: The Shadows' drummer Brian Bennett and guitarist Hank Marvin come face-to-face with their puppets at Stirling Road. Christine Glanville recalled that mimicking Bennett's drumming was one of the hardest parts of the puppetry on the film.

Far right: Sheet music for *Shooting Star*, the vocal number performed by Cliff Richard Jr and The Shadows.

Right: "What a terrific group!" Alan tells Penelope at the Swinging Star nightclub. Sylvia felt that the nightclub had a suitably 'with-it' name for 1966, but now admits that it sounds dated.

If one word was required to cover all these fantastically popular television programmes, many viewers, young and old, would think of the word . . .

EXPLOSION!

This is not surprising, for one of the first impressions created by GERRY ANDERSON'S fabulous TV series is the visual effects detonations.

But the word has other implications beyond that first vital point. Puppets, made from fibreglass, wood, wire, and wonderful magic, explode into life at the passing of each second.

Stories blast to new heights of dramatic adventure, like tongues of flame searing into the sky. Mechanical skill erupts to genius and brilliance as the cameras turn.

A dedicated and resourceful team has dynamited to success.

Yes-explosion is the right word to describe the growth in size and stature of a company that has become one of the largest television film producing organisations in the world.

Twelve months ago, the fuses were lit beneath another arsenal of gunpowder. The atom of an idea in the mind of Gerry Anderson was to burst into a project that had the force of an atomic bomb on the entertainment world.

Those smouldering fuses burned down to the flash point. Thunderbirds were ready to explode from the black and white television screen to the might of full scale cinema techniscope in vivid Technicolor. All systems read green . . . the firing button has been activated. The explosion is complete . . .

THUNDERBIRDS ARE GO!

Above: Derek Meddings prepares Craigsville for the crash-landing of the Zero X. He is appropriately dressed for the imminent pyrotechnics.

Right: The destruction of the Zero X, as illustrated in the *Thunderbirds Are Go!* special presented by *TV Century 21*.

2.4 LORD PARKER'S 'OLIDAY

teleplay by **Tony Barwick**
directed by **Brian Burgess**
first broadcast 23 October 1966

Parker and Penelope's visit to Monte Bianco coincides with a pioneering scheme to supply the area with solar energy. A lightning strike dislodges the solar reflector dish, leaving it in a dangerous position. The morning sunlight reflected from the dish now threatens to incinerate the whole town...

Gerry Anderson had first commissioned Tony Barwick to help him extend the 25-minute episodes of *Thunderbirds*. For the second series he gave him his first credited work. Barwick's script has structural problems, which include not knowing what to do with Penelope after she alerts International Rescue to the impending disaster, but it's redeemed by the farcical scenes set in the hotel. Parker and Penelope's fancy dress is wildly over the top, and Parker's pragmatic attitude to the disaster is in comic contrast to the local naysayer Bruno (Charles Tingwell), whose frequent predictions of disaster for the solar project turn out to be fairly accurate.

Penelope's instruction that Parker keeps the hotel guests distracted is a flimsy device (wouldn't it be more sensible to evacuate them?) but it affords us the opportunity to witness the chauffeur's hilarious reinvention as an aristocratic bingo-caller who at one point exclaims, "Hold on, hold on, Honest Lord Parker doesn't pay out until he's checked your card."

The principal plot, about the failure of an attempt to power a Mediterranean town using solar energy, strikes an unusually pessimistic note about the fallibility of clean alternatives to atomic energy.

One of the film's undisputed highlights was the ultimate destruction of the Zero X. There had already been around 300 visual effects model shots leading up to this point, but the Zero X crash would be Meddings' most spectacular sequence to date. United Artists' publicists were suitably impressed – a painting of the crash dominated one of the two Quad Crown posters designed to promote *Thunderbirds Are Go* in British cinemas.

The film's final surprise played out under the closing credits. Live-action footage of Drum Major Charles Bowden bellowing "Thunderbirds... are... go!" leads into Lieutenant Colonel F Vivian Dunn conducting

The Band of Her Majesty's Royal Marines in their rendition of Barry Gray's *Thunderbirds* theme. Lane had just one morning to shoot the sequence, setting his alarm at four o'clock so he could arrive early at the Royal Marine Depot in Deal, Kent. The time restrictions meant that the sequence's conclusion – a crane shot of the band in formation, spelling out 'THE END' – had to be filmed after a rain shower had drenched the parade ground.

Post-production lost more than 15 minutes from the running time – eliminating Kyrano from the film entirely – but added a previously unseen logo that proclaimed this to be Gerry Anderson's first on-screen venture under the company name Century 21. In November *Kinematograph Weekly* reported that Anderson had screened a cutting copy of the first reel at a recent meeting of the British Kinematograph, Sound and Television Society, where he pointed out that Techniscope was the only scope format with the necessary depth of field and argued that the picture definition was excellent.

Above left: More than 15 minutes was cut from *Thunderbirds Are Go*, including these three scenes. In the first picture, Jeff Tracy (in silhouette) broadcasts via the Trans American TV Network to explain why International Rescue can't comply with a request to safeguard the launch of the second Zero X.

Above centre: During the broadcast, the Hood makes telepathic contact with Kyrano, forcing him to reveal details of the mission should International Rescue go ahead.

Above right: This deleted scene found Penelope and Parker aboard a Fireflash, on their way to America to assist with security at the launch.

Below left: David Lane (pointing) with camera operator Alan Perry (centre) and focus puller Robin McDonald (right), filming the end titles for *Thunderbirds Are Go* at the Royal Marine Depot in Deal, Kent.

Below right: The Band of Her Majesty's Royal Marines spelled out the final shot of *Thunderbirds Are Go*.

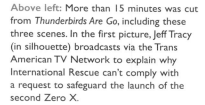

Above left: Gerry and Sylvia Anderson, with Lew Grade at the premiere of *Thunderbirds Are Go*.

Above right: Sylvia meets the press in the foyer of the London Pavilion. Cliff Richard remembers that the crowd outside the cinema was so dense that he struggled to get inside.

Far right: The front of the Pavilion was decorated with images of Thunderbirds 1, 2 and 3 for the film's premiere and West End run.

Right: Both sides of Barry Gray's ticket to the premiere.

PHONE: GERrard 2982

LONDON PAVILION PICCADILLY CIRCUS

WORLD CHARITY PREMIERE
IN AID OF DR BARNARDO'S
on MONDAY DECEMBER 12th 1966 at 8.30 p.m. (DOORS 7.45 p.m.)

GERRY ANDERSON'S

THUNDERBIRDS ARE GO

in SUPERMARIONATION and TECHNICOLOR

PRODUCED BY SYLVIA ANDERSON · DIRECTED BY DAVID LANE Released through UNITED ARTISTS

DRESS CIRCLE   **ROW A**   **SEAT No. 1**   **10 gns.**
ENTRANCE PICADILLY CIRCUS   Black Tie

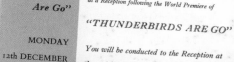

LONDON PAVILION

"*Thunderbirds Are Go*"

MONDAY 12th DECEMBER 1966 8.30 p.m.

The Deputy Chairman of Council, Dr. R. Ian Milne, and Council of Dr. Barnardo's request the pleasure of the company of

Mr. Barry Gray

at a Reception following the World Premiere of

"*THUNDERBIRDS ARE GO*"

You will be conducted to the Reception at the end of the performance, so please remain in your seat until you are fetched.

Please be sure to bring this invitation with you.

The premiere, on Monday 12 December, represented the peak of Gerry and Sylvia's meteoric career. The day had started well, when David Chasman, United Artists' European head of production, complimented Gerry on the film, adding, "I can't decide if it will make as much money as Bond or if it will make even more."

The event was held at the London Pavilion, where Gerry and Sylvia planned to arrive in a life-size replica of FAB 1. Unfortunately the car broke down, leaving them to complete their journey in a taxi. Making their way through the jostling reporters and photographers, they took their seats alongside their colleagues as The Band of HM Royal Marines introduced the screening with Barry Gray's famous music.

Gerry remembered that when the film finished David Picker, UA's managing director, leaned towards him and said, "Whatever subject you want to make next, Mr Anderson, it's yours."

Lew Grade was similarly appreciative, handing Gerry and Sylvia an envelope containing the keys to a villa in Portugal. Any hopes the Andersons may have had of moving in immediately were dashed when Lew's brother Leslie pointed out that he had already promised the villa to Tom Jones for a month. This must have been especially galling for the Andersons, whose recent efforts to persuade Jones to sing a title song for them had been blocked by Jones' manager on the grounds that they couldn't afford him.

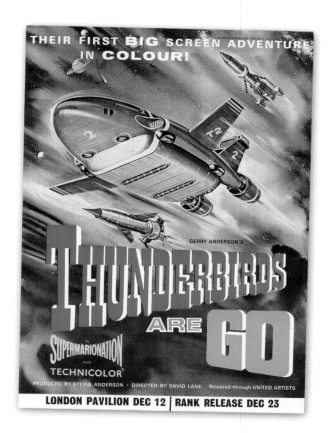

Above: A full-page advertisement from the 10 December 1966 issue of *Kinematograph Weekly*.

2.5 RICOCHET

teleplay by **Tony Barwick**
directed by **Brian Burgess**
first broadcast 6 November 1966

Tin Tin is enthralled by pirate television station KLA, but Alan doesn't share her enthusiasm for its smooth-talking disc jockey Rick O'Shea. Jeff warns that the orbit of the KLA satellite is occupying unauthorised space – an area that is later chosen as the detonation site for a malfunctioning rocket...

Ricochet's thinly veiled satire of mid-1960s 'pirates' such as Radio Caroline and their American-style DJs would be enough to make this episode noteworthy, but Tony Barwick's script also predicts the rise of MTV and the 21st century's superfluity of satellite channels with miniscule audiences. When Rick O'Shea (Ray Barrett) complains that Loman (David Graham) isn't quick enough with the ricochet sound effect that accompanies his name, the browbeaten engineer replies, "I doubt if anyone was foolish enough to be tuned in."

Flying High, the record that Rick dedicates to Tin Tin, is a song Barry Gray originally proposed for the end titles of *Thunderbirds*. The vocals are by Gary Miller (who previously performed *Aqua Marina* in *Stingray*), and backing singers include session musician Ken Barrie. Fifteen years later, Barrie would appear in another children's classic when he provided the voice of Postman Pat.

In an episode that boasts some of the funniest dialogue in the series, the best line goes to Brains. "I'm afraid music in the modern idiom is too repetitive for my taste," he tells Alan, "but I must admit it has a certain hypnotic effect."

THE LONDON WEEK

What's On IN LONDON

TOP GUIDE TO LONDON EVENTS

1/3

No. 1,622 DECEMBER 16, 1966

JEFF TRACY | VIRGIL TRACY | ALAN TRACY | JOHN TRACY | GORDON TRACY | SCOTT TRACY | 'BRAINS' | LADY PENELOPE

THEIR FIRST BIG SCREEN ADVENTURE IN COLOUR!

GERRY ANDERSON'S

THUNDERBIRDS ARE GO

SUPERMARIONATION AND TECHNICOLOR

ADULTS OVER 16 SHOULD BE ACCOMPANIED BY CHILDREN

PRODUCED BY SYLVIA ANDERSON · DIRECTED BY DAVID LANE Released through UNITED ARTISTS

ALSO "NAMU" THE KILLER WHALE

COLOUR by De Luxe

NOW LONDON PAVILION
PICCADILLY CIRCUS GER 2982
GENERAL RELEASE from DEC. 23rd

TORDENFUGLE MED GO

Left: The best-known *Thunderbirds Are Go* poster was designed by Eddie Paul and illustrated by Bill Wiggins. A two-colour representation of their artwork appeared on the cover of the 16 December 1966 issue of listings magazine *What's On In London*.

Below: The film's Danish press book.

The evening ended with a party at the Hilton Hotel, and the following day Gerry and Sylvia embarked on a nationwide tour to promote the film. The *Daily Express* review of 13 December was typical of the mixed notices that appeared that week. "The trouble is that, apart from Lady Penelope, her cockney servant, and Brains, the scientific genius of the rescue team, all the characters are lacking in originality," wrote Ian Christie. "The story too lacks imagination and at times I got the feeling that the scriptwriter was hard put to find enough ideas to pad the film out to its conclusion."

Writing on the same day, *The Sun*'s Ann Pacey was also underwhelmed. "Though the puppets are cleverly manipulated and their wires cleverly disguised, they do remain slow-speaking puppets with large heads, small

2.6 GIVE OR TAKE A MILLION

teleplay by **Alan Pattillo**
directed by **Desmond Saunders**
first broadcast 25 December 1966

Christmas is going to be especially memorable for a lucky patient of the Coralville Children's Hospital and a slightly less fortunate pair of robbers. As Jeff prepares to welcome young Nicky to Tracy Island, the criminals launch a sophisticated raid on the strong room of the Second National Bank...

Thunderbirds was successfully experimenting with its format right until the end. *Give or Take a Million* is a whimsical entry: the toys Jeff provides for Nicky (Sylvia Anderson) are models of the Thunderbird fleet and the story itself is the only one not to feature any kind of rescue. This is not to say that the episode is short on drama – Desmond Saunders' direction of Alan Pattillo's script wrings maximum suspense from the bank robbery scenes in particular.

One of the crooks, Straker (David Graham), would later share his surname with the hero of Gerry Anderson's live-action series *UFO* (filmed from 1969-70). Elsewhere, hospital benefactor Saunders (Jeremy Wilkin) is the last character to be

named after a member of the production crew. The director had already inspired 'Rue Desmonde' in *The Perils of Penelope*. Other notable examples include Bob Meddings (David Graham) in *Trapped in the Sky* and special effects man Brian (Ray Barrett) in *Martian Invasion*.

In the final sequence the cast gathers in the Tracy Island lounge as Brains' specially conjured snow settles on the palm trees outside. It's a suitably sentimental farewell.

bodies and little individuality in a film lacking sufficient imagination and invention to sustain interest for an hour and a half."

Clive Hirschhorn struck a more positive note in the *Sunday Express*, concluding that "Of course the cast are all puppets, the sets models, and the story unabashed nonsense. But it's great all the same. Your kids will take you, of course."

By the time this review appeared on 18 December, it was already clear that this wasn't going to be the case. United Artists' optimism had been confounded by near-empty cinemas. So why didn't *Thunderbirds Are Go* do better business? "Because I don't think it was a great film," says David Lane with disarming honesty. "And you couldn't compare it to James Bond. *Thunderbirds* was a children's show. Adults used to watch it on the television, but they wouldn't pay to see it at the cinema."

Top and above: The 30" x 40" Quad Crown posters issued to British cinemas were the responsibility of Downton Advertising, a London-based agency whose clients included United Artists.

Left: This Spanish handbill combined artwork from both of these British posters.

Above: Brains, the mastermind behind Skyship One, watches Alan depart Tracy Island in this picture from *Thunderbird 6*.

Top right: Derek Meddings' design for Skyship One specified that its topside should look as if it had been constructed from stainless steel.

Above right: Meddings checks the underside of a Skyship One model on a special effects stage at Stirling Road.

SKYSHIP **1** TOPSIDE TREATMENT STAINLESS STEEL

Despite this box-office disappointment, *Thunderbirds Are Go* spawned a sequel. Gerry Anderson maintained that a baffled UA commissioned a follow-up because they thought the failure of the first film must have been a fluke: "None of us – Lew Grade, David Picker, David Chasman or myself – could understand why the film hadn't succeeded, so it was decided to make another one."

Lane suggests, however, that ATV had the distributor over a barrel. "I think it was contractual," he says. "When United Artists saw some of the sequences we shot for *Thunderbirds Are Go* they commissioned another one straight away, before the first one had been released."

Gerry and Sylvia's screenplay for the new film was inspired by Desmond Saunders' recommendation that they should write a story about the ill-fated R101. "Des had a great interest in airships," said Gerry, "and he was always telling me how his ambition was to be involved with a picture that included them in the storyline. He fired my imagination and, as a result, I read a number of books on the subject, particularly the R100, the R101 and the Graf Zeppelin."

Thunderbird 6 would be set in the year 2068, however, and presented an entirely new design of airship. Skyship One was a luxurious, fully automated vehicle powered by Brains' revolutionary anti-gravity technology. The sets were created by Bob Bell and his two assistants Keith Wilson and John Lageu. Skyship One's Gravity Compensator Room is their greatest achievement, evoking the stylish functionality of Ken Adam's best work for the James Bond films.

The design that stuck in Bell's memory, however, was the Whistle Stop Inn – an alpine restaurant visited by Alan, Penelope and Tin Tin on their global tour as passengers on Skyship One. "That was one that taxed my brain, but it looked quite super on the screen," said Bell. "It was a restaurant designed as a railway station. The train came in with all the menus and the plates, and went round in a circle. It took a hell of a lot of calculation because we had the puppets in one scale and the trains in another scale but it all had to work together. The timing had to be absolutely perfect."

Above: The Gravity Compensator Room was a dramatic location for Alan's gun battle with the fake Captain Foster.

Below left: Meddings' sketch for the first of the Thunderbird 6 candidates Brains shows to Jeff.

Below right: Brains demonstrates the capabilities of the proposed Thunderbird 6 with this radio-controlled model, but his ideas are rejected.

Bottom right: Miniature trains deliver meals to the diners at the Whistle Stop Inn. The restaurant was one of Bob Bell's favourite designs from his time on *Thunderbirds*.

Below left: After visiting India, Penelope
dines with 'Captain Foster' aboard Skyship
One. Entirely new puppet heads were
created for *Thunderbird 6*, some of which
were slightly smaller than those that had
been used in the television series. In this
respect they represented a transition
in style from *Thunderbirds* to *Captain
Scarlet and the Mysterons*, which was shot
concurrently with *Thunderbird 6* in 1967.

Below right: A puppet-proportioned
model of the Tiger Moth is filmed at
Stirling Road.

Like its predecessor, *Thunderbird 6* was
shot in Techniscope and benefited from an
expansion of the Stirling Road studio in early
1966. The film would be made alongside
Century 21's new series, *Captain Scarlet and
the Mysterons*, and the espionage-themed
screenplay reflected that programme's
harder edge. It's particularly surprising to see
characters murdered in a *Thunderbirds* story,
and director David Lane now admits that he
is slightly uncomfortable about the casual
disregard for human life in certain scenes.

New additions to the cast included
John Carson, the voice of the Hamlet cigar
commercials, as the head of a gang that
ruthlessly commandeers Skyship One. Ray
Barrett was unable to take part in recording

sessions, so Keith Alexander (the voice of
television mouse Topo Gigio) played John
Tracy, while Gary Files deputised as the Hood,
even though the character is only ever referred
to by his code name 'Black Phantom'. Geoffrey
Keen, who at the time starred alongside Barrett
in the television series *The Troubleshooters*,
provided the voice of Jim Glenn, the president
of the New World Aircraft Corporation.

Thunderbird 6 was budgeted at £300,000
and began its four-month shoot on 1 May
1967. Lane's biggest headache was the vehicle
that would ultimately explain the film's
intriguing title – a 1940 De Havilland Tiger
Moth. The plane was piloted by Joan Hughes
MBE, a highly experienced instructor who
had flown Spitfires, Typhoons, Mosquitoes
and Lancasters for the Air Transport Auxiliary
during the war. Hughes had first lent her
talents to a film in 1964. "Joan was the pilot
that rang the bell on *Those Magnificent Men
in Their Flying Machines*," says Lane. "So we
knew we were on to a good 'un. You wouldn't
have thought she could ride a bike, but she
was a delight, and what a good-looking lady.
I absolutely adored her."

Above: David Lane films the sequence where the bodies of the original crew are dropped from Skyship One into the sea.

Right: The Stirling Road studio was expanded for the production of *Thunderbirds Are Go* in 1966. For the filming of *Thunderbird 6* the following year, a large part of this area was given over to a recreation of the English countryside as Thunderbirds 1 and 2 escort FAB 1 and the Tiger Moth towards their rendezvous with Skyship One.

THUNDERBIRD 6

screenplay by **Gerry and Sylvia Anderson**
directed by **David Lane**
first screened 29 July 1968 (Odeon Leicester Square)

Alan, Tin Tin, Lady Penelope and Parker are passengers aboard Brains' latest invention, Skyship One. The airship boasts an innovative anti-gravity system, but the ersatz crew are more interested in the secrets of International Rescue. Under directions from the mysterious Black Phantom, they prepare an elaborate trap...

Thunderbird 6 leaves Jeff, Gordon and John at their stations while some of the more endearing characters embark on a round-the-world trip that evokes the globetrotting glamour of the James Bond films. Some of 007's cold-blooded espionage also seems to have rubbed off – the murder of Skyship One's original crew, and the callous disposal of their bodies, are calculated acts of violence without precedent in the television series.

The unfortunate Parker is the butt of most jokes, and there is self-referential irony in the crudely constructed model that Brains uses to demonstrate the fire-fighting capabilities of a proposed Thunderbird 6. In *Thunderbirds Are Go* it was Alan who was heard humming the theme tune from the television series; this time round it's Parker who's astonished to hear it played by an Indian snake-charmer.

The film's juxtaposition of the high-tech Skyship One with a vintage Tiger Moth anticipates Gerry Anderson's final Supermarionation series, *The Secret Service*, but can't detract from the holes in the plot. *Thunderbird 6* is an elegant postscript from the series' creators, but evidence that their minds had already turned to other things.

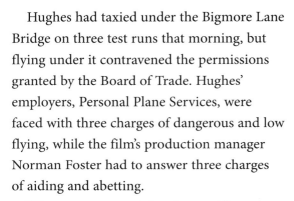

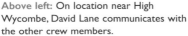
Above left: On location near High Wycombe, David Lane communicates with the other crew members.

Above right: Lane and Meddings brief Joan Hughes, who is dressed as Lady Penelope, before she takes off in the Tiger Moth. Dummies of Alan and Tin Tin can be seen on the starboard wing, and a dummy of Parker is attached to the undercarriage.

Below: Lane and his camera operator Peter Nash climb on top of a van in order to film Penelope's point of view as the Tiger Moth hurtles down the motorway.

On Sunday 21 May, Lane was shooting on a stretch of the new M40 motorway. The section of road, between Stokenchurch and Loudwater on the High Wycombe Bypass, was not yet open to the public. "Gerry had one of his brainwaves, and suggested that Joan flew the Tiger Moth under one of the bridges," says Lane. "I asked Joan if she thought it was possible, and she said yes. We were told that she could land and taxi under the bridge but not actually fly under it. I said to her, 'We've got three cameras on it. If you just happen to fly under the bridge, you can be sure we'll get it.' Of course she flew under the bridge and came out the other side."

Hughes had taxied under the Bigmore Lane Bridge on three test runs that morning, but flying under it contravened the permissions granted by the Board of Trade. Hughes' employers, Personal Plane Services, were faced with three charges of dangerous and low flying, while the film's production manager Norman Foster had to answer three charges of aiding and abetting.

"Norman represented us in court," says Lane. "He had a very smooth way with him. He went to Derek Meddings and asked him if he could build a really nice Thunderbird 2 model. At the court, Norman asked the judge if he had any grandchildren. When the judge said yes, Norman said, 'Would they like this as a gift?' and he handed over the model. The case opened, and Joan pointed out that it would have been too dangerous to taxi under the bridge because there was a crosswind and she had dummies of the *Thunderbirds* characters attached to the wings. She said it was actually safer for her to fly under the bridge, and they proved this."

The court hearing took place in March 1968 and lasted two-and-a-half days, during which

Hughes insisted that "There was positively no danger." The jury took just 40 minutes to reach a verdict of not guilty on all 13 counts of the indictment. While Century 21 awaited the verdict, Lane and Meddings found a new way to complete the Tiger Moth sequence.

"We built a motorway one-sixth scale in a field near Booker Airport [sic] and embarked on our first radio-controlled model," wrote Meddings in the April 1969 issue of *Film and Television Technician*. "There was a great risk of damage to these aircraft during filming and this, together with the fact that radio-controlled models were of a very sensitive nature, decided us to have six models built. As suspected, we started to lose them at the rate of one a day, and a shuttle service between the locations and the studio was set up to take the crashed models back and bring the new ones out. This took us six weeks to shoot because of the bad weather conditions, and we finally ended up with more personnel working at the location than were stationed at the studio. As

it turned out this part of the film was more exciting than had we shot it with the real Tiger Moth on the real motorway because of the antics of the radio-controlled model hitting the banks and bridges as it flew down our largest set-up to date. If we had used the real Tiger Moth not only would it have cost the company a small fortune in damage to the motorway, aircraft and bridges, but it would have been highly dangerous to the pilot... Nevertheless, a lot of exciting sequences with Joan flying were used in the picture and intercut with the radio-controlled model flying."

Above left: One of six radio-controlled Tiger Moth models that were used to complete filming when the shoot with Joan Hughes was brought to a premature end.

Above right: Meddings (centre) inspects one of the models on location at Booker Airfield.

Below left: Meddings (far left) supervises construction of a large model of the motorway and bridge for the filming of the radio-controlled models at Booker.

Below right: Meddings kept this photograph of the Tiger Moth flying under the Bigmore Lane Bridge as a memento.

Top left: The Quad Crown poster for *Thunderbird 6* was illustrated by *TV Century 21* comic artist Frank Bellamy.

Top right: *What's On In London* promoted UA's *Thunderbird 6*/James Bond triple-bill in the issue dated 26 July 1968.

Above: Skyship One looms over the International Rescue fleet on the cover of this Japanese press book.

Thunderbird 6 was certificated by the British Board of Film Censors in January 1968 but had to wait five months before its first press screening at the Jaceyland in Marylebone Street. Writing in the *Daily Mail* of 28 June, Barry Norman described it as "the most class-conscious film now to be seen in London... All the characters except one are meant to be either young, beautiful or rich. The exception is Parker – Lady Penelope's wrinkled old chauffeur – who represents the funny working-class prole as firmly as house servants did in drawing-room comedies."

Norman did go on to praise the film's "technical excellence", but despite this and other positive reviews it seems that United Artists were still smarting from the poor response to *Thunderbirds Are Go*. More than a month after it was reviewed in national

newspapers, *Thunderbird 6* was finally granted an experimental release. Exhibitors were offered the U-certificate *Thunderbird 6* for screening in the afternoons, and a double-bill of A-certificate James Bond films – *Goldfinger* (1964) and *Thunderball* (1965) – for screenings in evening or late-night shows. On Sundays, *Thunderbird 6* was dropped from the programme altogether.

The triple-bill was first shown at the Leicester Square Odeon on Monday 29 July. Kenneth Winckles, the managing director of United Artists' British division, told *Kinematograph Weekly* that this was "an exciting breakthrough in release patterns", but it must have come as little consolation to Century 21 that its new film was acting as a matinée support feature to a pair of reissues.

The package continued until the end of the school holidays in September, when

Thunderbird 6 disappeared from cinemas almost as quietly as it had arrived. For the Andersons, the *Thunderbirds* saga was over and they shifted their attention to the production of a live-action film, *Doppelgänger*.

"I'm happier with the second one," says David Lane, reflecting on the brief but eventful time he spent as one of Britain's youngest film directors. "I don't think we learned anything about filmmaking from the first one, but on the second one we had a more exciting script."

Sylvia Anderson has particularly happy memories of the publicity tour for *Thunderbirds Are Go*, but considers that the films were victims of bad timing. "The public really hadn't accepted that you could do a deluxe version of a television series," she says, "but everywhere that we went, Gerry and myself, we had the most wonderful reception. So the public generally didn't support it in the way one had hoped, but I still look upon both the films as a great success creatively."

Above: Alan, Tin Tin and Brains emerge from the wreckage of the Tiger Moth. Parker, who was hanging from the undercarriage, is presumed dead.

Left: The British campaign book for *Thunderbird 6* included a reproduction of a *Daily Sketch* article about Lady Penelope lookalike Penny Snow, who was hired to promote the film alongside a full-size replica of FAB 1.

Below: The new Thunderbird 6 announces the end of the film.

8

STRINGS ATTACHED

The location filming for the closing credits of *Thunderbirds Are Go* was graced by a very special visitor. "Barry Gray wanted to hear how his music sounded," says director David Lane. "I'm sure he didn't get to go on location very often. I think it was a fun day out for him."

His wish having been granted, the diminutive Yorkshireman stood behind camera operator Alan Perry as The Band of Her Majesty's Royal Marines gathered on the parade ground. As the shoot continued, Lieutenant Colonel F Vivian Dunn climbed onto the back of a Land Rover and prepared to wield his baton. Attached to the vehicle was a crane that suspended Lane and Perry as they focused on the band members below them. The camera started rolling, and Dunn led the men in a powerful rendition of Gray's *Thunderbirds* march – an instantly

recognisable tune that was fast achieving iconic status. "He was conducting so energetically that it was rocking the crane," remembers Lane. "I had to ask Barry to get him off the trailer because we were trying to film!"

At the premiere on 12 December 1966, Gray watched proudly from the dress circle of the London Pavilion as the band once again performed his music. At that moment very few people would have denied the huge contribution Gray had made to *Thunderbirds*, but fewer still could have predicted that his most famous theme would transcend the television series it was designed to serve.

Lane was also in the audience that evening. "Barry was a charming, charming man," he says. "And *Thunderbirds* was his best work, there's no question of that."

Above left: A dapper Barry Gray, photographed in the 1930s.

Above right: Gray was Vera Lynn's pianist and arranger from 1949. He maintained his association with the singer into the 1960s.

Below: In 1948 Gray co-wrote the lyrics of this song, which was included in the film *Noose* the following year.

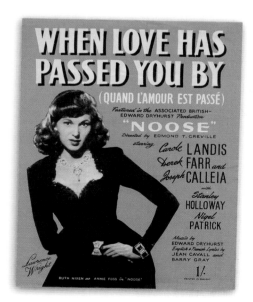

John Livesey Eccles was born in Blackburn on 18 July 1908. As a young man, his first great act of reinvention was to develop largely self-taught skills as a composer and arranger. The second came later when he changed his name to Barry Gray.

In 1932 Gray moved to London, where he began composing for theatre and radio, as well as arranging piano scores and orchestrations for B Feldman & Co. His first published work, *Somebody Else Took You Out of My Arms (But They Can't Take You Out of My Heart)*, was credited to Jack Eccles and issued by the company that year. After gaining further experience in Tin Pan Alley, Gray became a pianist and arranger for Radio Normandy in 1938 before joining the Royal Air Force in 1940.

Following his demob in 1946, Gray became Vera Lynn's pianist and arranger. It was the singer's association with author Roberta Leigh that led to Gray arranging, orchestrating and recording the music for *The Adventures of Twizzle* (1957-59) and *Torchy the Battery Boy* (1960-61). When Leigh and Gerry Anderson parted company, Gray was the catalyst for Anderson's first independent venture when he devised *Two Gun Tex Tucker*, the series that reached the screen as *Four Feather Falls*.

Throughout the 1960s and the first half of the 1970s the sound of Barry Gray was an intrinsic part of Anderson's classic productions. Aside from Gray's estimable skill as a composer, the secret of this success lay in a valuable piece of advice. "In the very early days of the Gerry Anderson shows it was Gerry's idea not to write kiddie music," Gray told *Soundtrack* magazine's Randall D Larson in 1982. "I should write as one would for a film, in the normal way, and this is always what I did. I never wrote down to children. I scored as I felt, or in other words I treated the puppets as if they were real people. And that was what we did more or less throughout the whole of those series."

The ground floor of Gray's house in Dollis Hill, London, was converted to create a recording studio and control room. Egg boxes were attached to the walls to baffle the sound and, in 1958, Gray installed an Ampex four-track tape recorder. The 'Barry Gray Studio' remained in service for demos, vocal numbers and other relatively basic sessions well into the 1960s.

Dollis Hill was also home to a large collection of electronic gadgets and instruments with such exotic names as a Clavioline, a Transicord and the Miller Spinetta. Chief amongst these devices was the Ondes Martenot. Gray used this complex-looking instrument to create wavering, Theremin-like noises that he manipulated by sliding a metal ring along the front of its six-octave keyboard. Gray acquired his Ondes Martenot in 1959 and spent a month in Paris with its creator, Maurice Martenot, learning how to operate it.

While scoring the 1961 *Supercar* episode *What Goes Up* Gray created an association between the instrument and scenes set in space. In 1962 the Ondes Martenot was prominent in

Above: A subtle tribute to AP Films' composer appeared in the 1964 *Stingray* episode *Tune of Danger*, which featured this close-up of a 'Greystein' piano.

Below left: Gray at the controls of the Ondes Martenot. Much like APF's studio at Ipswich Road, the ground floor of Gray's Dollis Hill home was soundproofed with egg boxes.

Below right: Gray was a talented artist, who illustrated this 1961 advertisement highlighting his skills at "electronic composition".

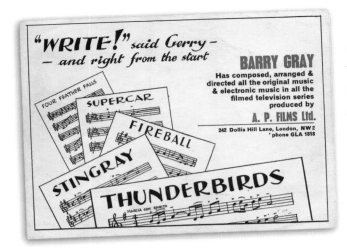

"WRITE!" said Gerry –
– and right from the start

BARRY GRAY

Has composed, arranged &
directed all the original music
& electronic music in all the
filmed television series
produced by

A. P. FILMS Ltd.

242 Dollis Hill Lane, London, NW 2
'phone GLA 1818

Above: Gray's hobbies included calligraphy, as seen in this advertisement from the *Thunderbirds* supplement of the December 1965 *Television Mail*.

Below left: Sheet music for *Aqua Marina*, the song Gray composed for the end titles of *Stingray*.

Below right: Gray leads the musical entertainment at the launch of the *Lady Penelope* comic on 18 November 1965.

Gray's music for *Fireball XL5*, which included a closing theme that reached the hit parade the following year.

Gray's interest in new musical technology and home recording suggests that his closest contemporary would have been Joe Meek, the maverick who wrote and produced the 1962 chart-topper *Telstar* in his London flat. The two shared the same arranger in Charles Blackwell, and in 1963 Meek produced an alternative version of Gray's *Fireball* hit by his group The Flee-Rekkers. There is, however, no evidence that Gray and Meek ever collaborated. Gray was a more musically conservative character whose pop compositions were rarely as accomplished as his television scores.

The urgency of Gray's theme for *Stingray* (1964-65) was designed to match the frenzied title sequence, but for the closing credits he contributed the ballad *Aqua Marina*. Joan Brown's eerie backing vocals recall the spectral wailing on John Leyton's 1961 'death disc' *Johnny Remember Me* – another single produced by Meek and arranged by Blackwell.

The recording sessions for *Thunderbirds* began at Olympic Studios in Barnes in December 1964. Gerry Anderson had vivid memories of hearing Gray's rousing theme performed by an orchestra for the first time. "I watched from the monitor room with sound engineer Eric Tomlinson," he said. "I'll never forget the incredible feeling I got when Barry conducted the first take. It sent shivers down my spine – I knew straight away that it was something special."

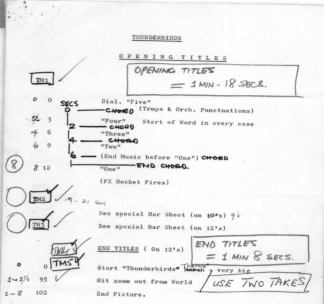

The sometimes frantic pace of the music meant that Gray could get overheated. "He'd stop for a second, put down his baton and then take off his shirt," said Anderson. "He'd conduct the rest of the session in his vest."

Ralph Titterton, one of the curators of the Barry Gray Archive, believes that the cinematic quality of Gray's music helped to elevate the AP Films/Century 21 shows of this era. "Many people describe the Gerry Anderson productions as children's series," he says. "They could be right or wrong, but in today's world children's television doesn't enjoy the degree of orchestration that you can hear in *Thunderbirds* and the other shows. In those days they had the budget, and the inclination, to create that sort of music, and I think it brought the programmes alive. It helped to transform them into epics."

Gray applied the Ondes Martenot to such *Thunderbirds* episodes as *Sun Probe* and *The Imposters*, but the instrument's distinctive electronic signature was most frequently heard in the theme that signalled the appearance of Thunderbird 5.

Despite his enthusiasm for such pioneering technology, Gray believed it should remain subservient to more traditional instruments. "I'm afraid that electronic music is mostly suitable only for visuals that are concerned with such things as laboratories, space, very weird and perhaps even strange situations," he said in 1982. "I'm not enamoured of writing orchestral music and producing it on synthesisers."

Above: Sheet music for Gray's *Thunderbirds* theme, with a cover promoting the first feature film.

Right: Lieutenant Colonel F Vivian Dunn (centre) conducted the theme for the end titles of *Thunderbirds Are Go*. He is pictured here with Gray and production manager Norman Foster during filming on 2 July 1966.

Below: Gray's copy of the tracks from the *Thunderbirds Are Go* soundtrack album, which was released by United Artists in March 1967. Gray conducted a 54-piece orchestra for the recordings, which took place at Olympic Studios from 29-30 December 1966.

In 1966, *Thunderbirds Are Go* offered Gray the chance to realise his ambition to conduct a much bigger orchestra. "Gerry called me into his office and he said, 'Barry, I'd like to get the real sound of a symphony orchestra for *Thunderbirds Are Go*. How many musicians would we need? So I said, 'Well if you want a real symphony orchestra sound you'll want about 120.' So, when Gerry had picked himself up from the floor, he said, 'Well, how many could you do it with?' I said, 'I'll do it with 70.' So it was decided there and then that I would have a 70-piece orchestra... I must say that it was a most enjoyable score to do, and we had most enjoyable sessions."

Later that year, Gray moved to a house called Red Gables in Esher, Surrey. The detached property had space for a larger studio and became a family home when, in 1967, Gray married Joan Cheeseman and adopted her children, Amanda and Simon. At Red Gables Gray composed music for the Century 21 films and television series produced in the remainder of the decade. The ominous drumbeat of *Captain Scarlet and the Mysterons* (1967-68) introduced a macabre chapter of Supermarionation, while the pulsing, guitar-driven theme from *Joe 90* (1968-69) evoked both the mind-altering subject of the series and the psychedelic experimentation of contemporary pop. Gray's final Supermarionation theme was his favourite – the title music from *The Secret Service* (1969) was a bizarre but irresistible homage to Bach and The Swingle Singers that formed the perfect accompaniment to Anderson's most eccentric format.

Ken Holt, the studio manager at Stirling Road, got to know Gray well during the late 1960s. "Barry was one of the boys," he says. "He came to the studio so much that we used to joke about setting up an office for him. He was a lovely, unassuming man. He had an accent, but I could never work out where he came from. He seemed quite posh, so we used to call him '50 bob', which was our way of saying that he was upper class. Fortunately he had a good sense of humour."

Gray was renowned among the studio staff for his collection of luxury cars, an indulgence made possible by royalties from the Anderson series and jingles for countless commercials. When Gray bought a Lamborghini with the personalised number plates LAM 1 it's said that he didn't take it home for fear of antagonising Joan. He was, however, quite happy to park it on Stirling Road, as Holt remembers. "He came in and said, 'I've got a new car. Would you like to come and have a look?' So I went outside and there was this Lamborghini. He took me for a spin, though I don't think we did much over 30 miles an hour!"

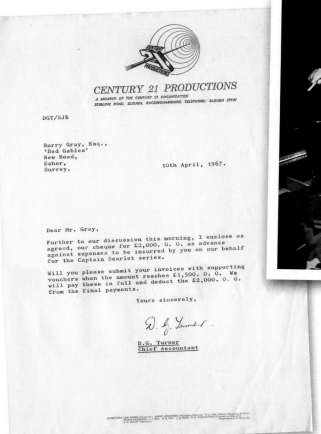

Above left: Shortly after completing the *Thunderbirds Are Go* record, Gray started work on Gerry Anderson's next series – *Captain Scarlet and the Mysterons*.

Top right: In February 1968 Gray directed his son, Simon, during the filming of close-ups for an episode of *Joe 90*.

Above right: Joe McClaine at the piano, in the corresponding sequence from *International Concerto*.

Below: Some of the *Thunderbirds* tape boxes retained by the Barry Gray Archive.

Original music composed, arranged & directed for Television & Films by
BARRY GRAY

"THAT DANGEROUS GAME" Orchestral version of a theme for the ATV Television Series "THUNDERBIRDS"	**"THE MYSTERONS"** Ominous slow theme based on the "CAPTAIN SCARLET" title (From the CENTURY 21 disc)
"SPACE 1999" Main title theme from new ATV Science Fiction series now being produced at Pinewood Studios	**"POP THEME"** from the "CAPTAIN SCARLET" episode "WHITE AS SNOW"
"THE SECRET SERVICE" Opening & closing title music from the ATV Television series. (A 3 part fugue in the style of J.S. Bach) Vocal by the Michael Sammes Singers.	**"THE DANGEROUS GAME"** Vocal version. (Words also by Barry Gray) Vocal by Ken Barrie. (from the PYE-CENTURY 21 record)
"FIREBALL" End title song from the ATV Television Series "FIREBALL XL5." Words also by Barry Gray, vocal by Don Spencer.	**"THUNDERBIRDS"** (March) Theme from the ATV Series (From the UNITED ARTISTES LP record)
"FORMULA FIVE" A theme in 5/4 time from one of the "FIREBALL XL5" episodes.	**"DOPPELGANGER"** Title theme from the UNITED ARTISTES feature film, starring Patrick Wymark, Herbert Lom & Ian Henry.
ELECTROMUSIC & ELECTRO-FX One or two examples from the "THUNDERBIRDS & "SPACE 1999" series. Space sounds, heavy steel door closing	**"STRANGE PLANET"** Ominous electromusic from the same feature film
AN EXAMPLE OF A CROSS-MIX from strange orchestral music to weird electronic music. (from the "SPACE 1999" series)	**"TRAITOR IN THE LAB"** Ominous orchestral section from the "DOPPELGANGER" feature film.
"ZERO X" Theme from the UNITED ARTISTES feature film "THUNDERBIRDS ARE GO!" (From the LP)	**"SLEEPING ASTRONAUTS"** Peaceful space section from the above film, featuring Mlle. Sylvette Allart playing the French electronic instrument, the ONDES MARTENOT.
"JOE 90" Theme from the Television series. (From the CENTURY 21 Mini LP.)	**"UFO"** Main title from the ATV TV series
"HI-JACKED" "Crooks & Heavies" theme from a "JOE 90" episode. (From the PYE record)	**"A MATTER OF LIFE & DEATH"** Orchestral section from the "SPACE 1999" series, a morose & tragic feel to a "death" chord.
	ORCHESTRAL SECTION from the "SPACE 1999" series. An ominous feel into a romantic & successful feel in the Commercial Break.
"CAPTAIN SCARLET" Title theme from the TV Series (From the CENTURY 21 Disc.	**OMINOUS DISASTER "SPACE" FEEL** from the "SPACE 1999" series
	"AQUA MARINA" (faded out, end of tape!) End title song from ATV Series "STINGRAY" (Words by Barry Gray, vocal by Gary Miller) Recorded on PYE label.

In 1970 the Gray family moved to Guernsey, where Barry completed work on *UFO* (1970-71). The first series of another Anderson production, *Space: 1999* (1975-76), proved to be Gray's final commission for film or television, but he continued to make public appearances in his later years. He conducted a 90-piece orchestra in a medley of his own compositions as part of the Royal Albert Hall's Filmharmonic 79 concert. He subsequently wrote and arranged music for the 1980 and 1981 Royal Film Performances.

On a more intimate level, from 1977 he was the resident pianist and organist at the Old Government House in Guernsey. In an interview with Radio Guernsey in 1983 he explained why he devoted so much time to the hotel. "I'm quite a gregarious person," he said. "I like meeting people, having a chat and a drink. I also enjoy playing. If I can't think of anything to play I just extemporise until I *can* think of something to play."

When asked whether his repertoire included any of his old television themes he cheerfully admitted, "I slip one or two in now and then."

Barry Gray died in Guernsey on 26 April 1984. Nine years later, Ralph Titterton and his partner Cathy Ford began the long process of cataloguing and restoring the Gray archive. "He liked to do things very carefully and very precisely," says Cathy. "All his scores are meticulously written. Other composers that have looked at them have been stunned by the care that he took."

As well as the tapes, scores and equipment retained by the archive, the notebooks offer intriguing clues about Gray's taste and personality. It is here that Gray preserved everything from an advert for built-up shoes to details of the factory that serviced his Aston Martin DB5.

The boxes also contain examples of Gray's handiwork with a pen – cartoons, caricatures and pages of exquisite calligraphy. A separate section is devoted to Gray's fan mail. "Many of the letters mention the fact that he sent kids recordings without any charge," says Cathy. "He would dub something from the master onto a cassette and just send it to them. He was generous with his time as well – some fans were quite regular correspondents."

In 2014 Ford and Titterton opened the archive to Ben Foster and his brother Nick when they were commissioned to compose the music for a new series of *Thunderbirds*. "There was never any debate about retaining Barry Gray's theme for *Thunderbirds Are Go*," says Ben. "Barry had a sound that was familiar not just from that show, but across all the shows. As an orchestrator as well as a composer I'm fascinated by the way he used trombones, a very small violin section and baritone sax at the bottom of his orchestral sounds."

Throughout his career, Gray underlined comic, romantic or dramatic sequences with a musical gusto that sounds naïve in comparison with modern soundtracks. "Sometimes the music has the same child-like innocence as the pictures, but on other occasions it acts as a counterpoint to some of the naïve material on screen," says Cathy. "But there was certainly nothing technically naïve about his music, which was beautifully crafted."

"Barry's music is phenomenally good, but it can seem a little bit 'on the nose'," observes Ben. "Some of the gestures seem a bit pantomime. I don't think that makes them irrelevant, but we felt we had to tone it down a bit. We tried to be reverential to what he did, but we had to remember that we were making a show for kids in the 21st century."

Ben is in no doubt about the impact Barry Gray made on the Anderson series. "When I was a kid, the fact the music was recorded by a live orchestra made me take it all very seriously. It was a big, symphonic sound, which made the models look better. Without that music, *Thunderbirds* would have been a very different show."

Top left: A variation on the sheet music for Gray's *Thunderbirds* theme. *Thunderbirds* is one of the most recognisable signature tunes in television history.

Top right: The theme from *Thunderbirds* was first released as a 7" single in December 1965. Sylvia Anderson, Peter Dyneley and David Graham performed Gray's composition for the b-side, the charming *Parker – Well Done!*

9

SALE OF THE CENTURY

In 1963, many professionals in the film and toy industries still needed the benefits of licensing explained to them. *Kinematograph Weekly*'s Supermarionation supplement introduced its readers to what it called "the value of merchandising" in a concise article on its back page: "The popularity of a property, whether it be a feature film or television series, is primarily created by cinema or television exposure," it began. "However, intelligent merchandising of the property – the marketing of toys, games, books and other by-products... not only provides a stimulus to the popularity of the film or television series, but also can be a useful source of royalty revenue."

Such ignorance was widespread when Keith Shackleton joined the staff of AP Films in 1960. "In the early days the concept and value of licensing were difficult for some to grasp, for reasons either commercial or philosophical," he says. The mechanics of this potentially lucrative business held no mysteries for Shackleton, as he would go on to prove.

Under Shackleton's guidance, *Thunderbirds* made a phenomenal impact in toy shops and newsagents during the latter half of the 1960s. The list of merchandise relating to the series is astounding – everything from ice lollies to watering cans and roller skates were licensed by AP Films (Merchandising) and its successor, Century 21 Merchandising.

Alongside confectionery and more eccentric novelties, the companies also sanctioned die-cast models and lavish comics. Acclaimed for their quality at the time, many of these items are now highly prized by collectors.

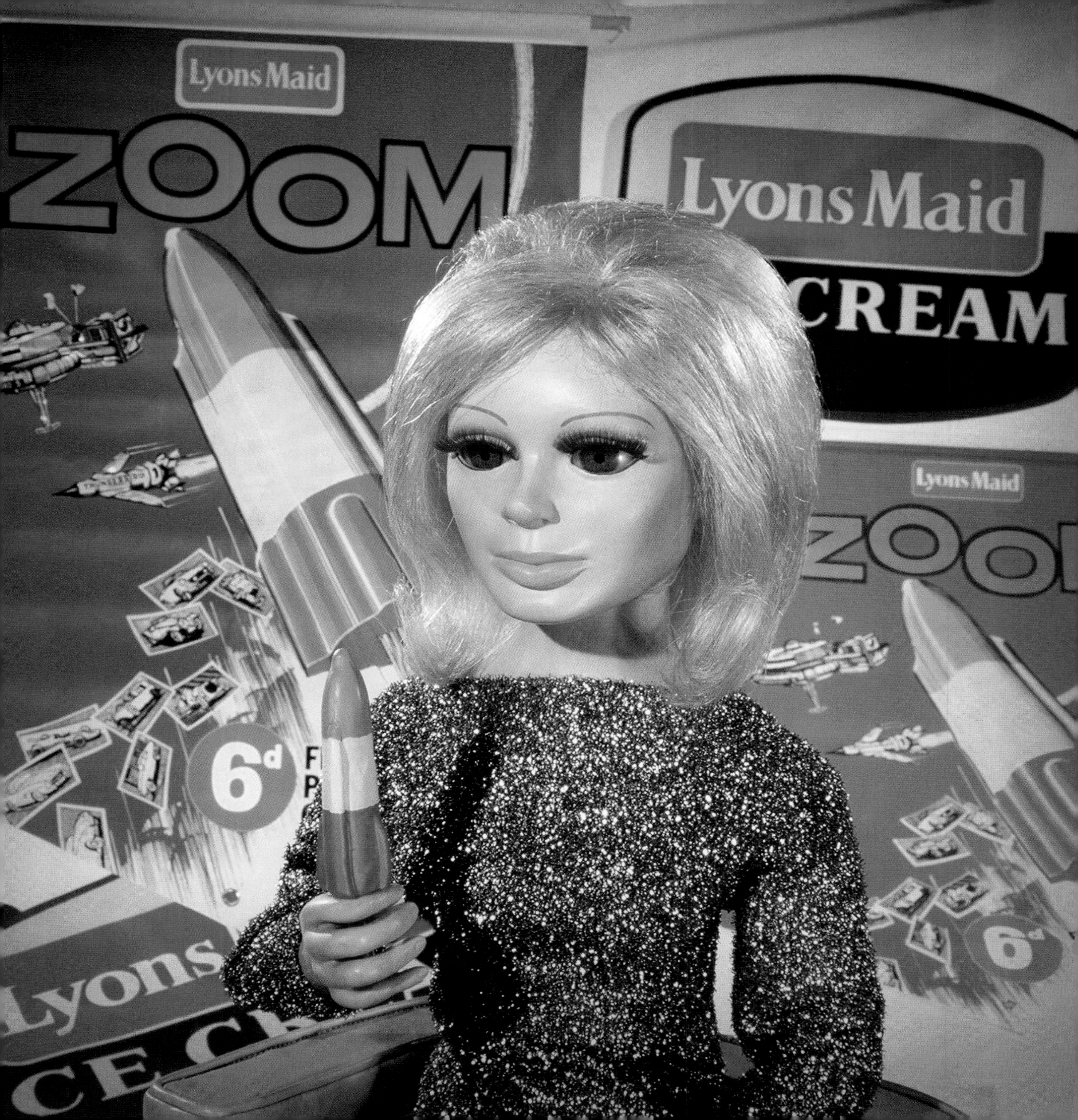

Lyons Maid
ZOOM
Lyons Maid
CREAM
Lyons Maid
6d
6d
Lyons

Above: Keith Shackleton in the early 1960s, when he was the managing director of AP Films (Merchandising).

Below left: The bowler hat Shackleton wore before he joined APF came in useful during the filming of *Thunderbirds* in 1965. The bowler appears on a hatstand in this memorable sequence from *30 Minutes After Noon*.

Below right: An advertisement from the 23 August 1962 issue of trade paper *Television Today*. *Supercar* was Shackleton's first major success for APF.

There is a popular misconception that the market for toys based on films and television series was created by Lucasfilm's ubiquitous exploitation of *Star Wars*, but the strategy had been pursued by numerous companies prior to the 1970s. Among them, AP Films was a pioneer.

According to the British Toy Manufacturers' Association, the value of annual toy output in the UK rose from £36.1 million in 1959 to £60.5 million in 1965. AP Films' marketing of *Supercar*, *Fireball XL5*, *Stingray* and *Thunderbirds* during that period made a significant contribution to that growth. The mastermind of this campaign was Keith Shackleton, the managing director of the company's merchandise division.

Shackleton met Gerry Anderson when they were both non-commissioned officers at RAF Manston in 1948. In between their national service duties they would share bicycle journeys to and from the local pub. "Gerry and I had quite different personalities, but we got on extraordinarily well," says Shackleton. "Gerry was quite a charmer, really. He liked the girls, I think we all did. We used to go dancing and drinking. We spent quite a bit of time together."

When Shackleton was demobbed he returned to his previous employment at soap manufacturer Lever Brothers before joining Industrial and Trade Fairs, a company owned by unlikely bedfellows *The Financial Times* and the *Daily Mirror*.

Shackleton's job took him to trade fairs all over the world, including Moscow at the height of the Cold War, but he kept in touch with his old friend throughout the 1950s. "Gerry and I used to meet once or twice a year for a pint and a chat. He kept nudging me, saying, 'Come and join our outfit.' He asked me several times and I declined, because I had such a super job with Industrial and Trade Fairs. But then I started having a difficult time with my boss, so the next time Gerry asked me to look after the commercial side of AP Films I said, 'Okay, I'll give it a whirl.' I then phoned my wife and told her I'd probably done something rather stupid!"

Shackleton made his first foray into the film and television business shortly after Anderson signed the deal with ATV to produce *Supercar*. He initially worked from an office at the Ipswich Road studio in Slough, but pointed out that he could do a better job in London. AP Films (Merchandising) Ltd – at that stage effectively Shackleton and his secretary – moved to the top floor of 9 Orme Court in Bayswater. The building's main tenant was Associated London Scripts, an agency whose clients included the surreal comedian Spike Milligan. "He used to come down the carpeted stairway with a golf club in hand, talking to himself while he practised his strokes," says Shackleton, smiling at the memory. "I can see him now. He was the most unusual man I ever met."

In 1961 Shackleton sold *TV Comic* the licence for a *Supercar* strip, which began in March. The strip was written by the deputy editor. "I remember the editor was the most unlikely man

to be the head of a children's publication," says Shackleton. "He used to keep what we'd now call adult literature in the top right hand drawer of his desk. If he'd been clever he'd have kept it at home, but then I suppose his wife might have found it... Anyway, his deputy was Alan Fennell, who was a great guy."

The Supercar Club, launched in September, was another big success for Shackleton. "That was one of my cycling inspirations," he says. "We came up with a badge, and the members got a Supercar pilot's licence. We took space in *TV Comic* to launch the club. The membership fee was half a crown, 2/6, and in three weeks we had 70,000 members."

Above left: Issue 509 of *TV Comic*, cover-dated 16 September 1961, was the first to give readers the chance to join the Supercar Club for 2s 6d. Members received a special pilot's licence and a gold-coloured badge, the latter manufactured by the Queen's ribbon-makers JR Gaunt and Son. A subsequent promotion with National garages offered club members an exclusive 7" flexidisc.

Above right: A selection of *Supercar* toys and other associated items. In June 1963 *Kinematograph Weekly* estimated that retail sales of *Supercar* merchandise had exceeded £750,000.

Right: The 7" EP edition of *Fireball*, performed by Don Spencer and fictitious backing group 'The XL5'. The *Fireball* single charted at number 32 in March 1963.

Below: This Fireball XL5 Spaceship toy was manufactured by Italian company Quercetti and released in summer 1963. The model was fired from an elastic catapult before Fireball and Steve Zodiac parachuted to the ground.

In January 1962 Como Confectionery Products introduced *Supercar* sweet cigarettes and had reportedly sold over three million packets by August. In the run-up to Christmas there were more than 50 *Supercar* licensees. Sales of Supercar models topped 250,000 units, amounting to a retail turnover of £100,000. It was this level of success that partly prompted Lew Grade to buy AP Films that December, and largely prompted Shackleton to advise Gerry Anderson against selling it to him.

"The reason Lew bought the company was that he realised the future was all about merchandise," says Sylvia Anderson. "Keith Shackleton started the merchandising for us, but ATV wanted to take it all. Because they knew that's where the money was. I'd seen whole factories doing just our stuff and nothing else."

In keeping with the futuristic style of APF's science-fiction subjects, the toys licensed by the company adopted modern methods of production – in the early 1960s Britain led the way in die-cast techniques for metal toys and various types of moulding for plastics. The replicas of Supercar would use them all.

Shackleton was not a shareholder in APF but received a profit-share that was boosted by the arrival of *Fireball XL5*. "For my money, the best *Fireball* toy was produced in Italy," he says. "It was a rocket that was launched from a foot-held catapult that pulled up to shoulder height. When you released it the rocket would climb some 50 feet in the air. It was lethal! You wouldn't get away with it today.

"I set up a meeting with the manufacturer in Turin and arranged to bring the first episode for them to watch. But first I had to make an eventful journey to Milan, where I was to stay. I travelled by train from Zurich, following a prior meeting, and when I got to the Italian border the customs officer confiscated the film can because he wouldn't believe it contained an episode of a children's series. We had an agent in Milan – it took him four days and I don't know how many lire to get the film released from customs. We screened it at the chamber of commerce in Turin, a splendid building with a cinema, and on the basis of that we sold a super toy."

The programme had already enjoyed some musical success with the 7" single *Fireball*, written by Barry Gray and sung by Don Spencer. "Don's agent was the Australian impresario Robert Stigwood," remembers Shackleton. "He had an office in an old pub at the bottom of Edgware Road. We put Don's song at the end of each episode and we got him into the charts!"

In 1959 ATV had bought a 50 per cent share of Pye Records. ATV's Louis Benjamin was installed as managing director, while Lew Grade and his brother Leslie took places on the board. The first collaboration between Pye Records and APF took place in 1962 with an LP that presented the soundtrack from the *Supercar* episode *Flight of Fancy*. A more formal partnership followed, with 44 titles released on Pye's Century 21 label between 1965 and 1967. Many of these were adaptations of *Thunderbirds* episode soundtracks on 7" 'mini albums' with picture sleeves that promised "21 minutes of adventure". Described by APF as "the only records made exclusively for children", the Century 21 EPs and LPs were distributed to newsagents as well as record shops.

Left: Century 21 Records launched a new range of 12" albums in April 1966.

Below left: Shackleton devised and produced *Journey to the Moon*, an original audio drama that became the first Century 21 record when it was released as a 12" LP in February 1965. The story followed the progress of NASA's Project Apollo as it worked towards landing a man on the Moon. The script was by Alan Fennell, and Shackleton hired television astronomer Patrick Moore as the consultant. Pictured here is the sleeve of the abridged 7" mini album, released in October.

Below right: Also released in October 1965 was *A Trip to Marineville*, an original *Stingray* drama written by Fennell and produced by Desmond Saunders.

"We were spreading our wings – we had a record company and the publishing side was beginning to grow," says Shackleton. "I always had a high regard for the *Eagle,* the leading weekly comic for children at the time, and it was this publication that provided the inspiration for what was to follow.

"I was seeing a lot of Alan Fennell, who used to put the annuals together for us – initially on a licensed basis and then we brought them in-house. I sat down with Alan and said, 'We're going to create something a bit special.' I described the new publication as a collection of everything we'd produced to date in a comic format. Alan was quite brilliant, and within a couple of weeks he'd produced a dummy magazine. I choose my words carefully there: 'comic' is the umbrella word for traditional children's publications, and doesn't really describe what we were trying to create."

The name Shackleton gave to this combination of strips and features was *Century 21.* His proposal followed a similar format to the *Eagle,* but softened that comic's educational subtext in favour of a contemporary approach aimed at boys fascinated by the Space Race.

The contents would depict the further adventures of *Supercar, Fireball XL5* and *Stingray,* as well as imports *Burke's Law* and *My Favourite Martian* that Shackleton had acquired during trips to America. Eight of the 20 pages would be in full colour, including a back page devoted to *Doctor Who*'s Daleks. The *Daleks* strip would be licensed from their creator, Associated London Scripts client Terry Nation, who collaborated with Fennell on a storyline revealing the machine creatures' origin.

"It was a natural thing for us to do our own comic," said Fennell, who had been a scriptwriter on *Fireball XL5* and had left his full-time job at *TV Comic* to write for *Stingray.* "Gerry immediately said yes, and then Sylvia said it was all right for us to do a comic as long as it was totally different from anything anyone had done before."

Gerry Anderson pitched in with a gimmick he felt would further distinguish *Century 21* from the competition. "My idea was that the comic should be a children's tabloid newspaper," he said in 2009. "This

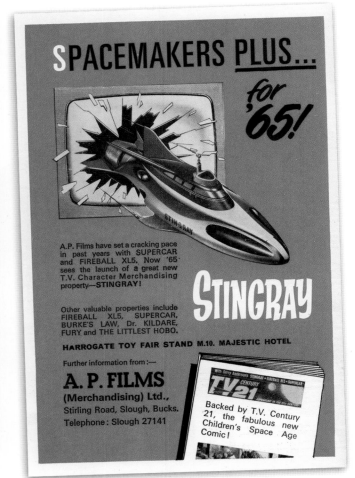

SPACEMAKERS PLUS... for '65!

A.P. Films have set a cracking pace in past years with SUPERCAR and FIREBALL XL5. Now '65 sees the launch of a great new T.V. Character Merchandising property—STINGRAY!

Other valuable properties include FIREBALL XL5, SUPERCAR, BURKE'S LAW, Dr. KILDARE, FURY and THE LITTLEST HOBO.

STINGRAY

HARROGATE TOY FAIR STAND M.10. MAJESTIC HOTEL

Further information from :—

A. P. FILMS (Merchandising) Ltd., Stirling Road, Slough, Bucks. Telephone : Slough 27141

Backed by T.V. Century 21, the fabulous new Children's Space Age Comic!

167 FLEET STREET, LONDON, E.C.4.
TELEPHONE: FLEET STREET 9971

met with a great deal of resistance because it was so unusual to print a children's comic that looked like a tabloid and had a tabloid approach. But I stuck to my guns, and my philosophy to not follow the crowd."

Shackleton asked Fennell to mock up an issue of *Century 21* that he could use to excite interest in the trade. "I remember doing the dummy in the sunshine, so it was probably around July '64," said Fennell. "I think Gerry decided that it should have news headlines on the cover, and the dummy had even more of that than we actually went with."

Even in its prototype form, Shackleton felt *Century 21* had potential. "There was a buzz about it, a vibrancy," he says. "You only had to flick through the dummy to realise that this concept was ready to fly. I thought we should publish it ourselves so I went to Lew Grade and asked him for some money. I showed Lew the dummy and told him we'd need £30,000 to launch the title. He sat back, took a puff on his cigar, and told me he thought we ought to license it instead. I was slightly disappointed, but went back and put the feelers out to various publishers."

Above: A flyer included in copies of trade magazine *Retail Newsagent, Bookseller and Stationer* in late 1964. The front previewed the cover of *TV Century 21*'s first issue, while the reverse promised generous terms to retailers and free gifts to purchasers.

Shackleton was turned down by his first candidate, a book publishing company, before briefly considering a proposal from a food manufacturer who would have created promotional copies to give away at retail. Shackleton next visited the offices of Sunday broadsheet *The News of the World*.

"At that time *The News of the World* was controlled by the Carr family, and I found myself talking to the general manager, Clive Carr. City Magazines was part of their group and there followed a meeting with Clive, the City Magazines general manager Clive Smith and myself. I came away with an offer that recognised the strength of the idea. I told Lew, and he bowled another fast ball at me. ATV and the *Daily Mirror* had several directors in common, and Lew asked me to

take the project to Hugh Cudlipp, the editor of the *Mirror*. I showed Hugh the dummy and talked about the deal that Clive had offered me. He said, 'We'll match it.' I thought that if they wanted me to take them seriously then they should have bettered it, and I wanted to go with *The News of the World* anyway. I told Lew all this, and we ended up going with *The News of the World*. It was an excellent deal that worked well for both parties."

Clive Carr and his colleagues at City Magazines were enthusiastic about the dummy issue but requested a change to its title. In order to emphasise the comic's strong television links it would be called *TV Century 21*. Fennell began production in August 1964, devising a universe that integrated characters and vehicles from *Fireball XL5* and *Stingray*. *Supercar*'s perceived obsolescence was reflected in its relegation to a humorous black-and-white strip.

From the outset, *TV Century 21* was seen as a promotional tool for the forthcoming *Thunderbirds*. Lady Penelope was given her own double-page strip which promised "Elegance, Charm & Deadly Danger" every week. The first instalment showed how Penelope recruited Parker, some nine months before the characters made their television debut. The Fireflash and *Pit of Peril*'s Sidewinder would also make their first appearances in the pages of *TV Century 21*.

"I wrote most of the early stories, but we had a staff of five people," remembered Fennell. "My episodes of *Thunderbirds* tailed off fairly rapidly when I started working on the comic."

The launch of *TV Century 21* was overseen by John Littlejohn, the circulation manager of City Magazines. "The first presentation to the trade was at a magnificent baronial hall somewhere in Cheshire," says Shackleton. "Board members from WH Smith, John Menzies and all the major distributors were present. The only person who didn't seem to be there was John Littlejohn, so we started the presentation without him. At the front of the hall were portraits of the family who originally owned the place. Suddenly, without warning, the huge portrait above the Jacobean fireplace rotated on a vertical axis, revealing John standing on a plinth. It was a wonderful opening to the proceedings."

City Magazines hosted launch events in Birmingham, Manchester, Leeds and Edinburgh. The largest party took place at the end of November, when Gerry Anderson joined Littlejohn and executives from the news trade at the London Planetarium. After serving a cocktail described as "TV Century 21 launching fuel", City screened an episode of *Stingray* in colour for the guests.

TV Century 21 was printed using the high quality photogravure process. This meant that the colour images in particular retained a detail and vibrancy, but the cost of the technique pushed the price of each issue up to a relatively expensive 7d. APF and City nevertheless gambled on a print run of 700,000 copies for the first issue. Shackleton visited the printers, Eric Bemrose Ltd in Liverpool, to press the button that set the presses rolling.

Above: Gerry Anderson, Cyril Bartle, John Littlejohn and J Baines, in a picture from *Retail Newsagent*'s report on the London Planetarium launch of *TV Century 21*. Littlejohn was the circulation manager of City Magazines, while Bartle and Baines were both executives from WH Smith.

Below left: On 20 January 1965 the *Daily Mirror* ran this full-page advertisement for *TV Century 21*.

Below right: *TV Century 21* and *Lady Penelope* were promoted alongside City Magazines' other titles in this advertisement from the 4 June 1966 issue of *Retail Newsagent*.

TV CENTURY 21

ADVENTURE IN THE 21st CENTURY

7D

No. 2 UNIVERSE EDITION   EVERY WEDNESDAY

DATELINE: January 30, 2065

STINGRAY ATTACKED!

AIR SEARCH ORDERED

By Our Special Correspondent

MARINEVILLE, 15.00 hours: A massive air search was started today when the 220,000-ton Submarine Aircraft Carrier S.A.3. vanished in the Pacific with her crew of 17,000 men.

The alarm was raised when the World Aquanaut Security Patrol vessel Stingray reported that she had lost contact with the carrier after being attacked by a Titan Terror Fish.

A grim-faced Commander Shore, Marineville's Chief, told reporters today that the S.A.3. was the third carrier to have vanished in a month.

For Full Colour Videoscan Report—See page 10.

GREAT NEW GIFT!

TV CENTURY 21 SPECIAL AGENT

SPECIAL AGENT BADGE AND SECRET CODED MESSAGE FORMS

FREE INSIDE!

New Asteroid Discovered!

SPACE City Head-quarters today buzzed with excitement at the news that Fireball XL5 has landed on an unknown asteroid in hyper-space.

At a press conference this afternoon, Commander Zero told reporters that Fireball made the discovery whilst hunting a mysterious space freighter.

FULL REPORT ON PAGE 4.

DALEK CITY IN RUINS

AFTER the accidental explosion of a neutron bomb on planet Skaro, it was discovered that the Dalek Capital City of Dalaza had been completely destroyed.

War Lord Zolfian and scientist Yarvelling were reported as the only survivors of the catastrophe.

See page 20 for full story.

CORGI MODEL CLUB NEWS — Page 19

TV CENTURY 21 ANNUAL

STINGRAY • FIREBALL XL5

SUPERCAR • BURKE'S LAW

MY FAVOURITE MARTIAN

TV CENTURY 21 ANNUAL

TV CENTURY 21 SPECIAL AGENT

Above left: The second issue of *TV Century 21* and its free gift – a plastic 'special agent' badge.

Above centre: The first *TV Century 21 Annual* was published by City Magazines and AP Films (Merchandising) in 1965. The cover included illustrations from *Fireball XL5* and *Stingray* alongside *Burke's Law* and *My Favourite Martian* – two American series that Shackleton had licensed for the UK.

Above right: The second annual was published in 1966 and included *Thunderbirds*.

At the beginning of 1965, City's stand at Olympia's Boys and Girls' Exhibition included a Dalek and a nine-foot model of Fireball XL5. *TV Century 21*, commonly abbreviated to *TV21*, received further promotion with a series of television commercials and a full-page advertisement in the *Daily Mirror* on 20 January.

The first four issues were offered to newsagents on a sale-or-return basis, but despite such favourable terms and the extensive publicity campaign, Littlejohn was dismayed to learn that less than 15 per cent of newsagents placed an initial order for the first issue. This betrayed not only a cynicism about the project, but a lack of faith in wholesalers to accept leftover copies.

The first issue was cover-dated 23 January 2065, but made available in newsagents over a hundred years earlier, on Tuesday 19 January 1965. "Gerry and I toured the newsagents in Slough and there were copies piled knee-deep," says Shackleton. "It was a disheartening sight. I thought we had a flop, but within a few days you couldn't buy a copy anywhere."

When Anderson visited the offices of City Magazines shortly afterwards he was greeted with Champagne and cigars: "I was the happiest man on earth."

Demand had greatly exceeded the limited supply available in shops, and retailers frantically revised their orders in the days to come. It's ironic to consider that the market-grabbing success of *TV Century 21* may have hastened the demise of the *Eagle*. "Everything has its day," says Shackleton philosophically. "The *Eagle* had done a super job, but we had the strength of television behind us."

For Shackleton, the next logical step was for APF to manufacture its own products, so in early 1965 he began negotiations with Jack Rosenthal, a former accountant who had joined the *Supercar* licensee Guiterman before founding his own toy company.

"Jack was doing quite well, but he wasn't making waves," says Shackleton. "It seemed to me that his company would fit quite neatly under our umbrella. We were in the position to buy the company for the sum of £55,000, which I had discussed with Jack Gill [ATVs financial director] and felt was about right. Robin Gill [ATV's deputy managing director] took over the negotiations and ended up paying twice what had originally been agreed. They offered Rosenthal performance-related terms, and of course their performance went through the roof because they started doing *Thunderbirds* toys."

APF announced its purchase of a controlling share in J Rosenthal (Toys) Ltd in July 1965. "Mr Lew

Grade is clearly at it again," remarked *The Financial Times* on 2 September, in reference to ATV's latest vertical merger. With *TV Century 21* selling half a million copies of each issue, and plans for a sister comic, the newspaper wondered whether the chairman of the Independent Television Authority should take note. "Altogether, it sounds as though the merchandising tail may wag the television dog, an event that might make Lord Hill think *Thunderbirds* was just one long advertisement."

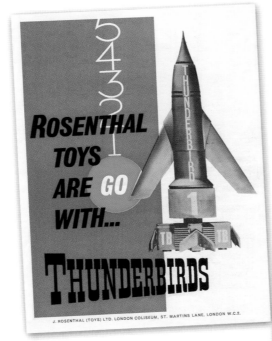

J. ROSENTHAL (TOYS) LTD. LONDON COLISEUM, ST. MARTINS LANE, LONDON W.C.2.

Below left: J Rosenthal (Toys) was part of the APF group by the time this advertisement for the company's *Thunderbirds* range appeared in the January-February 1966 issue of trade magazine *Toys International*.

Below right: Advertisements for Rosenthal's *Thunderbirds* toys appeared in numerous issues of *TV Century 21* during 1966.

Bottom left: Rosenthal produced two versions of Lady Penelope's Rolls-Royce, one battery-powered and one with a friction motor. The version pictured here sold for 14s 11d when it was launched in 1966.

Right: An advertisement for *Lady Penelope* from issue 53 of *TV Century 21*, cover-dated 22 January 2066.

Far right: The cover artwork from issue 15 of *Lady Penelope*, published in April 1966.

Below: A sunshade presented to retailers as a promotional item.

Bottom: This Monkees hat was a free gift with issue 89 in September 1967.

THE LATEST GREATEST COMIC FOR GIRLS! FOR GIRLS! FOR GIRLS!

Lady PENELOPE

7d

ELEGANCE...

CHARM...

FREE INSIDE! Lady Penelope's Fabulous signet ring

The MAN from U.N.C.L.E. BEWITCHED BEVERLY HILLBILLIES MARINA AND LADY P's EXCITING ADVENTURES

and DEADLY DANGER!

FOR GIRLS!

featuring
danger, mystery, intrigue and
adventure with
LADY PENELOPE
MAN FROM U.N.C.L.E.
SPACE FAMILY ROBINSON
MARINA
laughter, magic and spells with
BEVERLY HILLBILLIES
BEWITCHED
PERILS OF PARKER
7d ON SALE NOW!

Lady PENELOPE

7d

FAB CLUB GOES ON A PAINTING SPREE!

AND HER LADYSHIP'S LATEST ADVENTURES

Super COLOURING COMPETITION

ILLYA IN OILS! WHO HAS WON HIS PORTRAIT? SEE INSIDE.

PUBLICATION ISSUE 15 PAGE F/C COL.

Lady P. ISSUE 15. P.1   S/S

Lady PENELOPE EVERY WEDNESDAY

FREE WITH LADY PENELOPE
PRESENTED FOR GIRLS! FOR GIRLS! FOR GIRLS!

THE MONKEES APPEAR EVERY WEEK in LADY PENELOPE

I LOVE THE MONKEES

TV Century 21 upheld its impressive circulation, while providing an advertising showcase for APF's merchandise and previewing some of the highlights from *Thunderbirds*. "We certainly knew what we were doing," said Fennell. "We launched *TV Century 21* with *Stingray* and *Fireball*, knowing full well that sooner or later *Thunderbirds* would be coming along. And what a

tremendous boost that was, after the initial launch of the comic. We increased our circulation after the first year. And then we launched another comic, *Lady Penelope*, which initially outsold *TV Century 21*."

Lady Penelope was announced in the edition of *News Trade Weekly* dated 25 September 1965, just days before *Thunderbirds* made its first appearance in most ITV regions. Promoted as "The comic for girls who love television", *Lady Penelope* was given several espionage-themed launch parties in November. At one of these events, John Littlejohn told *Smith's Trade News* that "The comic comes out of the successful partnership we have with the producers of the series, Gerry and Sylvia Anderson. We found a successful formula with *TV21* and we think we can do it again with *Lady Penelope*."

The first issue arrived on Tuesday 18 January 1966 and proved Littlejohn correct. "We had one marvellous week when we sold 550,000 copies of *TV21* and 650,0000 copies of *Penelope*," recalled Fennell. "So it was 1.2 million copies in total. At that stage they were making more money than any comics had ever made. Not selling more copies than anyone else had sold, but making more money."

Above left and right: Issue 37 of *Lady Penelope*, cover-dated 1 October 1966, offered readers the chance to purchase a *Thunderbirds* charm bracelet plated in 22 carat gold.

Left: Original Frank Langford artwork from issue 41 of *Lady Penelope*, published in October 1966. The story, by Alan Fennell, saw Scott and Thunderbird 1 coming to the rescue of Penelope and Parker.

Above: Issue 52 was the first edition of *TV Century 21* to feature *Thunderbirds*.

Right: This Frank Bellamy-illustrated strip from issue 139, cover-dated 16 September 2067, depicts villains infiltrating Thunderbird 5.

The sustained success of these APF/City Magazines publications can be partly attributed to Fennell's insistence on hiring some of the country's greatest talents in comics. *TV Century 21*'s *Thunderbirds* strip began in January 1966 and was illustrated by a former *Eagle* artist that Fennell had been courting for over a year. Frank Bellamy was the doyen of British strip artists from this era, justifiably acclaimed for the dynamic presentation of both his characters and the panels they appeared in. Bellamy had been unhappy illustrating *Dan Dare* at the *Eagle* and was more interested in safari-themed stories than science-fiction. He eventually agreed to join the team after Anderson took him on a tour of the Stirling Road studio.

The greatest compliment that can be paid to Bellamy's distinctive work on *Thunderbirds* is that it now enjoys a similar level of acclaim as the television series it was based on. But *TV Century 21*, *Lady Penelope* and their spin-offs boasted many other outstanding artists, including Ron Embleton (*Stingray*, *The Man from UNCLE*, *Captain Scarlet*), Frank Langford (*Lady Penelope*) and Ron Turner (*The Daleks*, *Fireball XL5*, *Stingray*, *Thunderbirds*, *Zero X*, *Captain Scarlet* and *Joe 90*).

Above left and right: Original Frank Bellamy artwork from issues 153 and 181. *TV Century 21* was renamed *TV21* from issue 155, published at the beginning of 1968.

Left: This City Magazines flyer from 1966 is one of numerous sources that referred to the comic as *TV21* long before it formally changed its name.

Below: A *TV Century 21* free gift describing International Rescue's 'conduct code'.

The Bearer of this card is an associate of International Rescue.

I. R. Conduct Code.

1. I will help those in need.
2. I will honour those in command.
3. I will show courage in the face of danger.

Special Instructions to Holder.

For latest I. R. Bulletins read T.V. CENTURY 21 and watch the weekly telecasts.

Above left: Captain Paul Travers takes Zero X back into space in issue 211 of *TV21*, published in January 1969. This is original Mike Noble artwork, from a story by Angus P Allan.

Above right: Travers and his crew on the cover of issue 130. The *Zero X* strip was a regular feature from issues 105 (January 1967) to 241 (August 1969).

Right: The free gift in issue 141 was a pair of 3D glasses.

TV Century 21's most prolific artist was also one of its finest, maintaining a consistently detailed but vibrant style that played a large part in establishing the comic's high reputation. Mike Noble first appeared in issue six of *TV Century 21*, illustrating *Fireball XL5*. He would later become just as closely associated with the *Zero X* and *Captain Scarlet* strips. "I hadn't even drawn space stories before," he says, remembering his

earliest commissions from Alan Fennell. "I just had to get going on it. They gave me plenty of references and photographs, in black and white, of course. We also had a specification sheet for *Fireball*, which was in colour. I've still got that, but it's falling apart because I used it all the time."

Like many of his fellow artists, Noble worked from home. "Once a week I would take my completed pages to the station, where they would be sent down to London

by train," he says. "From there they would be picked up by a special courier and taken off to the publisher. Sometimes it was a bit hairy whether they'd arrive on time, but they always got there in the end."

Something else Noble had in common with the other artists was a dilemma about whether to remain strictly faithful to the characters' on-screen appearances. "Artwork is so much more flexible than puppets," says Noble. "On the earlier series in particular the puppets had rather large heads and that riled me because, as an artist, I was thinking, 'Oh God, it's all out of proportion.' And yet in a child's mind, when they see puppets they're really seeing people, aren't they? So I asked Alan, 'Can I make them more realistic?' He just said, 'I'll leave it up to you, as long as you keep the characters.' So that's how I approached it. In my strips the characters could walk, run, twist and turn. I mainly wanted to make the stories believable, no matter how weird and wonderful they were."

Aside from artwork, *TV Century 21* and *Lady Penelope* were illustrated with photographs that were specially taken at Stirling Road. "We had the luxury of a photographer called Doug Luke, who was on my payroll," said Fennell. "He started off working at the studio, but there was never really enough for him to do. Gerry wanted to switch his budget from the film company on to me, so Doug's brief became to shoot anything and everything that moved, for us to use in the comic. It was Gerry's idea to do that, but it wasn't because he wanted to help the comic – it was because he wanted to help himself, and his budget."

Above: Photographer Doug Luke and Gerry Anderson at Stirling Road during the production of *Thunderbirds*. Anderson dedicated this picture to Luke when they reunited to work on *Terrahawks*.

Below: Luke was the photographer on *Candy*, Century 21's comic for very young children. This *Thunderbirds*-themed story featured in issue 24, cover-dated 1 June 1967.

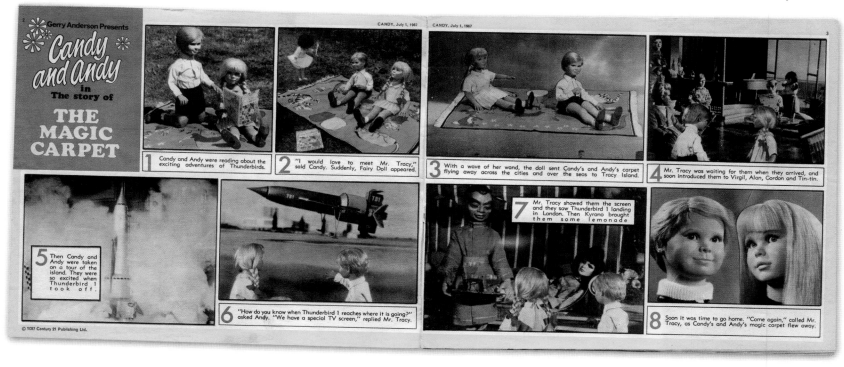

Above left: John Tracy and Thunderbird 5 appeared on the cover of this trade magazine.

Above right: An advertisement from inside the magazine. *The Man from UNCLE* was the most successful American import that Shackleton licensed for the UK.

Below: The die-cast FAB 1 was Dinky's first Gerry Anderson toy. The model was packaged with a missile and several harpoons.

The incredible success of *Thunderbirds* and its comics marked a turning point for APF. Shackleton admits that, like every Supermarionation series, *Thunderbirds* was at least partly created with licensing in mind. "Merchandise was on the agenda of every new series, as the income from licensing was an important item in the budget. The number of characters and the fleet of vehicles in *Thunderbirds* is evidence of this, but creative matters always took precedence. Strong storylines and believable characters were and are essential to the success of any series. *Thunderbirds* had everything – strong characters, groundbreaking hardware and storylines that appealed to all ages. That's why it's stood the test of time."

By the end of 1966 there were more than 120 *Thunderbirds* licensees, earning an estimated £6 million in retail turnover.

Some of the show's best-loved – and now most collectable – toys were the die-cast models manufactured by Dinky. The Liverpool-based company beat Corgi to a licence, launching their range in 1966 with a toy that was catalogue number 100. Lady Penelope's Rolls-Royce was, in some ways, a response to Corgi's bestselling replica of James Bond's Aston Martin DB5, released the previous year. The miniature FAB 1 included a rubber-tipped missile that could be launched from behind the hinged radiator grille, and plastic harpoons that fired from the rear of the vehicle. The model

was available in a variety of finishes and packaging until 1976.

"Lady Penelope's Rolls-Royce became their number one selling toy," says Shackleton. "I can't remember exactly how many they sold, but I know a set of die-cast tools used to last for about a million impressions. They got through two sets of tools."

Dinky's second Supermarionation toy was Thunderbird 2, catalogue number 101. At 12s 11d it was three shillings cheaper than FAB 1, but no less impressive. Dinky's Thunderbird 2 came with a detachable pod containing Thunderbird 4. The telescopic legs that were an engineering impossibility on screen were predictably challenging for Dinky's designers, who instead gave the

toy spring-loaded foldaway legs moulded in yellow plastic. From 1973 the toy was also available in blue, and a redesign in 1974 saw it enlarged and strengthened. This version was given the catalogue number 106 and remained in production until 1979.

Above left and right: These pages from Dinky's 1967 catalogue reproduced the box artwork for the FAB 1 and Thunderbird 2 toys.

Below: Dinky's original Thunderbird 2 was in production at the company's Liverpool factory from 1967 to 1973.

Above: A *Century 21 Merchandising News* supplement included with the December 1966 issue of trade magazine *British Toys*. By this time, Century 21 was obliged to represent other properties owned by parent company ATV. In the background is a letterhead from Century 21 Publishing.

Below right: Part of the four-colour film used in the printing of the boxes for Waddington's *Thunderbirds* jigsaws.

Below left: Waddington's colour proof of the four images that comprised the range.

The packaging of APF's toys and other merchandise underwent a subtle change when their copyright lines were adapted to reflect what would now be called a rebranding. The name Century 21 was originated by Shackleton and had been circulating since Anderson had proposed it as the original title for what became *Fireball XL5*. At Shackleton's suggestion, Anderson had registered the Century 21 Organisation at Companies House in 1962. Shackleton subsequently used the name for the comic in 1964, the record company in 1965 and the publishing company

in 1966. During that year, he expressed the view that the title AP Films had little resonance, successfully arguing that the whole company should now come under the Century 21 banner.

Trade magazines featured glowing endorsements of Century 21 Merchandising from licensees such as Chad Valley (who produced *Stingray* and *Thunderbirds* versions of their Give-a-Show Projector), Lone Star (who created a *Thunderbirds*-branded 'space gun') and John Waddington. "Never in this company's history have we noted such an initial impact for any of our lines as we did with our *Thunderbirds* jigsaw puzzles," wrote Waddington's sales director Mr K Page-Ritchie in 1966. "Sales were staggering and required considerable extra production capacity."

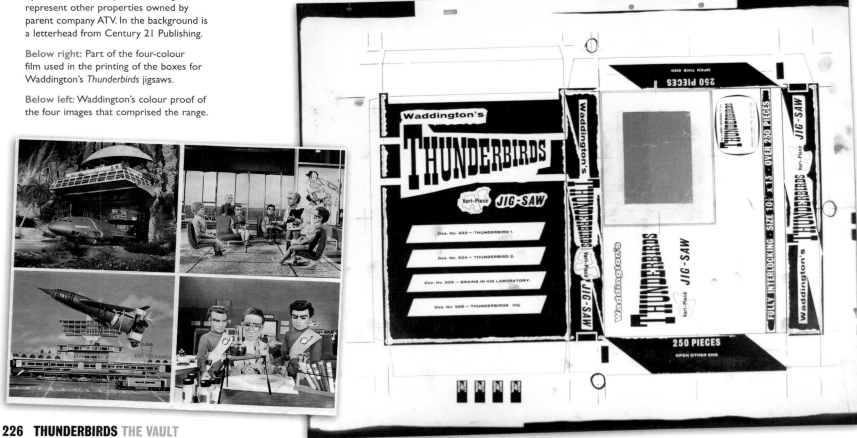

By this time, Shackleton's staff had grown to include Derek Cook, a former Chad Valley employee who became general manager of Century 21 Merchandising, Jim Watson, who also illustrated numerous strips for *TV Century 21*, and Roger Caton, who was originally recruited as Shackleton's personal assistant. The company needed a bigger office, so Shackleton asked if he and his staff could move from Orme Court to the nearby Bush House, in Aldwych. Lew Grade instead suggested that he looked at an office in May's Buildings, which was behind the ATV-owned Coliseum Theatre in St Martin's Lane. With the support of his business neighbours, Shackleton lobbied Westminster Council to change the title May's Buildings to May's Court. When the name AP Films was retired, Shackleton christened his new office Century 21 House.

In March 1967 Shackleton's team expanded further with the arrival of New Zealand-born licensing executive Richard Culley. "Richard was a good man to have with us," says Shackleton, "certainly when the time came for me to move on." Shackleton would become disenchanted, not only with the style of Anderson's post-*Thunderbirds* offerings but with the increasingly manipulative ATV.

"We knew that following the success of *Thunderbirds* wasn't going to be easy," says Shackleton. "And so it proved."

Above: Keith Shackleton (top left) with Sylvia Anderson, Barry Gray (centre background), Bob Bell and Gerry Anderson (foreground) at the Dorchester Hotel for the Television Society awards on 13 May 1966.

Below: Some of the most collectable items of *Thunderbirds* merchandise include the plastic figures given away inside packets of Sugar Smacks. APF filmed a television commercial to launch the promotion in 1966.

10
END OF THE ROAD

"This is the greatest puppet series ever made," Lew Grade told the *Daily Mirror*'s Ken Irwin during a preview of *Thunderbirds* in September 1965. "I predict it will take the country by storm. Everyone is going to love this stuff: the mums and dads, as well as the youngsters."

Genuinely enthused by the cinematic style of the new programme, he added: "The Americans now acknowledge that we are the best in the world at producing TV puppet shows of this kind. They just don't have the know-how to keep up with us."

The quality of *Thunderbirds* was self-evident, but the cost to ATV was huge – at an estimated £1 million, the budget for the first series was comparable to the money spent on international live-action hits such as *Danger Man* and *The Saint*. In the ATV boardroom, Grade was under pressure to balance the books on *Thunderbirds* with a sale to an American network. Unfortunately this was one deal the great negotiator couldn't close. Grade over-estimated the series' value in the US and, after a disastrous attempt to engineer a bidding war between NBC, CBS and ABC, he was forced to sell *Thunderbirds* into syndication.

Without a network on board it was no longer possible to justify such a costly enterprise, so the second series was brought to a premature end. In the 14 February 1966 edition of *The Daily Telegraph*, Grade tried to divert attention from his failure by claiming that the replacement for *Thunderbirds* would see the next great advance in Supermarionation. This time, Grade promised, "Every muscle of the puppets will move."

Above: The Martian Exploration Vehicle seen in the first episode of *Captain Scarlet and the Mysterons* (1967-68) had previously appeared in *Thunderbirds Are Go*.

Below left: The New York-based Physio-Chem Corporation promoted its line of imported *Thunderbirds* toys in this 1967 leaflet. The cover indicates that American broadcasters were offered *Thunderbirds* in colour and two different formats.

Below right: A 1967 television guide from the United States and a 1966 guide from New Zealand.

Keith Shackleton was in Gerry Anderson's office when Lew Grade called to explain that he'd just turned down NBC's offer of $7 million for *Thunderbirds*. "Gerry and I both felt this was a mistake," says Shackleton. "Lew felt he could walk on water, but this time he overcalled the hand. If NBC had picked up *Thunderbirds* I think it would have gone to a third or fourth series. Instead of which, Lew told Gerry he had to come up with something new."

Anderson's idea for *Captain Scarlet and the Mysterons* took its cue from the Martian exploration sequence in *Thunderbirds Are Go*. On the surface of Mars in 2068, a Zero X team of colour-coded officers from the Spectrum peacekeeping force misinterpret the first sign of life they encounter as an act of hostility. They open fire, destroying an alien complex in the distance. Sentient computers called Mysterons rebuild the complex in moments using their powers

of retrometabolism, but threaten a merciless retaliation against the Earth. Spectrum's Captain Black (Jeremy Wilkin and Donald Gray) is recruited by the Mysterons as the figurehead of this relentless campaign. Captain Scarlet (Francis Matthews) is killed and 'Mysteronised', but regains his loyalty to Spectrum. Now virtually indestructible, Scarlet leads the fight against his arch-enemy Black in the Mysterons' war of nerves.

In 1966 there was a feeling within ATV and Century 21 that the type of puppets created for *Thunderbirds* had become dated in their own lifetime. The *Captain Scarlet* puppets couldn't quite live up to Lew Grade's high expectations, but they were a suitably realistic-looking cast for the show's uncompromising premise. Anderson eliminated any trace of caricatured features, and was particularly pleased that developments in solenoid technology allowed heads to be created in the correct proportions to bodies for the first time.

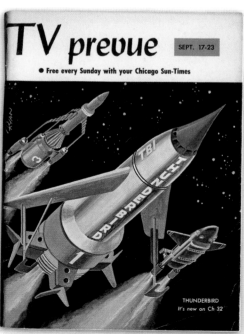

"Speaking as an operator, they were awful," said Christine Glanville of the new puppets. "The heads were very small and didn't have enough weight in them. You couldn't turn them very easily. They looked good on screen, and sometimes you had to look carefully to see whether they were people or not. But they didn't work like people. If you wanted them to turn their heads then more often than not there would be someone out of shot, with their fingers just above the puppet's head, actually turning it round."

Derek Meddings saw this as another step towards the realism he and Gerry were aiming for. "I thought they were very convincing miniature people," he said. "I know the puppets with big heads were probably more appealing, but that was the only thing you couldn't totally believe, really. The problem with the *Captain Scarlet* puppets was that

viewers couldn't identify one from the other. The heads were so small they didn't have any character to their faces."

Captain Scarlet and the Mysterons began production on 2 January 1967. Away from Stirling Road, the first cracks had started to appear in The Century 21 Organisation. A few weeks earlier, Gerry and Sylvia's publicity tour for *Thunderbirds Are Go* had run into trouble when the couple argued over Gerry's perception that Sylvia was trying to steal the limelight. She accused him of jealousy and threatened to cancel the tour. "I told her that if the papers got hold of this it would be a disaster," said Gerry, "and I was worried enough about the performance of the film already. The rest of the tour was thoroughly miserable, and by the end of it our hopes for the film had vaporised."

Above left: Colonel White (foreground) addresses his staff aboard Cloudbase in *Captain Scarlet and the Mysterons*. This was the first Supermarionation series to use puppets with perfectly proportioned heads.

Above right: This metal advertisement was produced by Lyons Maid in the late 1960s and included ice-lollies allied to three Supermarionation series – *Stingray*, *Thunderbirds* and *Captain Scarlet*.

Below: Dinky's die-cast model of *Captain Scarlet*'s Spectrum Pursuit Vehicle was manufactured from 1968 to 1976.

The couple separated shortly after Christmas 1966, but reunited in time for New Year's Eve and went on holiday to Paris. Early in 1967 Sylvia told Gerry that she was pregnant. "I had been quietly considering divorce," he said, "but at that moment I knew I was trapped."

Captain Scarlet and the Mysterons was first screened by ATV Midlands on 29 September 1967 and proved popular, if not the phenomenon *Thunderbirds* had been. "I think *Captain Scarlet* had an appeal for the *Boy's Own* stuff, but a lot of people found it too dark," says Sylvia.

Keith Shackleton also had reservations: "It had its own appeal, but the concept was too sinister for any significant licensing in the children's market. We soldiered on, recognising that we were not fulfilling our own or ATV's expectations."

Above: At London Airport in 1967, Gerry and Sylvia Anderson send Penelope and a selection of *Captain Scarlet* puppets on a promotional trip to Japan.

Below: A Spectrum Helicopter from *Captain Scarlet* takes the place of the stork in this congratulatory card designed by Reg Hill. Gerry and Sylvia's son, Gerry Jr, was born on 31 July 1967.

Right: Details of a gift to Gerry and Sylvia from the staff at Century 21's prop division.

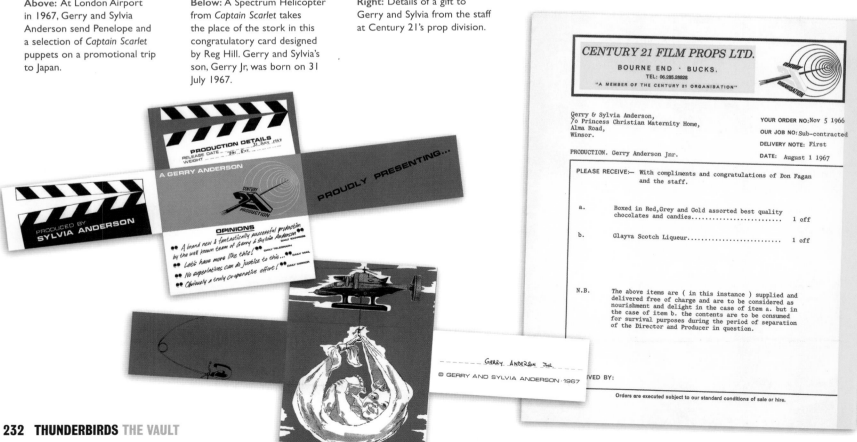

PRODUCTION DETAILS
RELEASE DATE ..... 31 JULY 1967
WEIGHT ..... 7lb. 8oz.

A GERRY ANDERSON

CENTURY 21 PRODUCTION

PROUDLY PRESENTING...

PRODUCED BY SYLVIA ANDERSON

OPINIONS
• A brand new & fantastically successful production by the well known team of Gerry & Sylvia Anderson — DAILY SKETCH
• Let's have more like this! — DAILY MAIL
• No superlatives can do justice to this... — DAILY MIRROR
• Obviously a truly co-operative effort! — DAILY EXPRESS

GERRY ANDERSON JNR
© GERRY AND SYLVIA ANDERSON · 1967

CENTURY 21 FILM PROPS LTD.
BOURNE END · BUCKS.
TEL: 06.285.28828
"A MEMBER OF THE CENTURY 21 ORGANISATION"

Gerry & Sylvia Anderson,
⁰/o Princess Christian Maternity Home,
Alma Road,
Winsor.

YOUR ORDER NO: Nov 5 1966
OUR JOB NO: Sub-contracted
DELIVERY NOTE: First
DATE: August 1 1967

PRODUCTION. Gerry Anderson Jnr.

PLEASE RECEIVE:— With compliments and congratulations of Don Fagan and the staff.

a.   Boxed in Red, Grey and Gold assorted best quality chocolates and candies........................... 1 off

b.   Glayva Scotch Liqueur........................... 1 off

N.B.   The above items are (in this instance) supplied and delivered free of charge and are to be considered as nourishment and delight in the case of item a. but in the case of item b. the contents are to be consumed for survival purposes during the period of separation of the Director and Producer in question.

...VED BY:

Orders are executed subject to our standard conditions of sale or hire.

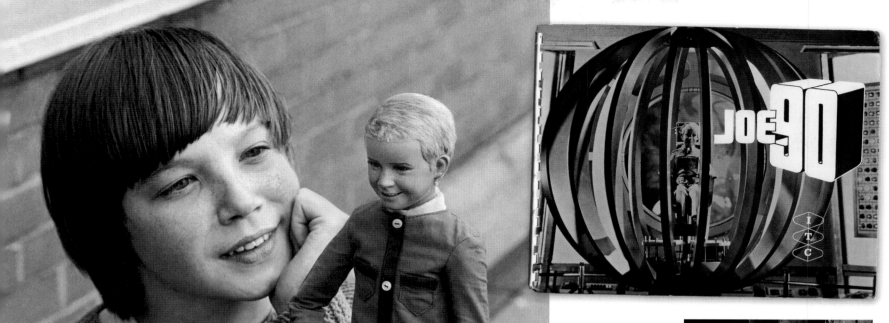

The new-style puppets returned in November 1967, when Century 21 began production on yet another series. For *Joe 90*, Gerry Anderson drew upon elements of the discarded proposal he had originally submitted for *Fireball XL5*. The revised version was set in 2012: electronics genius Professor Ian 'Mac' McLaine (Rupert Davies) reluctantly allows his adopted son Joe (Len Jones) to be recruited by WIN, the World Intelligence Network, in its operations against the Eastern Alliance and various criminals. Mac is able to grant Joe the knowledge and experiences of any expert whose brain patterns are stored in the BIG RAT (Brain Impulse Galvanascope Record And Transfer). When on a mission, Joe instantly accesses these skills by putting on a pair of glasses with built-in electrodes.

Joe 90 was relatively low on hardware compared to its predecessors, and represented a shift away from science-fiction to espionage adventures. The series was also a conscious effort to restore the characterisation and charm that had been sidelined in the militaristic *Captain Scarlet*.

Anderson's memories of the 1940s had a conspicuous influence on the first episode, *The Most Special Agent*. Joe receives the brain patterns of an accomplished pilot – the latest in a long line of characters inspired by Gerry's brother Lionel – and brings a stolen Mig fighter to land at RAF Manston, the base where Gerry and Keith Shackleton had been stationed during their national service.

The ITV regions gave *Joe 90* a patchy transmission from 29 September 1968. The series' format was ingenious, but Century 21 was now competing with itself – any new programmes had to fight for broadcasting space with repeats of previous Supermarionation shows.

SCRIPT EDITOR
TONY BARWICK

SUPERVISING FILM EDITOR
LEN WALTER

SUPERVISING SOUND EDITOR
JOHN PEVERILL

Top left: Len Jones with a puppet of Joe McClaine, the character he voiced in *Joe 90* (1968-69).

Top right: The cover of ITC's brochure for *Joe 90* showed Joe being prepared for a mission inside the BIG RAT's 'Rat Trap'.

Above: A proposal from the Stirling Road art department, suggesting a background and typography for *Joe 90*'s end titles.

Below left and right: Joe's special glasses and suitcase, photographed as reference for licensees.

JOURNEY TO
THE FAR SIDE OF THE SUN

©Universal Pictures Limited MCMLXIX
All Rights Reserved

Above: Outside the UK, Universal Pictures released *Doppelgänger* (1969) as *Journey to the Far Side of the Sun*.

Below left: The European Space Exploration Council (EUROSEC) launches a rocket carrying Dr John Kane and Colonel Glenn Ross in *Doppelgänger*. Derek Meddings supervised the filming of this six-foot model against a backdrop of real sky outside the Stirling Road studio.

Below right: Jason Webb (Patrick Wymark), the chairman of EUROSEC, with the results of Operation Sun Probe – the unmanned mission that reveals a previously undiscovered planet in the same orbit as Earth. Sun Probe was almost certainly inspired by the *Thunderbirds* episode of the same name.

The company had already grasped an opportunity to escape the ATV treadmill. *Doppelgänger* was a live-action feature film based on a science-fiction story Anderson had devised in the early 1960s: on the far side of the Sun, two astronauts (Ian Hendry and Roy Thinnes) crash-land on a familiar-looking planet that is in fact a mirror image of Earth. Universal Pictures backed the project on the strength of this promising idea, but ignored Anderson's recommendation that David Lane should direct. "They were right," says Lane. "When you're dealing with a feature film like that you want an experienced director who can handle artists. I was acutely aware that I wasn't in that league. At that point I'd never shot live-action. Gerry didn't seem to think there was any difference, but I told him *of course* there was."

Universal's finance was conditional on Century 21 hiring American director Robert Parrish, whom the distributor considered to be more bankable. Anderson found Parrish rather less malleable than Lane would have been. "Suddenly I came up against a Hollywood director who didn't want to play and we ended up extremely bad friends."

During one particularly heated dispute with the director, Anderson asked for John Read's support. Read replied that as director of photography his responsibility was to Parrish. "I said that if he felt he was in no way responsible to me, then he should not be a director of the company. Sylvia and Reg both supported me totally, but they didn't say a thing during the meeting. They left me to pull the trigger."

While *Doppelgänger* was shooting at Pinewood, Anderson put David Lane in charge of Stirling Road. Lane produced *Joe 90*, and the series that proved to be the final Supermarionation production. *The Secret Service* combined the most whimsical aspects of GK Chesterton's Father Brown with science-fiction technology and Cold War espionage. As if things couldn't get any stranger, the series' heroic vicar appeared as a puppet in close-ups and as comic actor Stanley Unwin in long shots.

"Gerry and I wrote the first episode [*A Case for the Bishop*]

at White Plains, Gerry's house in Gerrards Cross," says Lane. "We worked right through the night. He dictated it, and I would stop him now and then to make suggestions. Not only was I doing this with Gerry, but I was still filming and editing *Joe 90*. Gerry said he didn't want us to break after *Joe 90*, so we finished that on a Friday and started shooting *The Secret Service* a few days later. I was working 18 hours a day. I don't know how I did it."

Filming of *The Secret Service* began on 20 August 1968 and was well underway when Anderson screened the first episode for Lew Grade in December. Grade didn't even make it to the end, raising the lights as soon as he realised that Unwin was employing the gobbledygook language he was renowned for. Grade canned the series mid-production on the grounds that it wouldn't play in America. It transpired that *The Secret Service* would barely play in England either, with only a handful of ITV regions screening its 13 episodes.

Above left: ITC's promotional brochure for *The Secret Service* (1969), the final Supermarionation series.

Above right: Housekeeper Mrs Appleby (Sylvia Anderson) serves dinner to Father Stanley Unwin (Stanley Unwin) and his gardener Matthew Harding (Gary Files) at the end of *The Cure*, an episode of *The Secret Service*.

Below right: Stanley Unwin appeared in both human and puppet form during *The Secret Service*.

Below left: The Minimiser, the miraculous device Father Unwin keeps hidden inside a book in *The Secret Service*.

Above left: Commander Ed Straker (Ed Bishop) comforts Lieutenant Nina Barry (Dolores Mantez) in *Mindbender*, an episode of *UFO* first broadcast in 1971.

Above right: Moonbase – SHADO's first line of defence against the aliens in *UFO* (1970-71).

Below left: The cover of this ITC booklet featured George Sewell as SHADO's Colonel Alec Freeman.

Below right: A *UFO* annual was published by Century 21 Merchandising and Polystyle in 1970. One of the aliens' distinctive spinning spaceships appeared on the cover.

This curtailment was an ignominious end for Supermarionation, but Grade had already commissioned Gerry, Sylvia and Reg Hill to produce their first live-action series. While Century 21 waited for an underwhelmed Universal to release *Doppelgänger*, *UFO* went onto the floor at MGM British Studios in Borehamwood. Principal photography began on 28 April 1969, while the former puppet stages at

Stirling Road were subsumed by Meddings' special effects department.

In the 24 August edition of *The Sunday Telegraph* Sylvia tried to distance herself from Supermarionation ("We mustn't talk about the puppets, no more puppets") while the disturbing back story that she, Gerry and Reg devised for *UFO* appeared to disenfranchise Century 21's traditional audience of youngsters. In the early 1980s

SHADO (Supreme Headquarters Alien Defence Organisation) stands between the Earth and ruthless extraterrestrials intent on harvesting human organs for their own degenerating bodies. SHADO is commanded by Ed Straker (Ed Bishop), whose marriage has already collapsed under the weight of his top secret responsibilities.

By 1969, it was clear to many of the staff at Century 21 that Gerry and Sylvia's marriage was also in trouble. "They kept it hidden for a while, but it was very obvious when we were making *UFO*," says Lane. "Everybody who knew them intimately was

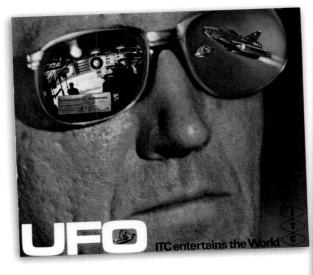

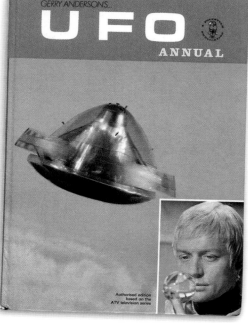

aware of it. When Gerry and Sylvia's marriage was coming to blows it was a very upsetting time for me. It wasn't that I was worried about my job, as in those days the world was your oyster. It was more that I didn't want them to split up because they'd been such a good team."

Things were also starting to unravel at Century 21 Publishing, as sales of the company's various comics declined. "I fell out with Louis Benjamin, who came in as the business manager," remembered Alan Fennell. "By that time Gerry had gone to Borehamwood to make *UFO*. He was still a director of the company, and still very closely associated with what I was doing, but sort of removed from day-to-day discussions. I just phoned him up one day and said, 'I can't stand this any more. I'm going to resign.' He told me to do what I had to do, and then said, 'Monday morning, I'll see you in Borehamwood.' At which point I became a contract writer on *UFO*."

Keith Shackleton was becoming similarly uncomfortable at Century 21 Merchandising. In his view, the success of *Thunderbirds* led to the increased scrutiny of Century 21 by certain ATV executives who wanted a piece of the action. "The honeymoon with ATV was marvellous, but the marriage was a disaster," he says. "The ATV board were not as

straightforward with each other as they might have been, so they thought everyone else was of the same ilk. When ATV started interfering we began to lose momentum. In 1970 I told Jack Gill that I'd lost all faith in what we were doing and that I was leaving. I metaphorically tore my contract up, and I think that suited his game."

When post-production of *UFO* came to an end the stages at Stirling Road fell silent. Derek Meddings and the other technicians were laid off. "We lost our team," says Sylvia. "We lost our family, if you like. When we went into live-action we became little fish in a big pool."

Stirling Road closed in early 1971. "I was the man that turned out the lights," says studio manager Ken Holt with more than a hint of sadness. "We'd already put what was left of the puppets and models into a skip. I locked the door and threw away the key."

Above: Lights out at Stirling Road – the studio doubles as the computer export division of Healey Automation in *A Case for the Bishop*, the first episode of *The Secret Service*.

Below left: A note to Barry Gray from Gerry Anderson's secretary Una Scott, written after Century 21 moved production of *UFO* to Pinewood Studios in 1970.

Below right: Reg Hill and Gerry Anderson, pictured during location filming for *Identified*, the first episode of *UFO*, in 1969.

Century 21 Pictures Limited

Pinewood Studios
Iver Heath
Buckinghamshire
telephone Iver 700

a subsidiary of
Associated TeleVision Corporation Limited

Barry,

Hope you can help with this one?

Luv
Una

Above: Gerry and Sylvia with Barbara Bain and Martin Landau on the Pinewood set of *Space: 1999* in March 1974.

Above right: A mid-1970s compliments slip from Group Three Productions.

Below: The first *Space: 1999 Annual*, published by World Distributors in 1975.

GERRY ANDERSON'S

SPACE 1999

ANNUAL

Authorised edition based on the popular Television Series

Before the dissolution of Century 21, Gerry, Sylvia and Reg Hill established a new company. Group Three Productions maintained close links with Lew Grade, initially operating as hired hands on *The Protectors* (1972-74), an adventure series starring Robert Vaughn, Nyree Dawn Porter and Tony Anholt. The action was brisk and glamorous, but the series belonged to ITC's increasingly homogeneous stable of thrillers and bore few of Gerry Anderson's hallmarks.

Group Three's next collaboration with Grade was a more logical extension of Century 21's work in the 1960s and the concepts developed for *UFO*. *Space: 1999* (1975-77) explored the challenges faced by a community of humans stranded on the Moon when it is blasted out of Earth's orbit. Led by Commander John Koenig (Martin Landau), Dr Helena Russell (Barbara Bain) and Professor Victor Bergman (Barry Morse), the crew of Moonbase Alpha undertake a dangerous odyssey, defending themselves from hostile aliens while searching for a new world to colonise.

Space: 1999 was hyped as the most ambitious television series ever created, and at £3 million it was certainly one of the most expensive. The stress of the production took a further toll on Gerry and Sylvia's acrimonious relationship, which finally came to an end when the first series wrapped in 1975. A second series of *Space: 1999* began the following year, but was dumbed down by ITC's New York office. This was the final time Gerry worked with Reg Hill and Lew Grade, his last remaining partners from the *Thunderbirds* era.

Reg pursued a new career as a freelance storyboard artist, while Sylvia joined the American subscription broadcaster Home Box Office. In the late 1970s Grade diversified into film production, but the failure of *Raise the Titanic* (1980) had a devastating effect on his reputation. He lost control of his companies in 1982.

Gerry Anderson was awarded an MBE in 2001, but without Grade's support his career produced uneven results. Some outstanding programmes were made during those years – notably the CGI remake *New Captain Scarlet* (2005) – but Anderson never found anything that captured the public's imagination in the same way as *Thunderbirds*. Anderson's dogged determination to keep working was only conquered by the debilitating illness that claimed his life on 26 December 2012.

"Dad was always one to move on once a project was completed, and for a long time I think he felt that *Thunderbirds* got in the way of that," says Gerry's youngest son Jamie. "I think that probably carried on until the 1980s, when he came back to puppetry with *Terrahawks* [1983-84, 1986]. It was around this time that he realised *Thunderbirds* could help him, and that people were still celebrating him after his divorce from Sylvia and after his career had declined."

For almost 30 years Gerry was frustrated in his ambition to make a new series of *Thunderbirds*. "It became the great unfinished project," says Jamie. "He got very focused on *Thunderbirds* and couldn't give it up."

At Gerry's funeral on 11 January 2013 his coffin was adorned with a floral display in the shape of Thunderbird 2. The mourners departed Reading Crematorium to the sounds of Barry Gray's famous theme tune. Newspaper, television and radio reports of the service summed up Gerry's long career

with the same few words – he was the creator of *Thunderbirds*.

Almost 50 years after it came to life, *Thunderbirds* was still recognised and admired by millions of people all over the world. The brilliant creation that Gerry had spent decades trying to resurrect had never actually been away.

Above: Gerry and Sylvia, pictured at the height of their success in 1966.

Below left: Floral tributes to Gerry outside Reading Crematorium on 11 January 2013.

Below right: The cover of the funeral's order of service.

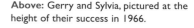

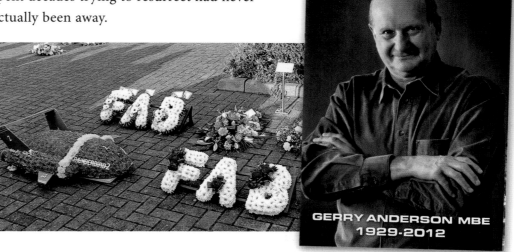

GERRY ANDERSON MBE
1929-2012

INDEX